DOGS SAVE

CRITICAL PERSPECTIVES ON ANIMALS: THEORY,
CULTURE, SCIENCE, AND LAW

CRITICAL PERSPECTIVES ON ANIMALS: THEORY, CULTURE, SCIENCE, AND LAW

SERIES EDITORS: GARY L. FRANCIONE AND GARY STEINER

The emerging interdisciplinary field of animal studies seeks to shed light on the nature of animal experience and the moral status of animals in ways that overcome the limitations of traditional approaches. Recent work on animals has been characterized by an increasing recognition of the importance of crossing disciplinary boundaries and exploring the affinities as well as the differences among the approaches of fields such as philosophy, law, sociology, political theory, ethology, and literary studies to questions pertaining to animals. This recognition has brought with it an openness to rethinking the very terms of critical inquiry and the traditional assumptions about human being and its relationship to the animal world. The books published in this series seek to contribute to contemporary reflections on the basic terms and methods of critical inquiry by focusing on fundamental questions arising out of the relationships and confrontations between humans and nonhuman animals, and ultimately to enrich our appreciation of the nature and ethical significance of nonhuman animals by providing a forum for the interdisciplinary exploration of questions and problems that have traditionally been confined within narrowly circumscribed disciplinary boundaries.

Why Veganism Matters: The Moral Value of Animals, Gary L. Francione

The Wake of Crows: Living and Dying in Shared Worlds, Thom van Dooren

Beating Hearts: Abortion and Animal Rights, Sherry F. Colb and Michael C. Dorf

Eat This Book: A Carnivore's Manifesto, Dominique Lestel

Flight Ways: Life and Loss at the Edge of Extinction, Thom van Dooren

Being Animal: Beasts and Boundaries in Nature Ethics, Anna L. Peterson

For a complete list of titles in this series, see the Columbia University Press website.

DOGS SAVE

STORIES OF CANINE REDEMPTION IN US CULTURE

KATHARINE MERSHON

Columbia University Press *New York*

Columbia University Press
Publishers Since 1893
New York   Chichester, West Sussex
cup.columbia.edu

Copyright © 2026 Columbia University Press
All rights reserved
Library of Congress Cataloging-in-Publication Data
Names: Mershon, Katharine author
Title: Dogs save : stories of canine redemption in US culture / Katharine Mershon.
Description: New York : Columbia University Press, [2026] | Series: Perspectives on animals: theory, culture, science, and law | Includes bibliographical references and index.
Identifiers: LCCN 2025047908 (print) | LCCN 2025047909 (ebook) | ISBN 9780231206969 hardback | ISBN 9780231206976 trade paperback | ISBN 9780231556743 epub | ISBN 9780231565301 pdf
Subjects: LCSH: Dogs—Religious aspects—Christianity | Dogs—United States—Anecdotes | Human-animal relationships—Religious aspects—Christianity | Human-animal relationships—United States—Anecdotes | LCGFT: Anecdotes
Classification: LCC BT746 .M46 2026 (print) | LCC BT746 (ebook)
LC record available at https://lccn.loc.gov/2025047908
LC ebook record available at https://lccn.loc.gov/2025047909

Cover design: Milenda Nan Ok Lee
Cover art: Laura Wright, *Onion*, acrylic on glass over acrylic on canvas

GPSR Authorized Representative: Easy Access System Europe, Mustamäe tee 50, 10621 Tallinn, Estonia, gpsr.requests@easproject.com

For Kevin

CONTENTS

Introduction: Redemption and the "American Dog"   1

PART I: ON CANINE ABSENCE

1. The Classic Canine Redemption Narrative   21
2. The Failures of the Canine Redemption Narrative   53

PART II: MAKING DOGS PRESENT

3. Relational Redemption   89
4. Troubling Redemption   123

Coda   153

Acknowledgments   163
Notes   173
Bibliography   211
Index   227

DOGS SAVE

INTRODUCTION
Redemption and the "American Dog"

I'm just glad you gave me a chance to redeem myself because you know that's the job, it's your establishment, you've got a thousand dogs you're trying to take care of. And you could've just fired me."[1] These words, spoken by Earl Moffett, a formerly incarcerated, middle-aged Black man from Louisiana, express the central conceit of the Animal Planet reality TV series *Pit Bulls & Parolees* (2009–2022). A typical episode pairs formerly incarcerated men with dogs in need, showing how the dogs and men rehabilitate one another. The series traces the highs and lows at Villalobos Rescue Center (VRC) in New Orleans, the self-described "world's largest animal shelter for abused and abandoned pit bulls."[2] It aired for thirteen years, with nineteen seasons, a testament to its immense popularity.[3] VRC is run by Tia Torres, a sixty-something-year-old white woman with a "dysfunctional" past and a formidable presence.[4] After witnessing her ex-husband's struggles to find employment after he was paroled, Torres decided to use her dog rescue to also help formerly incarcerated men find gainful employment. Torres supervises the shelter alongside her two daughters, her adopted twin sons,[5] their partners, and a cast of male parolees—including Moffett, a fan favorite.[6]

An episode from season 9 entitled "Redeemed" follows Moffett's struggles with an opioid addiction that he developed after sustaining an injury in prison. When he comes to work at VRC intoxicated, Torres places him on conditional leave and personally pays for his rehab. After he completes his program, she gives him his job back. In justifying these decisions, Torres explains, "We all know what's in Earl's heart. And now more than ever, it's what we really need."[7] Because Torres trusts that Moffett is a good person—she has watched his loving interactions with and commitment to the dogs—she gives him a second chance. Moffett affirms that the dogs will be essential to his continued sobriety. "These dogs don't care what you've done in the past," he explains. "They don't judge you for every mistake. They just want a little love, a little food, and you're their hero."[8] Because dogs have no concept of past crimes, they respond to the person they see in the present. By working alongside the dogs, Moffett regains both his sense of self and his VRC community. That is, through their ability to be present with the parolees—providing comfort that was withheld in prison and meeting them without judgment—dogs do healing work that humans simply cannot.

Pit Bulls & Parolees is equally about how people save dogs, specifically "pit bulls," referred to in the show's title sequence as "the world's most misunderstood breed of dog."[9] Pit bulls—a broad category for dogs who share a set of physical characteristics like smooth fur, muscular bodies, blocky heads—have a long and complex history in the United States.[10] Once known as nanny dogs and war heroes, they became negatively associated with "inner city" (read: Black and brown) people. Beginning in the 1970s, as "law-and-order" politics and policing took hold, the news media featured pit bulls in stories stoking white anxieties about rising crime in the inner city, thereby recapitulating racist tropes connecting Blackness to violence. Sometimes the dogs were protectors, but often they were "accomplices" in dogfighting matches. These sensationalized stories popularized scientifically incorrect myths about the pit bull, including their ability to lock their jaws down on prey, their unmatched physical strength, and their unpredictable behavior.[11] The goal of *Pit Bulls & Parolees* is to unmask these false stereotypes about both pit bulls and incarcerated people—though, as is common in the predominantly white space of dog rescue, Blackness is not explicitly named.

While the dogs enable the parolees' transformation into "productive" citizens, the canine side of the story is not considered successful until they are adopted into a home. An episode from season 8, "Second Savior," is a prime example of the kinds of dog rescue narratives the show celebrates. In this episode, the viewers meet a pit bull named Bullet, a Hurricane Katrina survivor.[12] When Bullet was first brought to VRC, his paperwork said he was found wearing a custom-embroidered collar. Clearly somebody loved him, but no one ever found his owner. Bullet lived at VRC for over a decade with no adoption prospects, likely because he was reserved around new people. Just when Torres had accepted that Bullet was going live at the shelter for the remainder of his life, she received an adoption application from a woman named Melody, who saw his photo in the "senior dogs" section of the Villalobos website.

At their first "meet and greet," a ritual in which the rescue organization assesses the compatibility between the potential adopter and dog, Torres sits down with Melody, a white woman in her seventies, to give her more background about Bullet before introducing them. "He is a true survivor," Torres remarks. "You know, he's just a tough little guy. And even though he's an older dog, he's like this innocent little child the way he is." This is a constant refrain in the show—pit bulls are both resilient and childlike. Melody is instantly charmed, relating to Bullet's shyness and his status as a "senior." At the end of the episode, Melody decides to adopt Bullet, stating, "It is rewarding for me to be able to give him a home, but I also feel like I'm the lucky one. And I have a new friend, and we're just going to be inseparable."[13] Bullet's story captures the other side of dog rescue: the power of humans to save dogs. After everything he went through—from surviving a devastating hurricane to losing his original family—Bullet finally has found a companion who accepts him as he is. Bullet may not be perfect, but he is perfect for Melody, as she is for him.

Stories like Melody and Bullet's are everywhere in US culture—on TV, in movies, on social media, and even on car bumper stickers. In *Dogs Save*, I show how these narratives are not only pervasive but also religious, drawing from Christian stories about redemption. My central aim in this book is to introduce the "canine redemption narrative" as the literary genre that explains these stories' popularity, reveals their religious underpinnings, and exposes unexamined assumptions about human-canine relationships.[14] In their most simple form, canine redemption narratives describe an individual person's or dog's transformation from evil to good, from social exclusion to inclusion. Crucially, in this genre this transformation requires suffering or punishment—violence—sometimes enacted through the state and other times through individuals. As *Pit Bulls & Parolees* exemplifies, stories of redemption are the defining cultural script for human-canine relationships in the United States.[15] Through close attention to the stories we tell about dogs, we can identify central themes and tensions at the heart of US identity.

Dog redemption narratives are so powerful because they invoke and contest core elements of American civil religion.

First introduced by the sociologist Robert N. Bellah in 1967, "civil religion" refers to the beliefs, symbols, and rituals that Americans recognize as holding transcendent value, regardless of their individual religious identities. As citizens, Americans participate in forms of public meaning making and political belonging that are essentially religious in character. Federal holidays like the Fourth of July, Veterans Day, and presidents' birthdays integrate local communities into the broader nation. According to Bellah, civil religion manifests outside of explicitly religious spaces—in football stadiums, in presidential inauguration addresses, and, as I show in this book, with dogs in animal shelters, prisons, training facilities, and homes.[16] Earl Moffett (the "parolee") and Bullet (the "pit bull" and canine Katrina survivor) embody American beliefs about the value of second chances—and they implicitly show that redemption is not available to everyone. As Bullet's and Earl's experiences also demonstrate, redemption is predicated on the rituals of suffering and punishment (either through rescue and rehabilitation for Bullet or incarceration and recovery for Moffett). And finally, Moffett's return to society via the dogs he cares for and Bullet's life with Melody show how dogs symbolize healing, unconditional love, and the completion of the American family.[17] Dog redemption narratives draw on familiar tropes within Christian redemption narratives but center interspecies encounters. By making dogs present in these stories, we can see how they do work that human beings simply cannot.

The redemption narrative in what is now the United States has a theological history stretching back to the sixteenth century and the rise of Protestant Christianity. In the landmark study *Redeemer Nation: The Idea of America's Millennial Role* (1968), Ernest Lee Tuveson argues that the vision of the United States as a "redeemer nation" is fundamentally religious in origin. As evidence, Tuveson turns to the Protestant Reformation, which heralded shifting approaches to biblical interpretation. More specifically, new approaches to the Book of Revelation play a central role in shaping the conception of the United States as a redeemer nation. The Book of Revelation describes a series of battles in which the Prince of Darkness (or Satan) is progressively defeated, based on God's preordained plan. After Satan's defeat, so the story goes, there will be a time known as the "millennium," a thousand-year reign of Christ on earth. In his interpretation of the Book of Revelation, the saint and theologian Augustine of Hippo (354–430 CE) famously wrote that the "mystic body of the faithful," also known as the "City of God," must live separate from worldly things, experiencing degrees of worldly persecution until the Last Judgment brings about the end of history. By implication, Tuveson argues, the Augustinian reading of the Book of Revelation suggests that prophecy must be read only allegorically and that the outlook for humankind in this world cannot be a hopeful one. This interpretation remained authoritative through the Middle Ages and the Renaissance but started to give way during the Protestant Reformation. Reading against Augustine, Protestant theologians began understanding the Book of Revelation in literal terms, arguing that "the millennium was to be an earthly *utopia*, an age at the end of all history, in which, not Christ in person, but Christians and Christian principles would really be triumphant." This millennium would be characterized by peace, justice, and mercy. While originally the source of evil was anything tied to "old papal corruption," (in other words, to Catholicism), over time the conception of evil expanded to include secular social and political behavior.[18]

This turn to the earthly realm also meant that God would work through specific nation-states. As the settlers living in the

American colonies "conquered" the wilderness and its Indigenous inhabitants, the language of the "chosen people" shifted from the Israelites of the Hebrew Bible to the Anglo-Saxons living in the United States. In this conception of redemptive nationalism, "God must use peoples, armies, governments to attain his ends. God had re-entered secular history as a participant."[19] That is, stories of redemption in the United States have a long history of being both religious *and* political.

The original Latin and Middle English roots of "redemption" provide additional context for contemporary understandings of the word. In its original Latin use (*redēmptiō*), "redemption" is defined as the "action of freeing a prisoner, captive, or slave by payment." As this etymology suggests, redemption brings together the themes of captivity, freedom, and exchange.[20] We see this history very clearly in animal shelter discourse, in which the recovery of a lost dog by her owner is called a "redemption."[21] A major function of animal shelters run by local governments is to collect and hold stray dogs. When stray dogs are brought to animal shelters, they are inventoried with a number instead of a name. The period of time an impounded animal is "held" by the shelter varies by state and county, but owners generally have between three and ten days to redeem their animal. If the owner materializes, they must provide proof that the dog is in fact theirs. If the dog's owner appears to claim "it," the dog is freed from a cage in a holding facility similar to a prison. This proximity to a human who can claim the dog allows them to regain a name and place in a family (becoming a "who" instead of an "it"). At the same time, the owner is usually issued a citation for their stray animal and must pay a fine.[22] Even when redemption occurs in animal shelters, there is still some form of punishment.

In many shelters, dogs who are not redeemed by a previous owner face a literal life-or-death situation: They will either die or be adopted into a home. Yet in order to be redeemed, the dog needs to be considered deserving of redemption in the first place. To be placed into a new family, the dog's worthiness needs to be constructed anew by a narrative that determines their potential to become a redeemable subject. For high-volume shelters with limited resources, such decisions are largely pragmatic, dependent on factors such as age, (perceived) breed, and physical and mental health.[23] As Harlan Weaver points out, there's a different dynamic at work for many shelter volunteers who have become attached to the dogs. For them, the greater the dog's suffering or proximity to death, the more redeemable they are. These dogs are often described by animal rescuers as being on "death row," again drawing explicit links between shelters and prisons. While narratives of death row dogs are compelling and heartbreaking, Weaver argues that they can also be dangerous; at this point, the dogs at risk of euthanasia often have deteriorated psychologically from shelter conditions.[24] Despite human rescuers' best efforts, some dogs are beyond redemption. This is a difficult reality to accept, particularly given the fact that the dog ended up at the shelter through no fault of their own.

The fate of unredeemed dogs is, to cite the euphemistic legal language of the state, to be "destroyed in a humane manner."[25] Destruction and humane behavior may seem to be contradictions in terms, but as Colin Dayan and Vicki Hearne remind us, state violence against dogs is often justified using the language of humanity. In both animal shelters and law enforcement, redemption carries the threat of violence, even or especially in the name of compassion.[26]

As a literary and religious genre that privileges the individual experience at the expense of broader social systems, redemption narratives cannot accommodate the reasons that someone did something bad or include the details about what happens after the redemptive moment. Returning to *Pit Bulls & Parolees*, my retelling of Moffett's redemption narrative leaves out the fact that, as we learn in later episodes, Moffett relapses again and gets arrested for driving under the influence. Recovery from addiction and the traumas of incarceration is nonlinear and cannot be confined to a single redemptive arc. Real-life narratives are not as straightforward or final as the genre insists. When dogs become part of these stories, it becomes even easier to see the problems built into the genre as a reflection of US identity. Certain dog breeds—notably, not pit bulls—are thought to be symbols with universal American referents, embodying the white, middle-class nuclear family. To make this assumption, however, requires ignoring white Americans' long legacy of weaponizing dogs against enslaved people, civil rights activists, and Black Lives Matter activists (to cite but a few examples).[27] It also means ignoring the ways in which dog breeds become racialized.[28]

The racial register of redemption in US history has a long history of its own. As historians like Carole Emberton point out, in the wake of the Civil War, the language of redemption became central to Americans' attempts to make sense of the war's catastrophic violence, resulting in competing redemption narratives that persist to this day. On the one hand, the coalition known as the Radical Republicans pitched their plans for Reconstruction as acts of atonement for "the sin of slavery."[29] In this account, "redemption narratives made the staggering loss of life more bearable, made the grieving meaningful, and in the eyes of some, demanded a reevaluation of the basic principles of American democracy." On the other hand, many white Southerners justified their continued violence against formerly enslaved people as punishment for what they believed was the rampant corruption wrought by Emancipation. Importantly, "redemption" became *the* operative term invoked by southern whites to describe efforts to take back their state governments from federal control. The use of the language of "redemption" was not coincidental but a reflection of white supremacists' savvy knowledge that other Americans would recognize the term's religious and political import and therefore take their claims more seriously.[30]

The Civil War also produced what Drew Faust calls a "culture of shared suffering" that served to unify the nation. However, this unity came at a cost to formerly enslaved people, for whom redemptive suffering was the gateway to becoming "suitable" citizens.[31] As Emberton points out, the legacy of redemption was fraught for formerly enslaved people: "They celebrated the end of slavery as a time of 'Jubilee,' the divinely ordained moment when their suffering would be redeemed." She adds, "Ex-slaves also invoked the violence they had endured as slaves and still experienced as free persons to make important claims as citizens." But this reliance on redemption narratives was a double-edged sword—one that also risked making suffering a precondition for freedom and basic human rights.[32]

In the present moment, we see this punitive logic of systemic racism embodied in the carceral state. The demand for the confession of one's sins and state-sponsored punishment are central to contemporary conceptions of redemption in US culture. As Aaron Griffith argues, evangelical Christians have been central in developing the religious culture pervading US courts and prisons today.[33] Within this worldview, crime remains attached to its Christian theological referent: sin. Therefore the only solution for incarcerated people is conversion to Christianity, which "requires sinners to ask God to transform their personal nature." Evangelicals focused on a racialized conception of crime as a social ill in order to reach a broader audience—one that was predominantly white and middle class. Still, as Griffith emphasizes, for evangelicals the only way to solve the crime problem is through individual transformation: "The heart, not redlined neighborhoods or segregated school systems, was the fundamental site of both sin's diagnosis and its hopeful solution."[34] If the problem of crime rests in the hearts and souls of individuals, then the responsibility for eradicating it becomes a matter of personal practice rather than collective accountability.

As figures in stories about individual and communal change, dogs make clear the punishing logic central to redemption narratives, as well as the liberatory potential in human-animal relationships. Over the past thirty years, a body of animal studies scholarship has drawn direct comparisons between human and animal oppression, best embodied in Marjorie Spiegel's *The Dreaded Comparison: Human and Animal Slavery* (1996) and Charles Patterson's *Eternal Treblinka* (2002).[35] Both these works compare the ideologies and technologies underlying the oppression of human and animals, making a direct comparison between human and animal genocide and enslavement. The dominant critique of these works—one I share—is that comparisons between oppressed humans and animals must be understood within a longer history of using such hierarchies to enslave and oppress African Americans.[36] In *Afro-Dog*, an in-depth study on Blackness and animality in the African diaspora, Bénédicte Boisseron argues for moving past the comparative approach to "focus on interspecies connectedness, [with] the main goal being to determine how the history of the animal and the black in the black Atlantic is *connected* rather than simply comparable, in order to reorient the discussion on black-animal relations toward an empowering frame of reference."[37]

Instead of thinking about Blackness and animality exclusively through the lens of shared abjection, Boisseron makes a case for also emphasizing moments of mutual empowerment. In *Bad Dog*, Harlan Weaver introduces the concept of "interspecies intersectionality" in order to "facilitat[e] understanding of the biosocial workings and political stakes of the experiences, identities, and ways of being that emerge through human and nonhuman animal interrelatings as processes connected to but not concretized in formations of identity."[38] Instead of imagining that dogs exist outside the realm of the political, Weaver shows how human and canine identities are co-created.

Dogs Save offers another category central to interspecies identity formation: religion. By bringing together dogs and religion, this book contributes to a growing body of scholarship in religious studies showing that conceptions of human religious life are incomplete without attention to animals.[39] While religious studies scholarship has demonstrated the importance of animals to human religious experience, the field of US religion is only beginning to explore this area. *Dogs Save* places animals front and center. In doing so, I hope to encourage other scholars to take up their own studies on animals and religion in the United States.

Because canine redemption narratives are so capacious and touch on so many aspects of US culture, this book's archive includes everything from contemporary American avant-garde film and literature to popular narratives about dogs and people written for the American public. While these authors come from different Christian denominational contexts, they all structure their relationships to animals in redemptive terms. I use the method of close reading because the canine redemption narrative is a story that is told over and over again. This repetition creates patterns in plot, themes, and images. The use of a literary approach thus allows me to first identify that the "canine redemption narrative" is indeed a genre and then to explain its structures, themes, and conventions. Through close reading, we can see that redemption narratives are about acts of transformation. In other words, redemption narratives *do* something in the Austinian sense.[40] By attending closely to their formal structure, we can see how redemption narratives use language to construct how we understand human and canine relationships. Finally, competing ideas about redemption have been rooted in different interpretations of the Hebrew Bible and New Testament, demonstrating how close textual interpretation (or hermeneutics) has always been central to understanding redemption.

The first part of the book is about canine absence, showing how canine redemption narratives use dogs as symbols of broader social harms at the expense of seeing the living, breathing dogs. In these stories, dogs are empty containers for human projection in both individual and national contexts. Chapter 1, "The Classic Canine Redemption Narrative," introduces what the canine redemption narrative looks like in its most canonical form. Through two books about the Michael Vick dog-fighting case—one written by Vick, one written about his dogs—I parse the literary conventions of the genre and demonstrate its religious and political stakes. Vick was the first African American quarterback to be the number-one pick for the NFL draft. In 2004, he signed a 130-million-dollar, ten-year contract with the Atlanta Falcons. Until his involvement in dog fighting was unearthed, Vick was ostensibly living the American dream. While other scholars have approached these materials from the perspective of critical race theory, gender and sexuality, and American studies, close attention to the role of religion in the Vick case allows us to see how redemption narratives embrace the carceral state and focus on individual change, obscuring larger systems like race, class, and gender.[41] By being quite literally trained into domesticity, Vick's former dogs sustain the fantasy that redemption heals past wrongs. At the same time, both narratives reflect the dangerous logic of the genre—that suffering is the precondition for redemption.

Chapter 2, "The Failures of the Canine Redemption Narrative," continues the throughline of dogs as symbolic sites of white racial anxieties at the expense of dogs as real animals, moving from focusing on dogs in US popular culture to Samuel Fuller's *White Dog* (1982)—a B-movie that has not been widely released in the United States because of its controversial subject. While the film's aim is to be antiracist, I argue that it is also an attempt to revise the dog redemption narrative by bringing together dogs and racism. The film is about a white female protagonist who rescues a German Shepherd and discovers that he has been conditioned to attack Black people. The woman finds a Black trainer, who commits himself to the project of retraining the dog. Initially, the film seems to allegorize the American failure to address the legacy of slavery, demonstrating that appropriate feelings and good intentions alone are not enough to remedy the larger structural problems built into multispecies relationships in the United States. However, the intersection of anti-Black racism and species difference in Fuller's film cannot be neatly or succinctly resolved within the genre of the redemption narrative. In other words, the film shows the limits of a highly formulaic narrative to offer a remedy for the problem of racism in American society. *White Dog*'s noted ambivalence as an antiracist project—and its failure—ultimately comes down to the fact that it can only conceive of moral responsibility in terms of the redemption of its white subjects and their symbols.

These first two chapters establish how redemption narratives deploy dogs as symbols of broader human social anxieties around race at the expense of the dogs, resulting in a form of canine absence. The second part of the book focuses on canine presence, examining canine redemption narratives that foreground the dog. However, as we will see, even when we are thinking about individual dogs, in telling stories about our relationships with them, we are also imagining them in symbolic terms. Because canine language does not translate to the page, it is difficult to get away from metaphor. Thus, the "dog as symbol" versus "dog as real animal" binary is more complicated than it may first appear.

Chapter 3, "Relational Redemption," takes on this tension between the symbolic and the real by focusing on dog training as a site of religious meaning making and practice that includes and then goes beyond institutional religions. The chapter begins by exploring the allure of the celebrity dog trainer Cesar Millan, whose television shows depict redemption as the transformation of a dog from demon to angel, restoring harmony to the home and preserving the dog's status as part of the family. While Millan's methods are temporarily effective, they also rely on outdated, punishment-based methods. Because violence and suffering are central to the redemptive transformation, however, the episodes conclude with what appears to be satisfying finality. Since most people are not well versed in canine body language and behavior, viewers fail to recognize Millan's training as violence in the first place. Unlike these immediate and transformational dog redemption narratives, the chapter then moves to more complex accounts of dog training that analyze the potential for redemptive intimacy between humans and animals. It foregrounds a relational model of redemption by exploring a collection of first-person narratives written by two white feminist scholars and dog lovers, Vicki Hearne and Donna Haraway. Although they draw on religious narratives and practices in different registers of Christianity (Calvinism and Catholicism, respectively), both describe their animal training experiences as a redemptive process that creates a form of interspecies communication, in which both the human and the dog are transformed.

Chapter 4, "Troubling Redemption," combines a discussion of national identity and individual, "real-life" relationships with dogs. I start by describing the 9/11 dog redemption narrative, a subgenre that deploys dogs as symbols of a triumphant nation and redeemers of its citizens from suffering. By way of contrast, I look at experimental art that engages with and unsettles the literary conventions of the canine redemption narrative: Laurie Anderson's *Heart of a Dog* (2015) and Eileen Myles's *Afterglow (a dog memoir)* (2017). Both use 9/11 as a moment that fundamentally changes their relationships to time, to the United States, and with their dogs. However, these works stage the dogs as metonymies for US war crimes—demonstrating a reversal of the dog-as-American-unifier in the traditional 9/11 stories. At the same time that Anderson and Myles are writing about 9/11, they are also grappling with the uncomfortable ethics of caring for a dying dog. Both are invested in the question of what we owe our dogs and how we can do our best to attend to their needs. Anderson offers Buddhism as a way into thinking about this question, and Myles draws from their Catholic childhood. Unlike earlier narratives featured in this book, here suffering is not redemptive.

As much as this book is addressed to scholars at the intersection of religion and animal studies, I am also writing for people who love dogs and who work with them. The genesis of this book came from my experiences volunteering at a municipal animal shelter, and I learned so much from the people and dogs I met along the way. Dog cultures in the United States—rescue, training, sports, veterinary medicine—are overwhelmingly white. While race, class, and religion shape the demographic makeup of these fields, racial politics are rarely interrogated in these spaces. By better understanding how dog redemption narratives work, dog lovers can be more aware of the power dynamics built into these stories and think about when and why they figure themselves as redemptive subjects. In other words, we cannot think about dogs without also understanding the religious meanings placed onto them—for good and often for ill. By becoming aware of these projections, I hope that we can begin to tell better stories about dogs, ones that hold together complexity, alterity, and love at the same time.

PART I
ON CANINE ABSENCE

1

THE CLASSIC CANINE REDEMPTION NARRATIVE

On April 25, 2007, local police raided a sprawling property in rural Virginia owned by the NFL quarterback Michael Vick. Upon arriving, authorities discovered sixty-six dogs, most of whom were classified as pit bulls. Many of them were chained to car axles, underfed, and bore injuries consistent with dogfighting.[1] Based on forensic evidence collected on Vick's property and the testimony of several witnesses, it was discovered that in addition to participating in illegal dog fights, some of Vick's dogs had been drowned, hanged, electrocuted, or beaten to death—actions in which Vick had participated. While authorities prepared charges against Vick and his partners in dogfighting, the dogs were held as evidence and placed at county shelters. Before this case called greater national attention to dogfighting, the standard practice was for the court to require that the dogs be held as evidence and then order their "destruction" at the case's conclusion.[2] As pit bulls, the dogs had even more stacked against their survival. Beginning in the 1980s, the propagation of sensationalized, racialized stories about vicious pit bulls spread myths about the breed. At the same time, a vocal movement of predominantly white animal welfare groups and pit bull advocates insisted that the dogs could be saved; they wanted to change the hearts and minds of the American public by demonstrating that the Vick dogs could be safely integrated into human homes.[3] The courts agreed to let them try. As the dogs received the resources needed to tend to their psychic and physical wounds, some even became "canine good citizens," serving as public representatives of their breed.[4] Before long, the Vick dogs became national symbols of the redemptive potential of dog rescue, no longer "Vick-tims" but "Vick-tory dogs."[5]

Michael Vick's "rags to riches" transformation—from a poor kid with big dreams to one of the few Black quarterbacks in the NFL—had been celebrated as a prime example of the American dream. Upon the public's discovery of his involvement in dogfighting, he became a pariah overnight. Many Americans, especially white animal activists, advocated for Vick to suffer the same cruelties that he had made his own dogs experience: beating, electrocution, and even hanging. These proposed racist acts of "retributive justice" suggested that Vick's cruel treatment of his dogs made him the "real" animal in this case. At the same time, Vick's defenders (most of whom were African Americans) denounced what they saw as his "lynching" by the American public.[6] His supporters argued that Vick had paid his debt to society by losing his NFL contract, endorsements, assets, and reputation, as well as serving nearly two years in prison. Vick also partnered with the Humane Society of the United States in an anti-dogfighting campaign. Nonetheless, many animal activists still feel that Vick's apologies were insincere and that he is fundamentally "irredeemable." Others believe that Vick is indeed deserving of redemption, including the NFL, which reinstated him almost immediately after he served his prison time.

What is central for this chapter—and by extension, for this book—is the ways in which Americans interpret both Michael

Vick and his dogs through the narrative frame of redemption. Stories about guilt, innocence, and redemption are everywhere in US culture—so much so that the "dog redemption narrative" is a genre in its own right. As noted in the introduction, canine redemption narratives bring together both explicitly Christian and secularized aspects of redemption that mediate complex US imaginaries of sinfulness, otherness, forgiveness, and inclusion across species but also, as we will see, across race.

This chapter focuses on the two most prominent books about this case, exploring how they deploy the religious and literary structure of the genre. The first book, *Finally Free* (2012), is written by Michael Vick and published by an evangelical Christian press.[7] The second book, *The Lost Dogs: Michael Vick's Dogs and Their Tale of Rescue and Redemption* (2010), is written by the sportswriter Jim Gorant and was published by a mainstream press and addressed to a secular audience.[8] These two narratives, which each focus on different actors and agents of this saga, provide the foundation for this book's study of the power that redemption narratives have in the American psyche, the symbolic role of dogs in these stories, and the punishment-based systems that redemption narratives reinforce.

"SERVING A GOD AND COUNTRY OF SECOND CHANCES": THE MICHAEL VICK REDEMPTION NARRATIVE

US redemption narratives refer to a transformational process that can be mapped as a series of steps. First, an individual does something bad. Second, an individual is punished for this action (if it is illegal, this punishment is enforced by the state). Third, an individual must face the consequences of this mistake during a period of moral condemnation and often physical imprisonment. Fourth, an individual must seek forgiveness from people and/or from God by explicitly confessing what they did wrong and apologizing to those they harmed (if possible). (Of course, the confession is a step in which dogs cannot participate, so their guilt must be narrated by a human.) Fifth, once the individual is brought back into the community, they begin life anew with resolve not to make the same mistake. And finally, the community is strengthened by the return of this individual. The final two steps are particularly important because they emphasize that while the individual needs to recognize their behavior and change for the better, an individual's redemption is not complete if they are not reintegrated into the community. And it's here that things grow tricky. Whether or not that individual has changed sufficiently is not up to the individual to decide. This person must be worthy of redemption, but who makes that call is often mysterious.

Michael Vick's book follows these steps with great precision. Accordingly, it is divided into three parts: "The Rise," "The Fall," and "The Redemption." In part 1 of the book, "The Rise," Vick describes his early childhood and teenage years, culminating in his ascent to the NFL. He uses this section to establish his fundamentally good character, emphasizing his close relationships with his family and his commitment to Christianity. Part 2, "The Fall," is Vick's confession. After achieving great financial and professional success, Vick describes how he turns away from his Christian values and becomes involved in drugs, gambling, and dogfighting. This naming of his crimes and sins is an essential step in redemption narratives.[9] Vick describes how he had to take accountability for these choices, which cost him everything: his dogs, his family, his career, and his freedom. Part 3, "The Redemption," begins with Vick's release from prison and details his efforts to reconnect with his family, return to the NFL, and partner with the Humane Society of the United States. Crucially, these reparative steps are part of Vick's process of returning to both his personal and professional communities. By following the genre's formulaic narrative structure, Vick's redemption becomes not simply probable but inevitable.

The Rise: A Solid Foundation

Redemption narratives are necessarily retrospective, written from the position of someone after they have sinned in order to make the case that they should be forgiven. Part 1 of *Finally Free* strives to show the reader that Vick really was a good person from the beginning—an innocent kid who later got caught up in bad things. As a way of giving a window into his life before the controversy, Vick opens the narrative with his childhood, describing how faith, family, and football shielded him from the violence in his neighborhood: "I grew up in the Ridley Circle housing project—unit 667—in the crime-infested East End of Newport News, Virginia. . . . Newport News is sometimes referred to as 'NewportNam'—a word twist on 'Vietnam.' The inference is that Newport News is a jungle-like war zone with pitfalls and traps at every turn. You just never knew when a peaceful situation would turn into a violent, volatile situation."[10]

The experience of spending one's formative years in a place compared to a war zone had a lasting effect on him. Vick explains that "you reach a point where you become immune to the violence and crime; the sounds of gunfire became white noise that faded into the background of our lives."[11] In order to survive, one had to develop an "immunity" to violence—to not be as affected by it. While Vick's narrative emphasizes violence and poverty, it is notable that he fails to mention race: Newport News, especially the East End where he grew up, was predominantly Black.[12] Scholars and activists have long documented the link between racist economic policies like redlining and crime, but Vick avoids anything that could be submitted to systemic critique, which is too complex for redemption narratives.[13] Furthermore, to turn to the broader context would risk sounding like he is not taking *personal* accountability for his actions, an essential component of redemption narratives.

Instead, Vick turns his focus to his family, emphasizing the strong women who raised him: his mother, "the rock" of his family, and his grandmother, who instilled in him a deep Christian faith. As an example of his childhood commitment to God, Vick describes not only reading from the Bible but sleeping with it under his pillow: "I know the other kids in the neighborhood weren't sleeping with the Bible under their pillows; they weren't reading their Bible at night. . . . The reason I say this is to highlight my solid foundation." His "solid foundation," a phrase Vick repeats multiple times in this chapter, is built on faith and family.[14]

Of course, the next ingredient is football, which protected Vick from the temptations in his neighborhood. In reflecting back on his involvement in football, he says, "I don't know what would have happened to me during my youth if I had not had the local Boys & Girls Club as a place to spend my time productively, participating in sports and other group activities. It was a sanctuary for me. It may have saved my life." Sports also connected Vick to men he described as the father figures he never had, including the man who ran the Boys & Girls Club in Newport News and his high school football coach Tommy

Reamon. Reamon in particular was instrumental to Vick's athletic success because, as he explains, they had a lot in common: "Like me, Coach Reamon grew up in the rough East End of Newport News, and he knew what it took to escape. He played college football at Missouri before being drafted in 1974 by the Pittsburgh Steelers of the NFL. . . . He later told me, 'You had to dream to get out of that neighborhood.'" Vick followed Reamon's advice, working hard and beating the odds to achieve athletic success. Instead of positioning his rise to the NFL as being motivated by the desire to achieve fame and wealth, Vick describes it as a matter of survival—a way of "getting out of that neighborhood."[15]

The remainder of the "Rise" section focuses on how Vick's strong work ethic and personal accomplishments led to the NFL. After landing a position playing college football at Virginia Tech, Vick fondly recalls spending countless hours lifting weights and studying plays with his coach, rather than partying with his teammates. When Vick describes his ascent to becoming a professional football player, he notes that he was the first African American quarterback in history to be picked first overall in the NFL draft. Vick characterizes this accomplishment as "a tremendous honor" and "something that will stand forever."[16] In one of the few moments when Vick mentions his race, he describes this experience as personally meaningful. However, Vick leaves the broader context unsaid: the fact that this achievement was a historic repudiation of racist claims that the quarterback position was the exclusive provenance of white men.[17] When race comes up—and again, it is rare—it is always within the context of Vick's desire to show the fruits of his personal hard work.[18] This selective colorblindness is a corollary to the individualizing thrust of redemption narratives and the way they focus critique on the self. In redemption narratives, it is the person and not the system that shaped them that must be redeemed. If Vick can make a case that he is fundamentally a good person—which he does through talking about his family, his faith, and the importance of football in building his moral foundation—then the public will be more likely to forgive him. At least that is the hope.

The Fall: Confession and Incarceration

After going to great lengths to establish his humanity and good intentions, in the section on "The Fall," Vick follows the next steps in the redemption narrative: He names what he did wrong, apologizes for it, and shows how he will take accountability for his actions. He starts this part of the book slowly, reserving the end of this section for the most controversial part of his story— fighting and killing dogs.[19] First, Vick lists comparatively minor lapses in judgment, such as when he was caught on TV giving some fans the finger. In reflecting back on that episode, Vick writes: "[I] wish I could apologize to those two men and to everyone who witnessed the incident. . . . The moment showed my immaturity and was probably a symptom of greater issues in my life." Vick goes on to give more context for his actions, attributing them to a nasty custody battle between his ex-girlfriend and himself. He explains that there were times when he was unsure of his son's whereabouts, which was terrifying for him. At the same time, and for the same reasons, Vick also acknowledges that he stopped applying himself in football and instead started partying, gambling, and hanging out with "questionable characters."[20] As he fell deeper into this world, Vick describes how he lost touch with his relationship to God and turned away from Christianity.

THE CLASSIC CANINE REDEMPTION NARRATIVE 29

But it's the section on the actual practice of dogfighting that is the most dangerous for Vick to talk about—and arguably the reason his book exists. While Vick received some negative publicity related to his other actions, it was his role in dogfighting that elicited such fervent public outcry and is what ultimately cost him everything.[21] The tone of this section is uneven; at times it sounds like it is written in a more legal or formal register, and at other moments it sounds much more colloquial. Given that this book was part of Vick's public redemption campaign, it makes sense that this part of his narrative would be carefully orchestrated.[22] One feels the mediated nature of the book in the chapter's opening, which reads as part legal disclaimer, part content warning:

> The subject matter I'm about to discuss is highly controversial and sensitive—and understandably so. I want to make it clear from the outset that in no way do I mean to glorify dogfighting or my involvement in it. But I do want to be candid about what happened, and my background with it, to answer any lingering questions that might exist. It needs to be shared because it is part of my story. And I will make it clear that such activity and behavior should be strictly avoided and not tolerated.[23]

To preface the most controversial part of his confession, Vick must strike a careful balance. On the one hand, he must acknowledge his direct involvement in fighting and killing dogs and to apologize for it. On the other hand, he needs to avoid delving into the gritty details and risk losing the readers' sympathy.

After this disclaimer, Vick returns to his personal experiences, emphasizing the conflicting messages he received about dogs growing up. Painting himself as a sensitive child, Vick explains that he always loved dogs, especially his childhood dog, Midnight: "Midnight had a really pretty black coat with brown dots above her eyes. She was a beautiful dog; I fell in love with her. Midnight was my companion, so I didn't want to do with her what I heard the other guys were doing with their dogs because I was emotionally attached to her."[24] In his recounting, Vick did not want to put Midnight in fights because he loved her; he knew her down to the brown dots above her eyes.

At the same time, human-canine violence was everywhere in his neighborhood. Vick witnessed his first dogfight when he was merely eight years old, right outside his home:

> One day, a friend and I stepped outside the building where I lived in the Ridley Circle housing project and saw kids and their bicycles surrounding a grassy area where we usually played football. But instead of a football game, about eight pit bull terriers were gathered. Most people don't know this, but back then, just as is the case now, I am scared to death of dogs I don't know. So my friend and I jumped on top of a mailbox to give us spectator seats at a safe distance from what was happening.[25]

It is hard to imagine the effect of walking onto the field where eight-year-old Vick played football—which was his safe space—and instead seeing it transformed into a canine battleground. Vick explains that while "[he] cringe[s] at the brutality of it all now," at the time, he "didn't realize how wrong dogfighting was. . . . It was just a way of life in the neighborhood. . . . It was going on almost everyday."[26] Without excusing it, Vick describes the brutality of dogfighting as being one of many forms of violence that he witnessed as a child. Remember, he previously described Newport News as a war zone.

While football saved Vick from getting deep into dogfighting as a child, as an adult, he noticed the similarities between football and dogfighting, which he came to regard as another sport. In his own account, what made Vick such an excellent athlete is also what drew him to dogfighting. As he grew more immersed in that world, before long, he "became better at reading dogs than reading defenses." Even though Vick notes that it makes him "sad to say now," but "it was that love and that passion for my wrongdoings [dogfighting] that led me to lose everything I had worked so hard for."[27] By implication, Vick's devotion to football and dogfighting were the same; the skills that were once his salvation had now become his downfall.

After establishing the influences that led him to dogfighting, finally, Vick must confess what he had long denied: the fact that he actually did kill dogs. He prefaces his confession by stating that no matter what happens in the future, his violence against the dogs will always be with him. "It's a day I would like to forget," Vick writes. "But I can't. It will always haunt me." Vick's conscience began speaking to him the moment he committed his most extreme act of violence—that he looked at a dog he killed and wondered if God would punish him for his actions. However, at the time, Vick justified his behavior because he believed that "*This is what these dogs like to do. This is why they're bred.*" Immediately after admitting that he had such a thought, Vick qualifies it. "I was so wrong," he says, demonstrating his current recognition of his past sins. Without excusing his behavior, Vick again situates his actions within the broader culture of dogfighting: "Everyone in dogfighting was doing the same thing: killing their dogs and getting rid of them when they lost. I had seen guys take the dogs right out of the fighting box and—*bam*—shoot them in the head."[28] Based on this logic, the rules of dogfighting were defined by their own violent rituals and norms. In this case, dogs are commodities, subject to death when they become unprofitable. While Vick partially hints at the broader economic context in which dogfighting emerges, he does not mention race at all. This is in dramatic contrast to the people who were his most vocal defenders.[29]

While Vick admits that he killed dogs, he goes into the most detail about his actions when defending himself against the most heinous allegation against him: that he used shovels to murder dogs. Again, Vick must walk a delicate tightrope: He must confess his crimes without alienating his audience. Immediately following his description of other people shooting dogs right after fights, he turns to a report about his own violent actions. "In January 2010, new documents emerged from the dogfighting investigation that my codefendants and I—among other things—allegedly killed dogs with shovels, but that's not true. Nonetheless, I understand that the killings were, and still are, sickening," Vick states.[30] That is as specific as Vick gets about his most violent actions—"the killings"; he describes what he did *not* do. He did not kill dogs with shovels or shoot them directly after a fight (at least that's what that example seems to suggest). On the next page of the book, there is an insert filled with images. The most striking one is what looks like an elementary school photo of Michael Vick; he is wearing a suit and tie and has a sweet smile on his face. This was likely taken around the time he was first exposed to dogfighting. It is almost impossible to view that innocent child—the same person Vick described in great detail earlier—as an inherently evil person. Those photographs do persuasive work that Vick's words cannot. The juxtaposition between this little boy and the man who killed dogs reminds the reader of Vick's humanity—that this child who slept with a Bible under his pillow will always be a part of him.

THE CLASSIC CANINE REDEMPTION NARRATIVE ❧ 33

Vick concludes the chapter by apologizing for his actions and acknowledging that he deserved punishment. While he apologizes many times throughout the chapter, this is his most complete statement of remorse and therefore worth examining in detail:

> Looking back, I'm deeply sorry for everything that happened and how it happened. I wish I could turn back the hands of time and do it differently. I understand that what I did was wrong. I especially wish I'd never talked to Tony [the dogfighting coach] that day in March 2001. But it was a choice I made. It was my fault.
>
> If I had the chance to take back one thing that I have done in my life, it would be what happened to those dogs. But I got caught up in that lifestyle and my own lies, and I didn't change or see that I needed to change at the appropriate time. The only thing I can do now is to try to make it right by seeking to help more animals than I have hurt by doing things like speaking to kids, schools, and groups through the Humane Society about the evils of dogfighting.[31]

On paper, these paragraphs are a prime example of what a confession in a redemption narrative looks like: Vick apologizes directly, acknowledges that what he did was wrong, and takes personal responsibility for his actions. In the specific context of this case, it is also important that Vick foregrounds how much he regrets harming the dogs—the key sticking point in his public redemption. He continues by emphasizing that the only way to make things right is to do better in the future, and he vows that he will do just that. Although he alludes to broader dogfighting cultures, he stresses that the blame is on him alone and that therefore only he can make things right. And yet, he uses the passive voice throughout, describing "what happened" as opposed to what he did.

While Vick says all the right things, is his remorse sincere? In one sense, it doesn't matter. As Peter Brooks notes, confession, "the process of rehabilitation and reintegration—if by way of punishment and expiation—can only begin when the suspect says the words, 'I did it.'"[32] By this measure, Vick did what he had to do, and therefore his audience has to take him at his word. But as scholars of Christianity are well aware, it is impossible for external observers to judge the authenticity of another person's internal conversion.[33] Peter Brooks speaks convincingly to this tension, arguing that the American public simultaneously demands and distrusts confessions: "Confessant and confessor (to use the significant language of the Church) engage in a fateful dialogue. The bond between them, like that of suspect and interrogator . . . urges towards speech. When it produces a confession, the confessor, and society as a whole, are reassured that they can pass judgment in good conscience. Yet the motives of confession are often far from determinate . . . unless the content of the confession can be verified by other means, thus substantiating its trustworthiness, it may be false."[34] Vick's reasons for confessing can be read in many ways—as opportunistic, as sincere, or perhaps somewhere in between the two. As the audience, we can never truly know. Either way, the burden of proof is on the individual seeking redemption, while the decision about their fate is made by other people or institutions.

It is here that prison enters the picture as a response to the question of Vick's remorse. While his audience may not know if Vick's confession is authentic, we (society writ large) can punish him. Vick himself endorses the necessity of his time in prison, arguing that his incarceration was a wakeup call from God, something that necessarily had to happen to make him the redeemable person he is today. After Vick describes the many lies he told during and after the dogfighting operation was revealed, he says that God intervened: "Eventually, it was as if God said, 'Kid, I offered you a chance to get this thing right. Now carry yourself to jail.' I know He didn't say it like that, but I can imagine Him saying, 'Go on. You need to do some time. You need to learn a lesson.'"[35] In Vick's retelling, it was necessary for him to serve time (eighteen months) in prison to understand how low he had fallen. As Daniel A. Grano argues in his analysis of the rhetoric of "genuine remorse" in the Vick case, "although occasional reference was made to systemic forces in the Vick case, it was the individual labor of redemption that (re)made the man as forgivable." As a result of this individualizing demand, Vick became both the spokesperson for the efficacy of incarceration and the engine of effacing broader systemic harms faced by people of color.[36]

Redemption: Faith, Family, and Football

The final part of Vick's autobiography, which he calls "The Redemption," is about Vick's personal quest to right his wrongs (as best he could) and to prove that he learned his lesson while in prison. In Vick's account, he did three things that mark his successful redemption: First, he returned to Christianity; second, he repaired the relationships with the people he hurt (especially his family); and third, he returned to the NFL. All three things come together in his relationship with the Black football coach and evangelical Christian Tony Dungy, a man who is heralded as "the moral compass of American sports."[37] Vick describes how Dungy visited him in prison to pray with him and to encourage him to show up for his children as a strong father figure. Dungy also played an instrumental part in helping Vick regain credibility with the NFL and in rehabilitating Vick's image after reentry.[38] In the words of Daniel Grano: "If anyone could get through to Vick by modeling an alternative and redemptive black masculinity and serving as an incorruptible medium between the league and the public, it was Dungy."[39] Without naming his Blackness explicitly in the book, Dungy's authorization of Vick's story in *Finally Free*'s foreword is enough to serve as evidence that Vick is worthy of redemption. Here Dungy makes a direct appeal to the audience, asking them to pause before casting judgment on someone else. "If you're like me," Dungy begins, "If you've ever done something in your life you wish you could take back—it will encourage you to learn that we serve a God of second chances and live in a country of second chances."[40] Dungy's address in the second person reminds readers that no one is immune to mistakes.

The redemption process for Vick culminated in a return to the NFL, which represents the public forgiveness of his sins. Vick describes his nervousness when he first met with NFL Commissioner Roger Goodell about his possible reinstatement. But to his surprise, Goodell is not interested in relitigating what already happened, instead telling Vick that "we're not here to talk about the past. We're here to talk about how you're going to change your life moving forward."[41] It therefore makes sense that *Finally Free* concludes with a painstakingly detailed account of Vick's successful 2010–2011 "comeback" season, complete with a nearly twenty-page chapter filled exclusively with his career playing statistics.

The implication, therefore, is that Vick's return to the NFL is essential to the US public's willingness to grant him redemption. While his proven profitability for corporate sponsors likely had a role in the NFL's willingness to reinstate him, Vick's narrative is particularly powerful because his personal redemption, an internal process, is made tangible and collective through the sport of football captured on televisions nationwide. By turning on their televisions and witnessing Vick's celebrated athleticism, Americans everywhere can vicariously authorize and participate in Vick's redemption.

This endorsement is solidified by the former president of the United States himself. In a passage toward the end of the book, Vick describes how President Barack Obama called the owner of the Philadelphia Eagles, the team Vick was playing for at the time, and praised their decision to sign him. While Vick does not have a direct quote from Obama, he says that the owner of the Eagles characterized their conversation as follows: "The President said that so many people who serve time never get a fair second chance . . . he was happy that [the Eagles] did something on such a national stage that showed our faith in giving someone a second chance after such a major downfall."[42] The praise from the president of the United States holds undeniable symbolic value as the collective, national endorsement of Michael Vick's redemption narrative writ large. Again, Vick's second chance—a phrase that recurs throughout his book—is only available to him after his prison sentence. Finally, Vick can now serve as a positive example for the community, marking the final step in his redemption.

READING RELIGION INTO THE AMERICAN PIT BULL

While it is clear why Michael Vick needed redemption, it may be less obvious why redemption is the primary frame through which his dogs are understood. Obviously, the dogs are not people, nor did they do something bad. Vick and his associates forced them to fight, and they were not good fighters, at that (which is why the handlers killed so many of them). Instead, Vick's pit bulls need redemption from the breed's entanglement with racist associations about "bad people," as well as prevailing assumptions that traumatized dogs—especially pit bulls—cannot be rehabilitated.

We must venture back to the United States of the 1970s and 1980s in order to understand how pit bulls, which were once known as "America's dog," developed a negative reputation linked to racism and classism.[43] There are many factors that led to this shift. To begin, in the mid-1970s, dogfighting started to gain the attention of US law enforcement, in large part because it tends to occur around other forms of cruelty and violence, including domestic and child abuse, and in connection with other types of illegal activity, such as drug dealing, firearm sales, and gambling.[44] As the police started raiding dogfighting operations and seizing pit bulls, the media began covering this growing subculture of guns, drugs, and gambling with greater frequency.[45] These raids did not occur in a vacuum but were part of the broader US moral panic about "crime," which was inseparable from white racist anxieties about "inner city" (read: Black) violence.[46] In this context, dogfighting became yet another way to surveil and police Black bodies, and pit bulls were caught up in the fray.

In addition to these reports about pit bulls and dogfighting, beginning in the mid-1970s there were an increased number of articles covering pit bull attacks, particularly against children.[47] As noted earlier, however, the visual identification of a pit bull is highly subjective, and newspapers took these individual breed identifications at face value. Soon, pit bulls came to stand in for all dangerous dogs. For instance, in 1986 alone, there were over

350 newspaper, magazine, and journal articles about pit bulls in the United States.[48] Indeed, the poet and dog trainer Vicki Hearne notes that as a result of the saturation of pit bulls in the media, "in the eighties Americans learned to recognize pit bulls where before they had only seen dogs."[49] The pit bull was understood to be no ordinary dog, but a beast possessing super-canine abilities that endangered America's (white) women and children.[50] And by association, pit bulls came to stand in for "dangerous" human beings, illustrating Harlan Weaver's claim that "the contemporary production of the pit bull in the United States as a kind of being frequently relies on, overlaps with, and connects to human racial categories."[51] As Weaver insightfully points out, this understanding of pit bulls as a "breed" defined by the visual perception of the viewer functions very much like the way that racial identification works in the United States. As a breed defined by visual perception, this means that people make assumptions about what a dog is like—about temperament and behavior—based on how the dog looks. These negative stereotypes about pit bulls thus draw from classist and racist conceptions of breed alongside anti-Black racism. Such stereotypes were very much still active in the US cultural memory in 2007, and it is these polarizing public perceptions of pit bulls upon which redemption narratives about the Vick dogs are based.

Public Response to the Vick Case: The Vick Dogs as Redemptive Subjects

Newspaper and magazine articles that appeared in the immediate aftermath of the Vick dogfighting bust reflect negative stereotypes that simultaneously dehumanize and personify the dogs, representing them as both monsters and dangerous criminals. Take one of the first of many similarly themed articles to appear on the Vick dogs, which was headlined, "Trained to Be Killers, Vick's Pit Bulls Now on Death Row."[52] As the sensational title suggests, the animal shelter is likened to a prison, and the dogs are personified as human inmates who are being held for committing a capital crime. Their "breed" and association with dogfighting offers the false equivalence that just as they had ostensibly killed other dogs, these pit bulls also would kill human beings. This article, like most that appeared in the immediate aftermath of the case, relies heavily on an interview with one person: Commander Sergeant Kevin M. Kilgore. Tasked with overseeing eleven of Vick's dogs while they were held as evidence at an animal control facility near Vick's property, Kilgore clearly cares about dogs. At the same time, he perpetuates stereotypes about pit bulls, particularly those caught up in dogfighting and confined to a stressful environment. Whether this was his intention, as an agent of the state whose job it is to oversee animal abuse cases, his perspective lends greater credence to these negative pit bull stereotypes. For instance, Kilgore describes how one pit bull "had chomped right through the heavy gauge metal door and escaped its confines," and next leadingly states, "imagine what that would do to human flesh," as though he were talking about a monster rather than a dog.[53] In contrast to this interpretation, most canine behaviorists would likely suggest that the dog chewed through the door out of anxiety, boredom, or frustration resulting from limited socialization and extended solitary confinement.[54] However, the officer instead assumes that the pit bull's violent actions toward something else (another dog, a gate) would automatically lead to its mauling a human being.[55] Articles like this one demonstrate how the logic of redemption for the Vick dogs cuts both ways: Because the dogs are represented in the media as being monstrous and criminal, the implication is that they are unfit for redemption.[56] At the same time, by associating the dogs with characteristics that are used for human subjects (however "guilty" they may be), the dogs are personified and therefore primed to become redemptive subjects.

Indeed, there are just as many accounts celebrating the Vick dogs' successful redemptions as there are those decrying the dogs, illustrating my claim that the negative stereotypes about the pit bulls are the first step in preparing them to become potential redemptive subjects. Only five months after it published a piece calling the Vick dogs "menaces," the *New York Times* featured an article entitled "Given Reprieve, N.F.L. Star's Dogs Find Kindness." As this article demonstrates, the dogs were quickly transformed from criminals to victims, whose human-perpetrated traumatic pasts are precisely what warrant their chance at redemption. Instead of describing nameless, aggressive pit bulls, the article begins with an innocent, wounded individual dog. This "pit bull mix" is named Georgia, and she is covered in "scars from puncture wounds [that] reveal that she was a fighter." The piece continues to linger on Georgia's broken body: "Her misshapen, dangling teats show that she might have been such a successful, vicious competitor that she was forcibly bred, her new handlers suspect, again and again."[57] Whereas previous descriptions of the Vick dogs also emphasized their physicality, this article locates Georgia's identity in her status as a victim of human abuse. Georgia is personified through her suffering, reflected in the "again and again" language, which implies that Georgia was not only forced to become a "fighter" but that she was a victim of rape, a crime usually limited to human beings. In this retelling of the Vick case, Georgia's scars do not signify her innate viciousness but instead her suffering and thus her right to redemptive justice.

Thus, redemption narratives around the Vick dogs rely on a personifying logic that emphasizes their suffering and victimhood. This reflects an important modification to the redemption process described earlier in relation to Michael Vick. God is absent from the canine redemption narratives, even though they share the same three-part structure as Michael Vick's Christian redemption narrative. Depending on one's perspective toward pit bulls, the dogs need redemption either because their breed makes them "bad" or because their trauma made them dangerous. In both cases, the Vick dogs' redemption narratives require that they achieve acceptance from the broader US public.

FROM VICK-TIMS TO VICK-TORY DOGS: THE CLASSIC CANINE REDEMPTION NARRATIVE

As we saw with Michael Vick's story, a central characteristic of the redemption narrative is its emphasis on suffering and punishment as a transformative and redemptive experience. In what follows, this chapter will show how Gorant's book functions as a canine redemption narrative—one that resembles but also departs in significant ways from the redemption narrative in Vick's book. Mirroring the same redemption narrative structure present in *Finally Free* without the explicit Christian evangelizing message, *The Lost Dogs* is divided into three parts: "Rescue," "Reclamation," and "Redemption." Part 1 begins with the dogs' experiences on the Vick dogfighting compound, part 2 details the complicated legal process of rescuing them from the dogfighting ring, and part 3 concludes with the dogs' individual redemption narratives.

Unlike Michael Vick's redemption narrative, which, as he notes throughout, is prompted by his own "sinful" actions, the dogs in Gorant's book are represented as inherently innocent—"Vick-tims," if you will. As this play on words (invoked by Gorant) suggests, the dogs' redemption requires a permanent association with Michael Vick. At the same time, this connection is both a liability and an opportunity. Animal advocates had to prove to the courts that the dogs could be safely integrated into family homes, despite the negative stereotypes associated with their breed and the enduring trauma of their upbringing.

Step One: Rescue

From its first pages onward, *The Lost Dogs* appeals to the readers' hearts, using pathos instead of Christianity as its tool of persuasion. The book opens with a long description of the kinds of frustration and sadness the dogs experienced while tethered outdoors on the Vick compound. "They can't run, they can't play, they can't anything. . . . they can never touch, planned positioning meant to frustrate and enrage them. For some it does; for many it simply makes them sad." This mixture of sensory stimulation and deprivation, signaled by the increasing proliferation of "can't"s, is not merely physical but also psychological. In addition to sadness, the dogs experience confusion, another relatable human emotion: "None of the dogs know what's happening around them, but they do know something isn't right. They've seen things they are not supposed to see. They've heard terrifying sounds and they've smelled fear and pain drifting in the air."[58] Even before the text recounts gruesome dogfighting scenes, the narrative depicts the dogs as conscious and feeling creatures, aware of their helplessness and preternaturally sensitive to the suffering around them. This canine knowledge, which is gained through the senses, leads to an awareness of their own plight and to an extrasensory moral acuity, the knowledge that "something isn't right." The text implies that, as dogs, they "are not supposed to" possess an awareness of evil, but they do through experiences forced on them by humans. This knowledge is what makes them more-than-canine, bringing the dogs closer to becoming redemptive subjects.

This particularizing emphasis is especially visible in the case of "the little red dog" who is beaten to death by Vick and his partners, an event that Vick, as we saw earlier, patently denies and that *The Lost Dogs* upholds as the pinnacle of canine suffering.[59] In an excruciating passage detailing the findings from an excavation of Vick's property, the little red dog becomes a sympathetic individual through her bruised and broken body:

> And then there was one body that stood out from the rest. It had signs of bruising on all four ankles and all along one side. Its skull was fractured in two places and it had four broken vertebrae. Brownie [Vick's groundskeeper] had said that all of the dogs that didn't die from being hanged were drowned, except one.
>
> As that dog lay on the ground fighting for air, Quanis Phillips grabbed its front legs and Michael Vick grabbed its hind legs. They swung the dog over their heads like a jump rope then slammed it to the ground. The first impact didn't kill it. So Phillips and Vick slammed it again. The two men kept at it,

alternating back and forth, pounding the creature against the ground, until at last, the little red dog was dead.[60]

While the little red dog is not saved, the singularity of her suffering and death justify the great efforts taken to redeem the surviving dogs. Her story is almost too much to bear. Although the little red dog's death prevents her from becoming a redemptive subject in her own right, the extremity of her undeserved suffering generates the kind of sympathetic identification usually reserved for human beings, therefore making it possible to imagine the other Vick dogs as potential redemptive subjects.

The idea that all the Vick dogs are individuals is a common refrain throughout the book (and in pit bull activism in general), but the text is particularly insistent on this point when the dogs' suitability as prospective redemptive subjects comes into question.[61] After describing the process of conducting temperament tests on each of the dogs in order to determine their potential to be rehabilitated, the book comes to the following conclusion: "The truth is, in the end, that each dog, like each person, is an individual. If the Vick dogs proved nothing else to the world, this would be a significant advance." The phrase "like each person" asks the reader to allow for the same kind of differences in canine personalities. This individualizing logic is essential to situating the dogs as redemptive subjects, as it distances the dogs from negative stereotypes around pit bulls and dogfighting and asks readers to imagine the dogs as being more human than canine. Indeed, the text makes this clear later when it says, "Suddenly they were no longer Bad Newz dogs or those pit bulls from Vick's place. They were Oscar and Rose, and Ernie and Charlie and Ray and Curly and forty-two others. They were no longer a story or a group or a commodity, they were forty-eight individual dogs in the same situation."[62] The dogs only become individuals after being recognized as such by human beings through the act of evaluating and naming them.

This moment of rescue also represents a transformation into whiteness, which is necessarily part of the dogs' redemption. Like Vick's book, *The Lost Dogs* also includes an insert of photographs in the middle that does powerful persuasive work. Bénédicte Boisseron's incisive description of these images speaks to the central role of whiteness in mediating the Vick dogs' redemptive process:

> Gorant's book is itself an attempt at salvaging the pit bull's public image. In it, Gorant includes pictures illustrating the rescue efforts. These pictures show white workers and volunteers (many women and children) in close physical contact with endearing looking pit bulls. In one of the pictures, a group of unidentifiable blacks are walking in the direction of the camera, alongside Vick's emptied kennels. The kennels look like a canine death row at the end of which a fenced door, the door closest to the camera lens, has been left wide open. The open door, certainly evocative of the very recent release of the dogs, also brings to mind the escape of a dangerous convict (or "con-Vick" as Gorant names Vick). Gorant's photographs attest to the inclination in America to perceive canine badness within a racial paradigm since the only blacks featured in Gorant's series of photos are associated with the pre-rehabilitation phase and the cement urban landscape of incarceration.[63]

Like *Finally Free*, *The Lost Dogs* is a redemption narrative that also does the work of public relations. It defangs the dogs by increasing their distance from Blackness (signified through Boisseron's point that the only Black people in these images are those on Vick's property) and giving them a new proximity to whiteness and domesticity (represented through the photos of them with white women and children). These images also reaffirm Colin Dayan's point that whether pit bulls live or die depends on the human with whom they are associated. Most are killed, except in "the rare and much publicized instances when an especially pitiable dog is chosen to be saved by a particularly compassionate person, usually a well-heeled white citizen."[64] The Vick case marks such an occasion where canine redemption is predicated on middle-class whiteness.

Step Two: Reclamation

After the state intervened and temporarily placed the little brown dog, who was introduced at the beginning of the book, at a county shelter, the animal control officers labeled her "Sussex 2602." Assigned the name of the county, just like all the other dogs, along with a unique number, her identity is both specific and generic: She bears a distinct number but remains a piece of property. Jasmine's experiences in the county shelter are again described from her perspective, in personifying terms: "She freezes and hopes that the man will leave. She's done this many times, and she knows that when she simply ignores them they will often go away. . . . He opens the gate. The brown dog's heart begins to race. . . . her body begins to tremble."[65] Although she is still referred to as a dog, Sussex 2602 is also described as being capable of memory and of future thinking. Her terror is also part of the text's rhetorical strategy. Emphasizing Sussex 2602's helplessness and fear makes her a sympathetic subject far removed from the vicious stereotypes about her breed.

Step Three: Redemption

In the "Redemption" section, which is the final part of Gorant's book, Sussex 2602's human rescuers give her a name, "Sweet Jasmine," and move her from the shelter to a family's home. Now that Jasmine is redeemed, the book ceases to portray the events from her point of view, instead focusing on the human rescuer's feelings. As this section makes clear, an essential part of the sentimentalizing logic of redemption narratives is the infantilization of the dogs. This phenomenon is made explicit in the relationship between Jasmine and Catalina (the woman who rescued her), which is described in terms similar to a mother and a child: "She cradled the dog next to her body and stood for just a moment, holding her, bouncing her a little, whispering soft wishes into Jasmine's ear. Catalina had always loved that name. She'd often thought that if she had another child and it was a girl, she'd name it Jasmine."[66] For someone reading this quotation out of context, one could safely assume that the text is talking about a human child rather than a thirty-five-pound dog, a connection that Catalina makes explicit. Jasmine is totally silent and still in this scene; there is no indication from the text as to how she feels about being held like a child. Everything is filtered through Catalina's experience and her personifying treatment of Jasmine as a little girl.

The importance of Jasmine's helplessness in solidifying her bond with her human rescuer, Catalina, is emphasized again later in the text: "As much as she [Catalina] gave to Jasmine, she had always felt that she'd gotten more in return and she'd never felt that more powerfully than now. She loved her children more than anything, and she felt like Jasmine was her third child, but because of her limitations she was different. She needed more and that somehow made their relationship even deeper."⁶⁷ Jasmine's redemption is ultimately just as much (if not more) about the effect she has on her human owner than about her own life. Jasmine's neediness, which was a result of her traumatic experiences on the Vick compound, structures the bond that Catalina forms with her. This moment reflects the broader logic of redemption at work in dog rescue, where the dogs' quality of helplessness—embodied in an abusive past—solidifies the human-canine bond. While I am not calling into question the fact that Catalina loves Jasmine, I am suggesting that Jasmine's troubled past and her current helplessness is what makes her uniquely suited for redemption. As Jasmine's case illustrates, the politics of care undergirding the redemption of the Vick dogs may be well intentioned, but they are not without power inequities.

THE LIMITS OF THE CANINE REDEMPTION NARRATIVE

While narratively satisfying, the generic structures of redemption narratives also limit the kinds of stories that can be told. Because redemption narratives require a focus on individual culpability, Vick's account of his fall scrupulously avoids a discussion of his race, obscuring an essential dimension of his identity.⁶⁸ But complexity is not what Vick is after here; redemption narratives do not allow for it. The omission of any discussion of his race allows Vick to highlight the challenges of being raised in a neighborhood with high crime rates without drawing attention to any broader socioeconomic factors that contributed to his formative childhood experiences.

This rhetorical move is consistent with what the scholars of race and religion Joshua Dubler and Vincent W. Lloyd state about the politics of punishment in the United States, arguing that the prison system "places people in an impossible situation and then demands that they improve themselves in that it leaves the penitent man or woman precisely *zero* room for social critique, for talk about justice beyond the procedures of the criminal justice system. All criticism must be directed inward."[69] In order to be redeemed, Vick cannot acknowledge that broader social forces shaped his life; his sinfulness must be entirely self-contained. Vick's public reentry and endorsement therefore bind him to the affordances and constraints of the redemption narrative. The process of regaining access to the NFL and the status of a respected sports star requires the elision of the structural forces of race that not only constrain Vick but other Black athletes. By attaching his success to the genre of the redemption narrative, Vick must perpetually perform his commitment to the power of individual action and punishment, which deflects structural critique.

As a counterexample to Vick, one might turn to the former NFL quarterback Colin Kaepernick, who made the news in 2016 for breaking NFL tradition by kneeling during the performance of "The Star-Spangled Banner." In a postgame interview, Kaepernick stated, "I am not going to stand up to show pride in a flag for a country that oppresses black people and people of color. To me, this is bigger than football and it would be selfish on my part to look the other way. There are bodies in the street and people getting paid leave and getting away with murder."[70] Because he violated the norms of how Americans are supposed to respond to the national anthem—and ignited a public debate about racist policing—Kaepernick lost his job. Kaepernick is currently a free agent and has devoted his time to civil rights activism. This exile from the NFL reflects the discomfort felt by many white audience members who do not wish to see politics bleed into football (as if the NFL is a depoliticized space to begin with). The legality of Kaepernick's actions is not what matters here. He was punished because he violated social norms that many Americans imbue with transcendent value.[71] Kaepernick's story cannot be integrated into the confines of a redemption narrative because he is pointing to wrongs larger and far more complex than his individual actions. The redemption narrative simply cannot contain the social problems Kaepernick is critiquing.

The story of the Vick dogs is also more morally complex than may appear at first glance. The end of *The Lost Dogs* concludes with Jasmine's accidental death. After all the work poured into saving her, she is hit by a car while Catalina is out of town. But instead of concluding on a tragic note, Gorant quickly moves past the material details of Jasmine's death to emphasize their religious significance. This focus on redemptive suffering is best expressed by Jasmine's guardians, who "believe that Jasmine had been sent to them for a purpose. They felt as though Jasmine had a mission in this life and having achieved what she set out to do, she had been free to move on. Jasmine was off to do something else, somewhere else, while the rest of us were left to follow our own paths." According to those who rescued her, Jasmine's death was not pointless but preordained. Her life was about teaching people a lesson about the indefatigable spirit of pit bulls, and once that moral was learned, her physical presence was no longer necessary, however devastating her loss may have been. The book doubles down on this sentiment, concluding with these words: "This is Jasmine's purpose. This is the story she tells."[72] According to Gorant, Jasmine's redemption is *The Lost Dogs* itself: She is redeemed through the book.

Critics of this way of thinking about human relationships to animals will draw attention to the ways in which redemption narratives are about people, even when dogs are their subjects. Because redemption narratives about dogs are ultimately about the humans who rescue them, the dogs are often rendered symbolic of human virtue, forever wedded to their abusive pasts. Furthermore, the Vick stories demonstrate that redemption is unequally granted. Try as one might to make redemption a personal problem, not everyone is as famous and profitable as Michael Vick. Most pit bulls are not given the publicity that Vick's dogs received—and even then, their redemption was conditional on their ability to assimilate into white, middle-class society. Even as these stories reveal the powerful grip that redemption narratives have in US culture, they also reveal a deeply limited vision of justice for humans and dogs.

2

THE FAILURES OF THE CANINE REDEMPTION NARRATIVE

When one thinks about "dog films," famous canine stars like Rin-Tin-Tin, Old Yeller, and Lassie likely come to mind, alongside the spate of dog movies that appeared in the early 1990s and beyond, including *Beethoven* (1992), *Homeward Bound* (1993), *101 Dalmatians* (1996), *Air Bud* (1997), *Marley & Me* (2008), *Hachi: A Dog's Tale* (2009), and *A Dog's Purpose* (2017).[1] Whether produced in the golden age of Hollywood cinema or today, these films celebrate common themes: the heroic faithfulness of a dog to his "master," often at the expense of his own safety or life; the unbreakable bond between dogs and children; the preternatural ability of dogs to judge human moral character; and the notion that dogs always come home to their families, be it in this life or the next. These films share the same themes and structure as the classic canine redemption narratives that I discussed in the previous chapter, which depict the power of suffering to change human and canine characters—through punishment for wrong actions, the inner transformation of their hearts, or salvation from death. While this change of heart may not result in a conversion to Christianity, these transformations bear the marks of Protestant Christian redemption narratives while combining them with secular influences.² In these films, the stories about the suffering and healing experienced by dogs teach the human characters to become "good people."³ By symbolizing stock traits like loyalty, bravery, and, most importantly, sacrifice, the dog serves as a model for human ethical behavior. Through their right actions in a universe where good and evil are always clear, the dog is the vehicle of moral instruction and collective unity. Closure in these films culminates in the completion of the American family: The dog comes home, the family learns a lesson about unconditional love or bravery, and the story ends.⁴ Crucially, whiteness is an unmarked category in Hollywood dog films; so too is anti-Blackness. Instead, the films exist in a sort of "colorblind" fantasy, in which race—and racism—are invisible.

The subject of this chapter, Samuel Fuller's *White Dog* (1982), challenges the conventions of the canine redemption narrative by featuring a dog who initially appears to be innocent but turns out to be deeply dangerous. Any suffering that occurs in the film fails to positively transform the people or the dogs; there is no satisfying closure. The film centers on Julie, a struggling actress and young white woman who rescues a dog, only to find out that he has been trained to attack and kill Black people. At Julie's bequest, the dog becomes the project of a Black anthropologist and animal trainer (tellingly) named Keys, who believes that "racism is learned" and that he can therefore reeducate the dog. The rest of the movie focuses on Keys's efforts to undo the dog's prior training. The film's title describes a historical practice by white enslavers and state actors to train what they called "white dogs"—canines who could track, capture, and kill Black people in the United States.⁵ While the enslavers believed that they could train their dogs to harbor racial animus against Black people, in practice, the dogs relied on contextual cues like the commands of their white handlers, the barks of other dogs, and the cries of those "racialized as prey."[6] *White Dog*'s conception of "canine racism" uses a slightly different understanding of white dogs that is also scientifically inaccurate, positing that dogs only see in black and white and can therefore be trained to attack based on the sight of Black skin. This legacy of the "white dog" as a weapon against Black people seeking freedom and self-determination is very much alive today—from the civil rights movement to the carceral state.[7] By depicting a relationship between a white dog trained to kill Black people and a Black trainer determined to deprogram him, the film asks whether racism can be unlearned in white individuals and, by extension, the nation.[8]

A RACIST DOG MOVIE? *WHITE DOG'S* PRODUCTION, RECEPTION, AND DISTRIBUTION

The film's backstory is important for understanding both how dog redemption narratives are used to secure a racist social order and the risk of undermining this central feature of the genre. The film was inspired by the Lithuanian-French writer and diplomat Romain Gary's eponymous short story, which appeared in *Life* in 1970.[9] Paramount Pictures picked up the story and commissioned Curtis Hanson to write the screenplay and Roman Polanski to direct the film. After Polanski fled the United States in 1977, the film's script was rewritten. In 1981, facing potential industry strikes, Paramount executives decided to fast-track the film, believing that it could be made quickly before the strike began. They brought in Jon Davison, the producer of *Airplane!* (1980) fame, who expressed concerns to

Paramount's president, Michael Eisner, that this was a "*Jaws on paws*' exploitation film that would be a marketing nightmare." Unable to get out of his contract, Davidson reached out to Curtis Hanson, who recommended Sam Fuller—a screenwriter and director known for his ability to make films quickly. A personal friend of Romain Gary, who had since died by suicide, Fuller signed on to the project. However, he had one requirement: that the film be grounded in what he called "a *nonracist approach*."[10] Fuller believed that the original script was racist because of the way it represented Keys (the Black trainer). In the original version of the story and the edited screenplay, Keys secretly retrains the white dog to become "a black dog" who attacks white people. At Fuller's insistence, Keys is rewritten as a "man of science" who harbors no ill will toward white people and genuinely wants to train the racism out of the dog.

Fuller's revision clashed with the aims of Paramount executives, who wanted a "suspense thriller that focused on a 'moving and emotional love story between a human and an animal.'" As the film scholar Lisa Dombrowski shows, Paramount executives wanted the film to focus on two themes: first, a female protagonist whose relationship with her dog teaches her to overcome her victimization by men; second, a racist dog who "could be presented as a loving helpmate whose violence is redeemed by self-sacrifice." The film executives not only did not object to the fact that the dog's violence was directed at Black people but were excited by this premise—as long as the dog's positive relationship to the white woman was protected. Dombrowski notes: "The narrative conceit of *White Dog* was a challenge from the start, as it suggested not simply '*Jaws* on paws,' but *racist 'Jaws* on paws.'"[11] In other words, they wanted a Hollywood dog redemption narrative that uses anti-Blackness to shore up white femininity and thrill its white audience.

The final script of *White Dog* keeps some of these conceits while discarding others. Like the original story and screenplay, the film is about the relationship between a young, aspiring white actress named Julie Sawyer (played by the child TV star Kristy McNichol) and a nameless white German Shepherd dog, whom Julie rescues after hitting him with her car.[12] Uninjured and seemingly without an owner, Julie brings the dog home, and the two begin to bond.[13] The dog becomes Julie's protector, competing with her boyfriend for her attention, as well as protecting her from a rapist. Up until this point, the film follows the traditional dynamics of a dog redemption narrative, in which the person and the dog rescue each other. All seems well until the dog attacks Molly, Julie's Black female coworker. After that incident, Julie seeks help from two professional animal trainers named Carruthers and Keys. Carruthers, a grizzled white man, believes that attack dogs cannot be retrained, going so far as to encourage Julie to euthanize the dog. Right after that conversation, the dog overpowers Julie and attacks a Black man at the training facility. Upon witnessing the dog's behavior, the other trainer, Keys, agrees to take on the dog. This is where Fuller's intervention comes through: As a Black anthropologist and animal trainer, Keys explains to Julie that this is no ordinary attack dog; he is a "white dog." Much to Julie's shock, Keys explains that the term refers to the historical practice of dogs being weaponized by white people to track, capture, and kill enslaved Black people, revealing that the dog's violence is not an aberration. The remainder of the film centers on Julie's awakening to racism and the question of whether Keys can successfully train the racism out of the white dog.

Even with (or perhaps because of) Fuller's "nonracist approach," Paramount executives grew increasingly nervous about a dog movie that foregrounds race. In the midst of its production, Paramount hired David Crippens, the vice president and manager of the local PBS station, and Willis Edwards, president of the Beverly Hills–Hollywood NAACP chapter, as consultants on the film's representation of race. Both men read the script and met with Jeffrey Katzenberg, the head of production at Paramount. Davison (the producer) and the actor Paul Winfield (who played Keys) also provided notes, considering how Black audiences would respond to the film while the nation was gripped by the continuing murders of Black children in Atlanta. While Crippens did not believe the script was racist, he suggested that it clarify the Black animal trainer's motivations. Edwards, however, worried about unforeseen readings of the film that "could cause a distribution problem if the Black population were to collectively voice an objection to the subject matter."[14] Such readings would misunderstand its irony and symbolic logic and instead take it literally. As a solution, Edwards recommended removing the racial component and instead creating a conventional horror film. This feedback, taken very seriously by Paramount executives, enraged Fuller.

When Paramount executives decided to go with Fuller's version of the film, the Los Angeles chapter of the NAACP organized a media campaign and film boycott led by Willis Edwards—the same person whom Paramount brought in as a consultant. Edwards contended that "when you train a white dog to kill black folks, that gives the KKK and other white supremacist organizations ideas."[15] For Edwards, the allegorical part of the story is irrelevant—the dog in this film could pose concrete dangers to people in his community. Paul Winfield (again, the Black actor who played Keys) publicly stated that "the protective stance of the NAACP and other well-meaning groups is actually a disservice to black people."[16] Even the production of the film reflects a reductive conception of race, as though all

Black people would interpret it in the exact same way. Edwards's and Winfield's different reactions also reveal competing interpretations of the dog, either as a symbol of racism or a dangerous living being.

While Paramount may not have changed Fuller's version of the film, they seriously curtailed its audience. After previewing the film in Seattle and Denver to overwhelmingly positive reviews, they opened it at five suburban and downtown Detroit theaters for a one-week test: Paramount characterized these reviews and box office profits as "not good." Even though there were requests to screen the film at major film festivals, Paramount declined all requests, "claiming it did not justify the expense of release." Instead, they decided to directly release the film to VHS and television. After paying $2.5 million for broadcast rights in January 1984, NBC backed out of its plan to air the film, viewing it as a liability worth the sunk cost. Fuller was so infuriated and disillusioned with Hollywood that he left the United States and remained in Paris for thirteen years, effectively ending his US filmmaking career.[17]

The film was not screened in theaters in the United States until 1991, and even then, it was limited to a short Sam Fuller retrospective festival in New York City. In 2008, the Criterion Collection released a DVD version of the film and received a film heritage award from the National Society of Film Critics for doing so.[18] The film can now be streamed online through the Criterion Collection (which requires a subscription) or purchased as a DVD, making it still difficult to access. This reception history (or the lack thereof) reveals how from the beginning, there were competing interpretations of the film and the dog's role within it. It also explains why most people, even Fuller fans, have not seen *White Dog*. And finally, the film's backstory shows how there are clear generic expectations for what a dog redemption movie should look like—and that violating these conventions exacts a financial and artistic cost.

WHITE DOG AS CLASSIC CANINE REDEMPTION NARRATIVE; OR, WHO RESCUED WHOM?

Before turning to the ways in which *White Dog* upends the dog redemption narrative, I first want to show how it invokes the genre made famous by earlier Hollywood films. The opening of *White Dog* hinges on two moments of violence followed by redemptive rescue that serve as a catalyst for the remainder of the events that unfold. Julie Sawyer, the white female protagonist, saves the dog, and in turn, the dog saves Julie. In line with typical dog redemption narratives, race—by which I mean whiteness—is not discussed in the first part of the film. At the same time that whiteness is invisible, Julie's status as a normatively pretty and childlike white woman shapes her treatment by the male characters in the film—all of whom have strong opinions about what she should do with the dog. Crucially, none of these suggestions align with Julie's sense of what is best for herself. Meanwhile, the dog has no say in the matter; he is merely an allegorical figure to mediate questions of suffering, guilt, and responsibility.

The film opens with a yelp and the screeching of brakes, the sound of the dog being struck by a car on the dark and winding roads of the Hollywood Hills. Julie immediately pulls over and inspects the dog with a flashlight; he is a white German Shepherd. While it is not initially clear if the dog is alive, she quickly reverses her car to where he is lying motionless, scoops his heavy frame into her arms, places him in the car, and speeds off.

The opening action is thus motivated by an individual act of violence and then rescue. Like the dogs in the previous chapter, the white dog is primed to become a redemptive subject: He has been injured, and Julie must respond to his suffering.

Although she did not intend to hit the dog, Julie does not hesitate to do everything she can to save his life, immediately rushing him to a veterinary clinic. The scene at the vet office sets up the film as one invested in the question of how to assign guilt and what accountability looks like in the wake of harm. When Julie explains that she hit the dog, the white male veterinarian's reply is terse: "Well, you brought him in, you'll have to pay the bill." Julie is taken aback by the vet's condescending reminder that she will need to pay for the dog's treatment, responding indignantly, "Of course I brought him in. I hit him. It was my fault," marking the second time that she acknowledges guilt in this single scene. Part of the vet's response is gendered; as noted earlier, he is the first in a line of white men in the film to infantilize Julie by implying that she is not properly caring for the dog. At this point in the film, Sawyer's moral universe is relatively uncomplicated: She injured the dog and therefore believes that she should be the individual responsible for paying for his care, whether she owns him or not.

After it becomes clear that Julie will not find the dog's owner that night, she brings him home. Following the conventions of the canine redemption narrative, a few days later, the dog saves Julie's life. It is important to note that the threat Julie faces is sexual violence; her status as a besieged and innocent white woman is central to how the film portrays her. In this scene, a white male rapist breaks into Julie's home and begins attacking her. The dog hears the commotion and sets himself upon the man, pulling him off Julie, who is able to reach the phone and call the police. When the rapist escapes out the window, the dog bursts through it, as glass shatters around him in slow motion. The dog bites and holds the screaming man down until the police arrive and drag him away. Shot from ground-level, Julie comes rushing to the dog, whose white fur is covered in the white attacker's blood—an image that recurs throughout the film—but this is the only time that the dog's victim is white.[19] The over-the-top nature of this moment undercuts the emotional impact of what would ordinarily be a terrifying event. It is scary, to be sure, but it is also mixed with comedy (mocking the rapist's ineptness) and action-type stunt work. At the same time, this scene sends an important message, namely, that the dog is the only creature capable of protecting Julie. If *White Dog* were to remain a traditional canine redemption narrative, the film would have next resulted in Julie adopting the dog, naming him, and the two of them living happily ever after. But the fact that this does not happen is what makes *White Dog* more interesting. While *White Dog* initially deploys elements from traditional canine redemption narratives, the lines between good and evil, victim and perpetrator, become increasingly blurry as the film progresses.

CRACKS IN THE REDEMPTION NARRATIVE: WHITE TEARS AND WILLFUL IGNORANCE

By following the dog and Julie's story after the rescue, the film moves past the redemptive moment at which dog movies usually end. Instead, it introduces the violence of racism into the narrative through the white dog, tracing Julie's psychological development from one of white innocence to white guilt. Julie's relationship with the dog exposes her to a world from which her white femininity and class status (based on her upscale clothing and housing) had previously shielded her. Her character also serves a pedagogical purpose as "the audience stand-in," reflecting how the film moves into a didactic mode, clearly trying to make a point to its audience about the dangers of racial hatred.[20] Like the dog, Julie is both a symbol and a person. Julie's "awakening to the horror of racism,"[21] as Fuller once described her character arc, is consistent with his general philosophy of film, which he called "the greatest educational medium."[22] While this may be the case, Julie—and by extension, the audience's—education happens at the expense of Black lives.

The first time Julie sees the dog's violent side against a Black woman, she does not realize he is a "white dog." The attack occurs as Julie is working on a commercial with another actress, Molly, who is Black. She brings the dog with her and ties him up while she performs. As soon as Molly speaks, the dog's ears perk up. He breaks free from his tie-up and launches himself on the unsuspecting Molly, knocking both her and Julie to the ground. As the dog mauls Molly, the camera closes in on Julie's tear-stained face, which dramatically contrasts with the blood covering Molly's. This scene concludes as Julie weeps—her primary mode of expression in the film.[23] This painful moment foregrounds the radical insufficiency of white tears to end suffering.

In the wake of the attack, Julie and her boyfriend, Roland, debate whether she should keep the dog—at this point, neither one knows about his racist motivations. This ethical dilemma crystallizes the complexity of the film's approach to redemption: Guilt and innocence are not so easily adjudicated. While the dog was previously useful as a potential protector, now he is a liability. Roland argues that the dog cannot be reformed, but Julie refuses to acknowledge that the dog is dangerous.

Although this denial may be based on her emotional attachment to the dog, it also reveals that she can be dangerously reckless. In response to Roland's insistence that the dog not only cannot be cured but should be killed, Julie erupts: "Then they [the people who made him violent] should be put to sleep, not the dog!" This childlike outburst reflects Julie's unwillingness to take responsibility for the fact that she owns a dangerous dog. She believes that she has what it takes to cure him—and if not, she will find someone else who can, regardless of the costs.

Motivated by naive optimism—and still oblivious to the racist motivations for the attack—Julie brings the dog to an animal training facility owned by two men: Carruthers and Keys.[24] She first encounters Carruthers, an older, cantankerous white man. The specific way Julie describes the problem she is facing with the dog is important, asking Carruthers if he could "unteach [the dog] something bad that he's been taught to do." The euphemism "something bad" reflects the fact that Julie does have some knowledge that harboring a dangerous dog is morally wrong. A pained look comes over Carruthers's face as he registers what Julie is saying. "Good friend of mine had a German Shepherd for eight years," he recounts. "Lived with him. Slept with him. Hunted and fished with him. Did everything with him. Then one night that dog turned and chewed my friend's jugular out. That dog was an old attack dog," he whispers, the camera turning to the dog's muzzled face. "Can you help him?" Julie pleads. "Can't . . . can't nobody can unlearn a dog. Nobody." In Carruthers's experience, dogs like this one cannot and should not be trusted. Like Julie's boyfriend, Carruthers believes that the right thing to do is euthanize the dog. This is the third time that Sawyer is told by a white man that the dog can neither be saved nor changed.

Before Julie leaves the premises, she learns that her dog is not only an attack dog but a white dog. This realization marks the beginning of Julie's education about white supremacy—and once again, her knowledge comes at a cost to a Black character's physical safety. As Carruthers opens the door to his office to see Julie and the dog out, the viewer sees a Black man named Joe working outside. Mirroring his behavior with Molly, the dog launches himself on top of Joe and begins attacking him while he screams. This time, however, there are several witnesses present to recognize that this attack was racially motivated. The first person to try to explain his status as a "white dog" to Julie is Carruthers. Viscerally upset by the attack on Joe, Carruthers screams at Julie: "That ain't no attack dog you got! That's a white dog!" Julie does not get it. "Of course he's a white dog," she replies, referring to his physical appearance, not understanding the import of Carruthers's statement. He responds with frustration: "I don't mean his color. He's taught to attack and kill Black people!" Julie initially rejects the possibility of anti-Black violence occurring right before her eyes—a world in which overt racist attacks like that one occur is a vestige of the past. Instead of pausing to listen, she snaps back at Carruthers, calling the idea of a white dog "crazy" and something she "[doesn't] believe." This refusal to affirm Carruthers's statement is a classic response by a white person who is faced with the reality of race (much less racism). As Robin DiAngelo describes in her famous book on "white fragility," white people display "emotions such as anger, fear, and guilt" when confronted with racism's reality.[25] Julie is the epitome of the fragile white woman.

The next person to try to convince Julie that white dogs exist is Joe. In response to Julie's charge that it is crazy to call a dog racist, Joe stands up and appeals to empirical evidence and personal experience. Unwilling to tolerate Julie's ignorance, he responds directly to her: "What the hell you mean, huh? You see this scar, lady? You see this goddamn scar?" The camera zooms in on a large mass of scar tissue on his calf: "Well I got it when I was fourteen years old. A white dog did it. I'm going to call the police. I'm going to tell them we got a goddammed white dog here."[26] As Joe explains, white dogs are a historical reality that persists to this day. In Joshua Bennett's words, white dogs are "dogs that, as a result of those who claim ownership over their flesh and employ it, exploit it toward white-supremacist ends that are more or less inextricable from hegemonic whiteness as a set of sociopolitical protocols."[27] In other words, white dogs are inseparable from a racist hierarchy that places whiteness at the top and through violence, canine and otherwise, keeps Black people at the bottom.[28] There is nothing symbolic about this description here—for Joe, that particular white dog is an immediate threat.

It is at this pivotal moment that the film's hero, Keys, intervenes, arguing against calling the police and proclaiming that he can cure the white dog of his racism. He bends down to the dog's level, studying him carefully, as the tethered and muzzled dog barks and lunges toward him. The film cuts to Julie's tearful and dusty face. This is the first time that someone other than her has suggested that the dog could be retrained, but what retraining looks like has shifted dramatically for Julie. What initially seemed like the general problem of aggression, a behavioral issue familiar to Julie, becomes about racism. Still staring at the dog, Keys impassively says to Joe: "Take five weeks' vacation, Joe. If I don't break him, I'll shoot him." As Keys makes this promise to Joe, and by implication to the dog, the camera cuts to a close-up of Julie's stony face. She remains silent.

From this point forward, the responsibility for the white dog has been passed from Julie to Keys. The camera then turns to a close-up shot of Keys's eyes, then to a counter-shot of the dog's eyes, and then to a close-up shot of Keys and the dog face to face, their eyes locked on each other, foreshadowing their many battles and resembling western-style showdowns. Through these cinematic effects, *White Dog* goes to great lengths to make it clear from the outset that Keys's promise of redemption is going to end in violence for at least one of them.

Once Julie knows what white dogs are, the film addresses the question of how this knowledge will shape how she responds to Molly, the Black actress whom her dog attacked. Now that the dog is Keys's problem, Julie goes to visit Molly, whose injuries were so severe that she is recovering in a hospital. While Julie was perfectly capable of confessing her culpability when it came to hitting the dog with her car, she refuses to take accountability for her role in a racially motivated attack. Race haunts the conversation but is not named, because Julie refuses to talk about it. At the beginning of the scene, Molly is stretched out in a hospital bed, with large white gauze bandages on her left

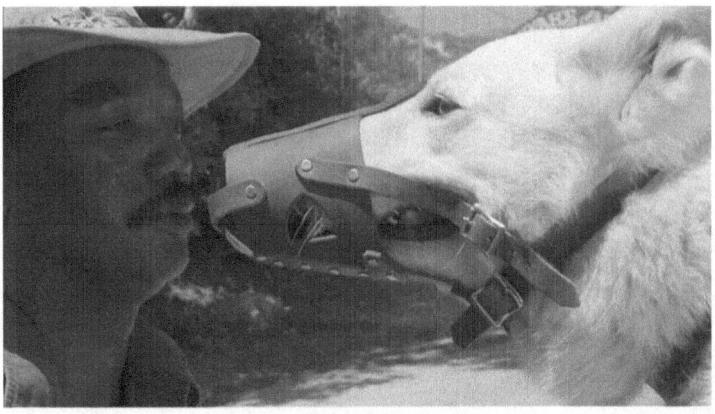

FIGURE 2.1. Keys encounters the dog for the first time.

Source: Screen grab.

cheek, neck, and arm. "I hope you didn't bring that damn dog with you," she quips, remarkably good-natured about what has happened. Julie brings flowers and places them alongside the dozens of other bouquets that line the windowsill. Turned away from Molly, she says nothing.

At first, it seems like Julie might confess the truth to Molly. Julie slowly turns around and looks at her friend with a wounded expression on her face, as though she is about to start speaking. Molly sees her expression and tries to comfort her: "[Julie] Sawyer, don't make me feel any worse with that long, guilty face of yours. It wasn't your fault. It was an accident." This is the perfect moment to admit her guilt, but instead Julie accepts comfort from the Black woman she harmed. Julie's white feelings are once again the center of the scene.

This is now the third time that the responsibility for facing the dog's racist violence has been placed on a Black person—first Joe, then Keys, and now Molly. "Molly—" Julie interjects, seemingly about to confess her guilt to Molly, but she is interrupted. "Sawyer," Molly says, "Don't ask if there's anything you can do for me. You've done it. You're here." This statement, "you've done it," can be read on two levels: To Molly, it refers to Julie's presence at the hospital, but to Julie it might also refer to her role in causing Molly's injury. At this point, Molly finally asks Julie the dreaded question. "You know," she muses, "I've gone over it in my head a hundred times. What do you think spooked that mutt?" The camera turns to a close-up of Julie's expressionless face, cloaked in the shadows. "I don't know," she lies.

This scene reflects an important critique of white liberals like Julie who fancy themselves on the "right" side of history while willfully denying that racism exists the moment they are implicated in it. As Susanne Schwertfeger notes, "[Julie's] behavior illustrates Toni Morrison's observation on the habit of ignoring race in social or literal discourse or research, as being (mis)understood as a graceful or liberal gesture. As a consequence, not only is the black body again enforced to 'invisibility through silence,' but '[a]ccording to this logic, every well-bred instinct argues against noticing and forecloses adult discourse.'"[29]

Julie will not admit the truth because she is so invested in preserving the appearance of her own white innocence. Molly, forced to submit to white liberal conceptions of politeness, does not push back. If the film were to align with the traditional pattern of redemption narratives, this scene would have depicted Julie tearfully confessing her guilt to Molly, who in turn would forgive her. But to apologize would require that Julie acknowledge not only her individual culpability but also her inheritance of the structural privileges that come with her whiteness, including the fact that this is the first time she has seriously thought about racism.

Furthermore, even if Julie were to confess her responsibility for the racially motivated attack, it is not clear that this would have led to redemption, the cleansing of her own guilt. In this respect, redemption narratives share a feature of the melodrama, which Linda Williams describes as a "compulsion to 'reconcile the irreconcilable'—that is, its tendency to find solutions to problems that cannot really be solved without challenging the older ideologies of moral certainty to which melodrama wishes to return."[30] Redemption is fundamentally inadequate because dismantling racist structures requires a willingness on the part of white people to sit with moral ambiguity—that even if our intentions are good, we still participate in and uphold racist systems.

WHAT DOES IT MEAN TO TRAIN A SYMBOL? OR, THE OVERDETERMINED WHITE DOG

Dog training and the possibility of redemption are intertwined in Fuller's film. The relationship is fundamentally negative: It is about ridding the dog of a sin (racism) that is manifest in a form of behavior (mauling Black people), not necessarily the cleansing of guilt. The film also does not explore the potential for this individual dog to live a fulfilling life with a human being. Although there is a personal relationship between Julie and the dog, that relationship is inseparable from canine violence. It is also at this point in the film, right after Julie visits Molly and when Keys begins training the white dog, that the dog's symbolic status is foregrounded. He is less an individual than a metonym for the legacy of chattel slavery, what James Madison and countless politicians after him refer to as "America's original sin."[31] The film emphasizes the dog's status as a symbol by his remaining nameless (neither Julie nor Keys name him) and his being referred to via his literary counterparts (Jekyll and Hyde, the Hound of the Baskervilles), mythical creatures (a monster), or ontological status (a white dog).

The didactic quality of the film is made explicit in a conversation between Julie and Keys in which, once again, Julie receives a lesson about racism from a Black character. "I don't understand," she says. "One minute, he's gentle as a lamb. The next minute, he's a monster." Keys has a different take: "He's not the monster. He was made into one by a two-legged racist," echoing Julie's earlier conversation with Roland about punishing the person who made the dog violent. In Keys's interpretation, white people are the monsters, racism is a disease, and the dog is simply the instrument for their crimes. As an instrument, the white dog can be retrained, and the results of this experiment might potentially deter people from trying to create white dogs in the first place. Julie is still skeptical, refusing to accept Keys's perspective: "You know, I don't understand how that can happen. I really don't. How could someone turn a dog into a racist?" Here, Keys provides the historical context that Sawyer sorely lacks: "Well, over a hundred years ago, they raised dogs to catch runaway slaves. Then they progressed. To track down runaway black convicts." Julie absorbs the information and then somewhat sheepishly asks: "What about runaway white convicts?" The camera pans to Keys's face, as he tilts his head sideways and chuckles, not even bothering to respond to a question that only a sheltered white woman like Julie would pose. Instead, Keys continues with his history about the creation of white dogs in the United States: "Well, almost overnight, they graduated to a vicious breed of watch dogs trained to tear apart any blacks within sight." "Does he attack any other color?" Julie asks, still unwilling to believe that a dog could be trained to embody and enact US racism. "No," Keys answers. "Dogs live in a black and white world. Unlike us, they live in it visually, and not racially." In the universe of the film, dogs can literally only see in black and white, making it easy to train them to attack a single color. The fact that this is scientifically inaccurate does not matter; the film is not actually interested in the details of canine perception.[32]

Because it is true that dogs were used to hunt runaway enslaved people, it might seem like *White Dog* is accessing this real history. But in fact, this distorted version of canine perception both misunderstands how dogs work and displaces the solution for systemic racism onto educating individuals. Keys's description of how white dogs are trained to "hate Black skin" is important for understanding how the film positions the dog in relation to racism. As Keys explains: "Find a black wino who desperately needs a fix... then pay him to beat that dog of yours when he was a puppy.... As that dog grew up, that methodological seed of beating by blacks planted the seed of fear in him. And that fear became hate and that hate conditioned him to attack the color black before..." "Before a black can attack him," Julie chimes in, slowly understanding how this process works. The creation of the white dog thus depends on Black disenfranchisement and desperation. The Black individuals involved must also actively participate in the creation of the weapons that will later be used against them. As a way of "deconditioning" the dog, Keys then needs to desensitize the dog to Black skin, which he does by putting his own body at risk, slowly exposing more and more skin and seeing how much it takes for the (muzzled) dog to attack him. Based on his logic, Keys explains that if racists learn that white dogs can be untrained, then they will be less likely to create them in the first place. Perhaps. But this premise does not account for the other ways in which racism inserts itself in US society, as though racists would not (and indeed do) find other means to wound and kill Black people.

This description of how the white dog is "programmed" captures the ways in which race in the United States is constituted in the binary terms of black and white.[33] There is no indication that well-meaning individuals like Julie can perpetuate racism even while seeking to overcome it. Bénédicte Boisseron describes how Keys's training methods—and the film itself—rests on this highly reductive understanding of race: "Keys exposing his bare hand in order to teach the dog how to disassociate black skin from the feeling of aggression demonstrates a literal form of racial discourse. The dog becomes the essentialist voice of racism in the film. The animal returns to basics, ultimately presenting race as a natural component rather than a social

FIGURE 2.2. Keys "training the racism" out of the white dog.
Source: Screen grab.

construct."³⁴ Furthermore, this training method also places the actual labor of antiracist training, and the inevitable violence it involves, on the Black person. In the universe of the film, Julie is not involved in this training process and incurs no personal risk. Redemption in *White Dog* thus involves the overcoming of the United States' racist past by creating a world free of racism—all represented in the drama between Keys and the white dog.

CHRISTIANITY AND ANTI-BLACKNESS

Although Keys has his plan for training the racism out of the dog, the dog does not go along with his plan and escapes from the facility. His first action is to locate a Black man and kill him. This dramatic attack is particularly important because it occurs in a church and is a damning critique of Christian institutions' participation in racist violence. Susanne Schwertfeger also locates a religious dimension to the training itself, referring to Keys's training as "a secular equivalent of the religious practice of exorcism."[35]

As the dog trots down a long sidewalk after his escape from Keys's training facility, the camera pans to a head-on close-up of a man wearing dress shoes and a suit. The audience cannot see his face or the color of his skin initially. Then we hear the dog growling, and the camera quickly pans up to a close-up of a Black man's face. The order of this shot is important, demonstrating how the film asks the audience to focus on identifying race as they try to anticipate how the dog will react—there is a kind of spectatorial satisfaction when the audience realizes they were "right" even about something so horrible.[36] As the camera shifts from the man's terrified expression to the dog's snarling face—paralleling Keys's earlier showdown with the dog—the man turns and sprints away, the dog following behind him in close pursuit. Desperate, the man darts into an empty church, and the dog leaps upon him in the doorway. We see the dog tearing at the man's legs and neck as he screams and tries to writhe away. Instead of capturing the bloody attack, however, the camera pans up to the various saints lining the church walls, who are silent and immobile witnesses to the attack.

As the man shrieks in agony, the camera settles on the altar, above which is a huge stained-glass window of St. Francis of Assisi, complete with a white dog by his side. While arguably melodramatic, the insertion of the white dog into the stained-glass window symbolizes the enmeshment of Christianity and anti-Blackness. Here the figural white dog is portrayed at St. Francis's side at the same time that his literal instantiation murders a Black man. The dog is not the rescuer like he was with Julie but instead the attacker. There's suffering, but it is not redemptive, because the man is Black. This is another reminder of the ways in which redemption is not available to everyone.

FAILURES OF THE CANINE REDEMPTION NARRATIVE ○ 75

FIGURE 2.3. St. Francis and the white dog.
Source: Screen grab.

Next the viewer does not see the man himself—only Keys's horrified reaction as he stands over the man's body, the camera moving around him to capture his expression, as he breathes heavily, sweating and weeping. The camera zooms in to get a close-up shot of Keys's tear-stained face until all we can see are his eyes and nose, as he looks at the result of his experiment. In this film, tears are a sign of the futility of individual action against larger social systems. And here Keys is forced to recognize the fact that his good intentions led to the loss of human life—another Black victim sacrificed in the name of his experiment. And yet, like a mad scientist, Keys sedates the dog and brings him back to the training facility, unwilling to give up.

SANCTIMONY AND WHITENESS

The question of culpability returns in the penultimate scene of the movie, in which Julie meets the man responsible for training the white dog. This is another moment of big white feelings, but this time, Julie expresses self-righteous anger rather than tears. The white dog's owner catches Julie right as she is rushing out of her house to watch the final test to determine whether the white dog has been cured. Instead of the racist monster she imagined, Julie is greeted by a grandfatherly white man holding a box of chocolates, flanked by his two young granddaughters. The man is full of smiles and social graces, tipping his hat while introducing himself and his granddaughters, both of whom sweetly lisp, "Hello, Miss Sawyer" in unison. Even though Julie is impatient to get to the dog, she is visibly charmed by the girls. Explaining that she's in a hurry and must leave, one of the girls inquires quietly, "Where's my dog?"

This question stops Julie dead in her tracks, the camera behind her and closing in on her face as she slowly turns around, looking at them with an entirely different expression than before, as she registers the juxtaposition between the family's respectable appearance and their abhorrent beliefs. The grandfather seizes this moment to continue: "The SPCA says you have our dog, Miss Sawyer. He ran away from the trailer park. We're very grateful you took such good care of him. We brought you some chocolates," stretching out his hand in offering. The fact that the dog was raised in a trailer park adds an additional social commentary by connecting class status to racism, providing a contrast to Julie's conception of her own polite liberal beliefs.

Julie pauses for a moment and asks the man if he trained the dog, the camera zooming in on his smiling, bespectacled face. "I sure did," he says with folksy pride, "since he was just a puppy." There is a pause, and Julie softly replies, "To be a white dog," the camera turning to a close-up of the man's face. His

FAILURES OF THE CANINE REDEMPTION NARRATIVE ❧ 77

FIGURE 2.4. The racist man who trained the white dog, with his two grandchildren, seen from Julie's point of view.
Source: Screen grab.

smile falters for a moment, and the camera moves between shot-countershots of Julie's questioning face and the man as he figures out what to say. Recovering his smile, he responds: "And the best of the lot!"

At this admission Julie explodes in a fit of rage, throws the chocolates and screams: "You bastard! You sick son of a bitch! You got two puppies there, you gonna teach them to be as sick as you are? Do you know what your grandfather did to that dog? He turned that dog into a monster, a killer! Don't let him turn you into monsters either. Don't listen to a damn word he says about anything. Not a damn word!" In analyzing this scene, Susanne Schwertfeger argues that "those little children again stress the topics of education and socialization, as the omnipresent motif of the animal training, and thus the viewer is inevitably reminded of Keys's notion that the racist training starts with the puppies."³⁷ This charged confrontation also allows Julie to reoccupy the moral high ground she lost after lying to Molly, which she does through a heavy-handed species inversion: The children are strongly identified with animals ("pups") who have yet to be trained into their grandfather's racist ideology, whereas the dog operates as a symbol for white human racists.

Julie's confrontation with the white dog's trainer reflects a striking contrast to her interaction with Molly in the hospital. In both cases the dog has hurt—even killed—people under Julie's supervision. Whereas that moment in the hospital could have been an opportunity to have a real, albeit uncomfortable, conversation about anti-Black racism and culpability, which Julie loses by lying to her friend, here Julie screams at the man with dramatic righteousness and distances herself from any individual guilt. While one might be tempted to read this second moment as redemptive for Julie—as an expiatory scene where she not only tells the man that he cannot buy back the dog from her but also that she has found a way to cure the dog—that would be an overly simplistic interpretation of redemption, one that lets Julie off the hook. It is insufficient for Julie simply to call out the racism of others when she is unwilling to interrogate her own internalized racism or to be held accountable for her own actions.

WHEN REDEMPTION FAILS

The conclusion to the film reflects the strain that the dog redemption narrative experiences when the dog is used to address a complex social phenomenon like anti-Black racism. After countless days of hard physical labor retraining the dog, through which Keys increasingly reveals more of his skin to the unmuzzled dog while feeding him hamburgers, Keys achieves success. The dog no longer tries to attack him. Keys takes his experiment a step further, asking another (random) Black man to face the muzzled dog again, wearing protective body armor. The dog does not try to attack him, much to Keys's delight. He believes that he has successfully ridded the dog of his racism. For his final experiment, Keys brings Julie and Carruthers (Keys's business partner) into the facility, asking them to see the fruits of his work.

In an elaborately staged moment, the dog is given an opportunity to prove that he is no longer racist by approaching Keys without aggression. Keys has Julie and Carruthers enter the training ring. The dog is unmuzzled. As other critics have pointed out, this scene, which occurs in a large circus ring surrounded by the Hollywood Hills, is reminiscent of the ending of Sergio Leone's spaghetti western *The Good, the Bad, and the Ugly* (1966), complete with the same musical composer for the soundtrack.[38] The scene begins with a low-angle shot where one can only see Keys's feet as he stands facing the dog head-on, recalling a classic western shootout, as well as mirroring the sidewalk confrontation that led to the death of the Black man in the church. These effects prime the viewer for an epic showdown that both cues expectations of violence and also distances the audience from "the real" by drawing from the western genre.

Keys and the dog are positioned at opposite ends of the ring, ready for their face-off. When let loose, the dog sprints directly toward Keys; the camera turns to Julie and then to Carruthers, both of whom look terrified. The dog barrels toward Keys in slow motion, his mouth bared in a snarl, and Keys, realizing what might happen, grabs the pistol in his pocket—he is the only person armed and therefore responsible for protecting everyone. As the dog approaches, his face slowly morphs from a snarl into a friendly expression, his eyes soft and mouth open. Despite the troubling beginning of the experiment, in which it seems like the dog might attack Keys, Julie is convinced that the dog has been cured: "You did it, Mr. Keys!" she exclaims, appearing more childlike than ever.

At the sound of her voice, however, the dog whips around toward Julie, growling and baring his teeth. In a long shot, the dog charges toward Julie, again filmed in slow motion, as Keys readies his pistol. Still in slow motion, the dog slackens his pace and stops in front of Julie and starts barking at her in excitement, his face transformed as he recognizes her. She then bends down and wraps her arms around him and buries her face in the dog's neck, visually mirroring the earlier scene where she hugged him after he saved her from the rapist. As Julie embraces the dog (she is the only character to have this kind of physical contact with him), the camera zooms in on his expression, which changes as he sets his sights on

FIGURE 2.5. Keys readies his pistol to shoot the dog.

Source: Screen grab.

Carruthers—who closely resembles the old white man who "trained" him. In another slow-motion shot, the dog pulls away from Julie and charges toward Carruthers, forcing Keys to ready his pistol once again. Julie slowly rises, realizing what is about to happen. In a ground shot, the camera pans to the dog's body as he leaps onto Carruthers and begins tearing at his flesh as Carruthers screams out Keys's name. Filmed from Carruthers's point of view on the ground with the dog on top of him, the viewer sees Carruthers's bloodied hands and the dog's red mouth.

Keys readies his pistol and fires twice—the music stops, and the viewer hears the same pained canine yelp that opened the film—and then everything goes silent. Julie runs toward the dog in slow motion, screaming though no sound exits her mouth, unable to save the dog or prevent him from attacking Carruthers. In silence, Julie and Keys lift the dog's outstretched body off Carruthers, who is gravely injured but alive. As they

FIGURE 2.6. The white dog breathes his last breath, as Julie and Keys rescue Carruthers.

Source: Screen grab.

FIGURE 2.7. The final image of the white dog.
Source: Screen grab.

place the dog on the ground, he is still breathing, his mouth curled in a threatening grimace. The dog then turns his head and looks directly at the camera, which zooms on his face as he lets out a last breath and then dies.

The film closes with a helicopter shot of the arena as Julie and Keys help Carruthers limp away, an arm over each of their shoulders. The dog, stretched out in the middle of the ring, is abandoned. The camera zooms in on a shot from above of the dog's face and neck, riddled with two bloody bullet holes. The dog's mouth is covered in blood, his face is still frozen in a snarl, and his eyes are blank and open. The film concludes with a shot of the dog's corpse, stretched out in the center of the arena. It then zooms out to the arena and the surrounding Hollywood Hills, silent witnesses to his death. From there, the credits begin to roll, the soundtrack starts up again, and the background fades to black and white, returning to the dog's ostensibly binary world.

ON THE DEATH OF THE DOG

While the white dog's death is upsetting, it is much less so than the canine deaths in other dog redemption movies. There are several reasons why this is the case. First, the allegorical conceit of the film makes it difficult to connect to the dog as an actual dog. He does not have a name and seems more like a human's weapon than a sentient being. Second, the dog is never depicted as wholly innocent—he is always on the verge of a violent eruption. What is usually so heartbreaking in films that stage canine deaths is the fact that the dogs were innocent; this is not the case in the world of *White Dog*, which suggests that if he could not be reformed, he had to die. This shifting back and forth between the dog as real and allegorical contributes to the film's contradictory ending: The dog is always both. As such, the audience cannot experience the same degree of pathos for him.

The film also rests on another crucial slippage: between the human and the canine. In a 1982 interview, Fuller describes his conflicting attitudes toward his canine star actor in a revealing way: "The dog . . . I directed him like a human being. It was an attack dog. There was a signal for him to pounce. You had to be careful on the set because the slightest noise that sounded like the signal could make him attack . . . me! I talked to him like an actor. Did you notice the close ups of his eyes in the film? I looked him right in the eye. I wanted the dog to be shown as a thinking being. Me, I hate movies like *Lassie*."[39]

This statement reflects a tension that troubles the entire film. In one sense, the dog is a human—a "thinking being" whom Fuller treats as an individual in his own right by "talk[ing] to him like an actor" and "look[ing] him right in the eye." As Fuller's statement also reveals, when the dog is an individual, a human being, he is not allowed to be a dog. Fuller's concluding claim that he "hates movies like *Lassie*" suggests that the dogs in those films are the opposite of the white dog: not thinking beings. At the same time, Fuller acknowledges the fact that the dog is very much not a person: "It" was trained to attack, and his identity as a dog makes him a potential source of danger to Fuller himself.

ON FAILED REDEMPTION

Is this still a dog redemption narrative? My answer is no. There is no sense in the film that the dog's death is a sacrifice that provides any redemptive resolution for humans or canines. Instead, the film organizes itself in such a way as to refuse to take on a "real" version of white labor or accountability. It uses the dog and the Black man as ways of evading any suffering in which white persons actually have to "stay with the trouble" by registering their own capacities of harm or exploring what justice might look like.[40] If truly grappling with the legacies of slavery and white supremacy would mean fully coming to terms with what that entails, we have a split second in which things slip from allegorical to real, when the white characters actually encounter the white dog's aggression and might imagine the violence of being attacked by the dog. But the film quickly retreats from that impulse and kills the dog. As Bénédicte Boisseron argues, "*White Dog* was a graphic materialization of what American consciousness was not yet ready to face, namely a deeply ingrained history of violence—and even more trouble—some 'canine' violence against its black population."[41] Accordingly, the dog has to be killed as a scapegoat to save Carruthers's life. This death undoes the experiential knowledge that the white audience briefly felt during Carruthers's attack, letting us off the hook from further imagining ourselves as the dog's victim.

Ultimately, *White Dog* relies on producing emotions rather than actions. The white audience members can therefore "feel good" about the fact that we learned something about racism without doing anything to change our behavior. This set of limitations built into the film's structure suggests that redemption narratives, with their emphasis on the moral transformation of the individual, cannot provide the tools for dealing with the legacies of US chattel slavery and systemic racism. And in failing to engage with those legacies, they are harmful to humans and canines alike.

Like conventional redemption narratives, *White Dog* focuses on individual reformation through suffering or punishment in lieu of collective structural change. The film's wager is allegorical: If the racism can be trained out of the individual white dog, then other racist Americans can also be reformed. Antiracism, therefore, is a matter of retraining individual hearts and minds.[42] But at the same time that *White Dog* adopts some of the themes and structures of the dog redemption narrative, it also subverts the generic conventions by introducing a dog who is not only dangerous but racist—and whose death represents a moral failure. The film rests on both a historical reality (white dogs did exist) and also an incorrect understanding of canine perception (dogs did not attack Black people based on the color of their skin, nor do they have a conception of race). This dynamic demonstrates how the film demands that the dog be a symbol of white supremacy and an actual dog at one and the same time—a theme that recurs throughout this book. In blending historical realism with allegory, *White Dog* ultimately produces contradictory messaging. On the one hand, the recourse to US history makes it possible to imagine the dog as an actual dog—a descendant of this racist national lineage. On the other hand, the film's return to the allegorical enables the displacement of racism to be perpetuated, evading the question of how white people should hold ourselves accountable for our role in perpetuating racist violence.

PART II
MAKING DOGS PRESENT

3

RELATIONAL REDEMPTION

On April 10, 2024, the celebrity dog trainer Cesar Millan participated in a tower lighting ceremony at the Empire State Building as part of his press tour to celebrate the twentieth anniversary of his Emmy-nominated reality TV show, *The Dog Whisperer*.[1] Before hitting the switch to light up the tower, Millan gave a short speech. In his remarks, he explained that only in the United States, and only through dogs, could a previously undocumented Mexican immigrant like him experience such a meteoric rise to success:

> I can't thank enough the dogs of this world because they gave me such a beautiful opportunity just like God did with this incredible mission, but the dogs have definitely opened the doors of a great country in the world, and that's one member of society that keeps us united. No matter where I go in the world, as soon as there's a dog in it, everybody talks about a dog and everybody neutralizes the conversation, and then they just ask me "Cesar, what should I do right now?" Money, fame, power really doesn't matter if you're low income, middle class, super wealthy. The dog doesn't understand that concept.... Now more than ever we need our animals to live with healthy humans, to live with

happy humans, and to live with humans that have a good heart and maintain the hope as high as you can.²

Speaking in the midst of a 2024 presidential election campaign characterized by Donald Trump's xenophobic rhetoric and political polarization, Millan claims that dogs are not only the key to his personal success but to national unity.³ In other words, Millan emphasizes the role that dogs play in upholding and contesting what Robert N. Bellah called "American civil religion": the beliefs, symbols, and rituals that Americans recognize as holding transcendent value.⁴ While these values can serve as a point of connection that transcend difference, they also reveal areas of dissent, fracture, and exclusion in US society.⁵ Millan's remarks suggest that dogs are seen as apolitical and can therefore exist separate from identity politics.⁶ But at what cost to the dogs?

Millan's brand is rooted in a form of dominance-based training where the human must become their dog's "pack leader."⁷ This training philosophy—which involves kicking, choking, and forcing the dog into a state of "learned helplessness"—has long been criticized by veterinary behaviorists, trainers, and people in the animal welfare community, who point out that the "pack leader" concept came from flawed studies of wolves in captivity.⁸ In 2009, five years after the first season of *The Dog Whisperer* aired, the American Society of Veterinary Behavior went so far as to release a position statement denouncing dominance-based training.⁹ Despite these expert interventions rooted in evidence-based science, Millan's "pack theory" took off, with words like "alpha dog" and "pack leader" becoming part of the US vernacular.¹⁰ If we consider the appeal of Millan's training methods through the lens of redemption, the draw of TV shows like *The Dog Whisperer* comes into sharper focus.

Millan's methods provide the audience with the outcome that the dog redemption narrative primes us to expect: the transformation of the dog (ridding him of his problem behaviors) and the restoration of multispecies familial harmony.[11]

Indeed, Millan's TV episodes are mini–dog redemption narratives themselves, in which the dog is miraculously transformed and familial peace is restored—all within the confines of a single episode. Every episode of Millan's show takes on an extreme case of a "problem dog": someone who is aggressive toward people or other creatures and/or who has intense separation anxiety that manifests in destroying the house or other severe behavioral issues. Invariably, these issues produce intense conflict between human family members that lead to ultimatums and threats of divorce, shaking the family's foundation to its core. Millan does not work with dogs who are in need of basic manners training—the dogs he meets are far past that point. Instead, Millan arrives when he is the family's last hope: If he cannot retrain the dog, then the dog may need to be rehomed, dropped at a shelter, or even euthanized. While these examples are extreme, the ultimate goal is always the same: to teach the humans how to become "alpha" dogs and to train the dogs to adjust to the family's expectations of peaceful domestic life. This is also a deeply masculinist and anthropocentric vision of dog training that privileges the "alpha male" as the natural leader of the household.

What is so captivating about Millan's shows is the seeming ease with which he rids dogs of their problems through an (allegedly) straightforward formula: "exercise, discipline, and affection, in that order." Through this succinct prescription, Millan sells the fantasy that all disobedient dogs can be "cured."[12] This redemptive vision conforms with Millan's own "rags to riches" life story, supporting a masculinist, masterful ethos that offers a bootstraps version of dog training. But the kind of redemption that Millan sells in the form of an instantly well-behaved dog relies on punishment-based training techniques. The fact that Millan is so popular raises important questions about the kinds of relationships people in the United States want with their dogs and about what we are willing to accept in exchange for the appearance of "obedience."

Millan's fame also highlights how dog training and redemption have become part of US mass culture, offering a form of dog redemption as a formula that is narratively complete and emotionally satisfying. Like the structure of classic dog redemption narratives described in earlier chapters, Millan's shows always conclude with a happy ending, with one crucial difference: The redemptive moment occurs not when the lost dog returns home to her family but instead when the bad dog is reformed and therefore able to remain at home. Even though these episodes are surely heavily edited, the fact that each one follows the same narrative formula suggests that this form of redemption is the primary cultural script for how Americans understand their relationships with dogs. Or at the very least, the show speaks to the strong human desire for relationships with dogs that are uncomplicated and easy. If dogs become vessels of unconditional love and loyalty, then they require very little in return—but such a formulation of dog-human relationships is far too simplistic. As canine behavior experts have noted in their forceful repudiations of Millan's methods over the past twenty years, the forms of training he promotes produce short-lived effects.[13] What looks like training is human violence; what redemption masks is canine suffering.[14]

Millan and his work provide an entry into the US public's investment in redemption narratives about dog training. The texts that are the subject of this chapter, Vicki Hearne's *Adam's*

Task (1986) and Donna Haraway's *Companion Species Manifesto* (2003) and *When Species Meet* (2008), are less well known outside of academic spaces, but they offer more nuanced (and at times confounding) corollaries to the dog redemption stories seemingly made possible through Millan's training methods. The dog training worlds frequented by Hearne and Haraway are also filled with predominantly white women with time and money, demographics that Hearne and Haraway acknowledge and problematize. These limiting socioeconomic factors might offer another reason why Millan's methods are more popular: They are transferable to everyone because they require a lower time and financial investment.

Although dog training is the practice through which redemption is made possible for both Hearne and Haraway, they draw from different religious sources to orient their theologies of training—Calvinism and Catholicism, respectively. In *Adam's Task*, Hearne describes a form of what I call "relational redemption" that allows for the restoration of a prelapsarian language between humans and animals, a recovery of a time before humans sinned against God and subsequently lost their authority over animals. In contrast, Haraway's vision of training looks less like a linguistic process of command and response and more like the affective merging of the flesh and the spirit made possible through play—what she calls a "material-semiotic" process that allows dogs to express their full potential and people to escape the isolation of the human condition.

Instead of building toward a redemptive conclusion like Millan's television shows, both Hearne and Haraway emphasize instances when training fails—when the dog and human do not understand what the other is trying to communicate. These moments warn us of the dangers of assuming that training is about teaching dogs to be more humanlike, as well as remind us of the potentially generative lessons that arise from moments when interspecies communication falters. In Hearne and Haraway's accounts, training is a nonlinear process—a feature that disqualifies them for entertaining television but is truer to the experience of training. Rather than using dogs to mediate human social conflicts (*White Dog*) or to offer a universal training formula for domestic harmony (Millan), Hearne and Haraway focus on specific dogs: Salty the German Shorthaired Pointer and Ms. Cayenne Pepper the Border Collie. While Haraway is troubled by the unequal power dynamics in human-canine relationships, Hearne views them as part of the divine order outlined in the Book of Genesis. For this reason, training for Haraway looks different than it does for Hearne, whose methods are more aligned with practices endorsed by Millan.[15] In Hearne and Haraway's versions of training, it is a transformative process that makes possible the creation of an interspecies language that merges human and canine ways of knowing and being. Both authors strive to make the dogs present as actual dogs—or at least, that is the goal.[16] Through what I call "canine presence," relational redemption is possible, transforming both human and dog.[17]

AFTER THE FALL: VICKI HEARNE'S COVENANTAL THEOLOGY OF TRAINING

From the outset, Hearne insists that her audience take dogs seriously as intelligent, judging, and thinking creatures who are formed with and by humans. In *Adam's Task: Calling Animals by Name* (1986), which has become a foundational text in animal studies,[18] Hearne focuses on dog training as the bridge between theoretical and practical knowledge.[19] Hearne's unique claim that there is an intrinsic relationship between philosophy and dog training motivated her to write a book that strives to bridge these two seemingly disparate fields. Through her own experiences, Hearne observes that the philosophers who theorize animal life and the animal trainers who work with "real" animals have not found meaningful ways to talk to one another. In her experience of academia, it was frowned upon to use any sort of anthropomorphic language that attributes a "concept of self" to animals. In contrast, Hearne's experiences as a trainer of dogs and horses were filled with people who used "highly anthropomorphic, morally loaded language." As she explains, trainers speak of animals in such a way that recognizes that "animals are capable not only of activities requiring 'IQ'—a rather arid conception—but also of a complex and delicate (though not infallible) moral understanding that is so inextricably a function of their relationships with human beings that it may well be said to constitute those relationships."[20] Although she acknowledges that dogs are decidedly not human, Hearne maintains that dogs possess vibrant inner lives that warrant attention, care, and love.

As signaled by the title *Adam's Task*, the Book of Genesis is crucial for understanding Hearne's "theology" of animal training and the types of training practices she advocates. In her exegesis of the creation stories in Genesis 1 and 2, Hearne states that "Adam gave names to the creatures, and they all responded to their names without objection, since in this dominion to command and to recognize were one action. There was no gap between the ability to command and the full acknowledgement of the personhood of the being so commanded."[21] Hearne thus reads this prelapsarian moment (i.e., before the Fall) as an instance of what animal training should aspire to: a relational process of mutual recognition between the human and the animal, or, as Hearne puts it, between "persons."

And yet, as anyone familiar with the Adam and Eve story is well aware, this idyllic interspecies arrangement does not last. In her reading of Genesis 3, Hearne argues that as a result of Adam and Eve's primordial act of disobedience, most animals "turned pretty irrevocably from human command . . . refus[ing] to come when called, to recognize our naming." In Hearne's terms, the Fall broke down the mutual recognition between humans and animals—and this communication breakdown is linguistic in nature. Hearne describes the Fall as a kind of reverse domestication: "The tiger, the wolf and the field mouse as well as, of course, the grasshopper refuse to come when called, to recognize our naming. One may say that before the Fall, all animals were domestic, that nature was domestic. After the Fall, wildness was possible, and most creatures chose it, but a few did not. The dog, the horse, the burro, the elephant, the ox and a few others agreed to go along with humanity anyway."[22] In Hearne's retelling of the creation story, domesticated animals like the dog and the horse chose to have the capacity to respond to human commands—but this capacity to respond, to restore what was lost in the Fall, can only happen through training.

For Hearne, the act of naming makes the human-canine relationship possible in the first place. The creation story in Genesis is therefore central to the importance of naming for her theology of training:

> My talk of the change from utterances such as "Belle, Sit!" to "Belle, Go find!" is an example of names projecting the creature named into more glorious contexts. . . . But I think our impulse is also conservative, an impulse to return to Adam's divine condition. I can't imagine how we would do that, or what it would be like, but linguistic anthropology has found out some things about illiterate peoples that suggest at least names that really

call, language that is genuinely invocative and uncontaminated by writing and thus by the concept of names as labels rather than genuine invocations.²³

Naming becomes a problem for Hearne only when it is done in the service of labeling a dog, treating "it" as a passive object or abstract category ("the dog").²⁴ In contrast, Hearne foregrounds the importance of naming because it gives "the soul room for expansion"—it opens up the possibility of an animal's being recognized as an individual subject who enters into a relationship with a human being through training.²⁵

As Hearne explains, the distinction of a name being an invocation versus a label is a matter of life and death for dogs. In an anecdote about a friend who works in a shelter, Hearne describes how the shelter manager instituted a mandatory training program that required potential adopters to complete at least some rudimentary dog training before being granted the privilege of naming the dogs. The kind of training that interests Hearne is that which allows the dogs to find their own names, which can only happen in relationship with other people—through canine presence. When a dog is given a name, the possibilities for an interspecies language between the human and animal deepen, moving from simple commands like "Belle, sit" to opportunities for greater canine creativity and independence, reflected in the command "Belle, go find," which would be given in the context of canine sports like tracking or nosework.²⁶ In each of these instances, the command is part of a larger grammatical structure linking the act of naming to an imperative command: Through human utterance, the dog learns to recognize his or her name. In this process, the dog's world expands, and they become present as an individual dog alongside their human companion.

In Hearne's reading, therefore, the redemptive possibility of training is covenantal in nature, characterized by a sacred contract formed between a human handler and a dog, a contract that holds the possibility to restore interspecies communication. This covenant between the dog and the human is thus required to make dogs present *as dogs*. Through training, Hearne argues, "dog and handler, having learned to talk, are now in the presence of and are commanded by love.... The dog's apparent command of human language may be limited, but his respect for language commands him now, with his handler, as deeply as only a few poets are commanded. In this sense, command of and by language and respect for language are one."[27] Dog training creates an interspecies language—one that requires both the person and the dog to learn how the other communicates, in the process creating a relationship bound by mutual responsibility, love, and respect.

However, this interspecies language does not mean that the human-canine relationship is equal. This language of "command" recalls the language of covenant used in the Hebrew Bible: It involves two parties who agree to mutually bind themselves together through an oath, but the stronger partner expects the weaker one unilaterally to obey commands in exchange for protection.[28] The covenant implied in Hearne's retelling is not between God and the people of Israel but between the human and the dog. As is the case with the Israelite covenant with God, in Hearne's terms, relationality between dogs and humans does not amount to equality; the dogs must hold up their end of the contract in order for an interspecies language—and in turn, for redemption—to be possible.

Hearne's vision of human redemption is therefore dependent on her sense that dogs are intelligent, spiritual creatures, that their ability to answer and respond to human commands is what makes relational redemption achievable. In this account, human beings can find redemption through a mutual process that unfolds in the material space between human and animal, in the work of training.[29] Hearne again uses language from the Hebrew Bible to help elaborate her understanding of training's redemptive potential:

> So, the imperative "Joe, Fetch!" commands the dog (and the handler), not as Newton's laws were understood to command the behavior of falling bodies, but as God's laws command some. "Fetch!" cannot be said meaningfully unless it is said with reverence. Its coherence requires that retrieving be sacred for both members of the community. But here is the paradox: the trainer must speak as if the sacred spoke through him or her, as though training were prophecy, even while knowing that it is mostly impossible, that the gap between the sacred and our knowledge of it is ineluctable.[30]

By opening up the possibility that dogs have an interior life with their own thoughts, desires, and motivations, Hearne argues that dogs are endowed with the ability to respond to human beings. In Hearne's understanding of dog training, the sacred involves mutual attention, responsibility, and respect. A covenantal relationship endows the human handler with something akin to divine capacity vis-à-vis the dog.[31] While the dog can refuse to comply if the trainer's methods are "profane," in Hearne's account, the human is still acting in a position similar to God, with all the responsibilities that accompany great power.

Hearne's relationship with an irascible Pointer named Salty best reveals the redemptive possibilities of training to make dogs present, as well as the gap between Hearne's theological aspirations and training practices. In the first scene, Hearne introduces her experience of curing Salty of her predilection for digging holes in the yard as an example of what she calls the "theology" of dog training. To discourage Salty from this habit, Hearne must move past her own initial exasperated reaction at the sight of her destroyed lawn. As with most people, a yard riddled with holes violates Hearne's sense of what a well-tended domestic space should look like. However, in Hearne's reading, hole digging for Salty is much more than an irritating habit: It is a religious ritual. "Hole digging is sacred," Hearne cryptically states, noting that "in the activity [of digging holes] the secret significance of everything reveals itself."[32] While recognizing that Salty partially digs holes out of boredom, Hearne believes that the ritual of hole digging is sacred because it connects Salty to a transcendent realm inaccessible to humans—a different conception of the sacred than the one offered earlier. Hearne never goes so far as to tell the reader what "the secret significance of everything" might be, likely out of the recognition of her limited ability to inhabit Salty's mind. But fully understanding the act's sacred significance for Salty is not what is important for Hearne—which is perhaps why there's considerable slippage in what she means by "sacred" across the book. What matters for Hearne is the recognition that this act has religious meaning for Salty in the first place, which requires Hearne both to try to experience hole digging as a religious ritual in her own limited human terms and to make sure Salty sees her efforts.

This identification of Salty's hole digging as a religious act is central to how Hearne decides to go about training Salty out of this practice. She finds that her initial impulse to "yell, scream, deliver 'Out!' corrections" and to "wallo[p]" Salty have no effect. As Hearne describes it, "any corrections and punishments are just part of the fun, accepted like a dedicated athlete accepts aches and injuries. I don't mean [Salty] *likes* being walloped, but she is not deterred by walloping as she was deterred when the matter of puddling on the rug came up: puddling on the rug wasn't sacred."³³ Hearne doesn't elaborate as to why for Salty urinating in the house is not a sacred act whereas hole digging is deeply religious. My hypothesis is that the distinction for Hearne has to do with the ritualistic force of Salty's hole digging, as opposed to the casual way she "puddles" on the rug, something she might be doing for a variety of reasons (e.g., she is still learning where it is and is not appropriate to eliminate, she might be territorially marking the house, and so on). While Hearne believes that using verbal and physical corrections when Salty was urinating in the house might have been effective training tools for that type of behavior, which is rooted in a failure to recognize human domestic norms, not all negative corrections are the same. This is also a decidedly idiosyncratic interpretation of Salty's behavior. It is common knowledge among trainers that dogs dig holes for a variety of reasons, including to have fun, to hunt, to expose cool dirt to sit in, to hide, and more—things that were surely in Hearne's training toolkit. In these instances of problematic digging, the generally accepted training solution is to create a designated "digging area" for the dog, either in your yard or in something like a dog sandbox.³⁴ I am guessing that Hearne was aware of these theories and perhaps agreed with them but felt they didn't get to Salty's root motivation, which transcends the material realm.

Instead, Hearne has a very different interpretation of hole digging, which is best described as a religious ritual with the possibility of opening up a shared religious life between Hearne and Salty. Therefore, the first step in training Salty out of this behavior involves Hearne's showing Salty that she also understands that hole digging is sacred: "So I submit my myself to the holy discipline of hole digging. Dressed in gardening clothes, I go into the backyard and discover the Hole. I rejoice. I dance a jig around the Hole in celebration of the Mystery. I congratulate Salty on the Hole and, still dancing, get out a spade and shovel with a view to make this perfect thing even more perfect. Salty is delighted and helps me dig the Hole. We perfect its Form, making it diamond- or heart-shaped."[35]

Turning hole digging into a sacred act for Hearne means to participate in the creation of the hole alongside Salty with the same religious devotion and fervor displayed by the dog. However, Hearne's behavior that marks hole digging as sacred differs from Salty's ritual, in that it is consecrated by the behavior and language reserved for human religious rituals: Hearne therefore "rejoices," "dances," and "celebrates" all that is the Mystery made manifest in the Hole. In doing so, Hearne must leave behind her anthropocentric judgment that holes should not exist in backyards and instead try to experience this activity on Salty's terms, even if she cannot fully understand its "secret significance" outside of her own human framework.

It is only after becoming a devotee to Salty's sacred practice of hole digging that Hearne can reassert her authoritative status as a trainer and move toward creating a covenantal relationship between the two. This training method not only involves becoming a fervent religious believer alongside Salty, but according to Hearne, it also requires that she assert her power over Salty through physical force. After jointly finishing their hole-digging ritual for the first time, Hearne describes how she fills the hole with water, and then, "still rejoicing . . . put[s] Salty's head in the Hole." In response to this undesired and unexpected baptism, which solidifies this moment as a religious rite of passage for Salty, "Salty emerges quite quickly (she's a very strong, agile dog), gasping in astonishment and outrage," decidedly unconverted by Hearne's first training attempt. In response to Salty's shock and discomfort, Hearne says, "I am surprised and say, 'But I thought you loved hole digging,'" displaying an even greater devotion to the Hole than Salty and feigning incomprehension as to why Salty would have a such a negative response to her head being forcefully submerged in water.[36]

Hearne goes on to describe how she and Salty participate in this religious ritual every day for two weeks until Salty begins to hang back upon hearing Hearne humming her "hole-digging hymn" as she gets ready to fill a new one with water. In order to support her interpretation of this moment as a success, Hearne gives human language to Salty's affective experience of this moment: "Her face begins to say something like 'Christ! She's crazy! Hole digging is not fun!'"[37] In Hearne's narrative account of Salty's experience, the process of establishing a human-canine covenantal relationship can be confusing and decidedly "not fun" for the dog. Hearne believes that this unpleasant ritual is necessary until Salty understands her message. Only then can the door open for communication of a higher order between the two of them. While physical punishment may not be Hearne's goal, it is a necessary step in training that is geared toward a larger purpose: a covenantal relationship and the creation of an interspecies language between the human and dog.

Not all dog trainers would interpret Hearne's training methods as being religious; some would not only call them profane, but cruel. The trainer Suzanne Clothier, known for her "relationship-centered" approach, gives voice to this perspective by revisiting the Salty story. This time, however, Clothier asks the reader to occupy the position of the witness:

> See the dog's surprise when the woman grabs her and pushes the dog's head into the hole where the water is still chasing itself around. See the reflexive arching of the dog's body upward, away from the shock of the cold muddy water that has covered her head, splashing into her ears and up into the surprised nostrils before survival instincts take over and stop the intake of breath. When the dog fights free and looks into the woman's eyes, tell me what you see in the dog—trust? joy? the poetry that Hearne tells the reader exists in the dog's soul?[38]

In this passage, Clothier implores the reader to occupy the experience as a passive bystander, portraying Hearne's training methods are disturbing at best and abusive at worst. By focusing on the concrete details of the scene—Salty's fear, shock, and surprise—Clothier interprets this moment as one of coercion, exploitation, and broken trust. When written from the point of view of an onlooker with a greater focus on Salty than on Hearne, Clothier suggests that this approach to training is violent and perhaps even abusive, characterized by a punishing human and a victimized dog.

Anticipating criticisms like Clothier's, Hearne emphasizes that this training ritual is a matter of understanding what is sacred for Salty and then adjusting her own anthropocentric belief system accordingly. She reiterates that *"this has nothing to do with either punishment or authority, and if it is corrupted by either then it becomes cruel.* . . . *If I get the idea that this is a battle of ego and stamina, I'm doing punishment, not dog training."* According to this logic, dog training becomes a form of punishment—rather than a sacred practice—when actions like submerging a dog's head in water are motivated by a hubristic desire to exert power over the dog.[39] In order for her training methods to work, Hearne cannot fake her devotion to this practice but must truly believe that it is a sacred act. She expands on her theology of training as follows:

> Trainers tend to talk about the importance of connections being impersonal, especially the out-corrections I discussed above. That's right, though the term is a bit misleading; it would also capture something to say that corrections should be as personal as possible, that they should be expressions, not of opinions, but of the trainer's nature. You simply become the sort of animal who, as it were, helplessly gives certain corrections in the face of certain crimes. This is something like the impersonality of the law, having to do with our sense that the law ought to be sacred to judges, but it also has to do with our sense that a good judge, or a good teacher, is not so much someone who is good at slipping into the imperative mode as someone who can do it without expecting that with obedience can or ought to come obeisance as well.[40]

Hearne thus bestows the lesson on Salty like an impersonal god in order to create a shared language. Training in Hearne's formulation is not about exercising her totalizing authority over Salty but about inhabiting Salty's sense of the sacred and then teaching her to devote herself to more appropriate religious practices. As Hearne insists, obedience and obeisance are not the same thing; obedience can be compelled, but obeisance cannot, because it involves respect, a more complex concept that involves internal judgment. Although Hearne's training methods were initially frightening, Hearne believes that Salty ultimately responds to her commands because Hearne has made them coherent to her, not because Salty fears what will happen if she digs another hole. Salty's religiosity in Hearne's account happens through their shared language, which makes it possible for them to participate in new activities together. In such instances where humans take undesirable canine behaviors personally rather than administering an impersonal correction, Hearne acknowledges that dogs have been drowned. But despite these concerns, she maintains the appropriateness and efficacy of her methods.[41]

After ridding Salty of the hole-digging habit, Hearne describes the process of teaching Salty to participate in the elite canine sport of retrieving, which exemplifies what relational redemption looks like once a dog and handler are both ready for it.[42] The important training distinction here is that instead of teaching Salty to *refrain* from participating in an activity that is destructive, Hearne is training her to *participate* in a sport that harnesses the same kind of tendencies that Salty poured into hole digging and redirecting those tendencies toward a human-canine sport. In order to teach Salty to retrieve, Hearne must first create a ritual with Salty, much as she did with the hole-digging activity, involving Hearne commanding Salty to sit and stay and then gently placing a dumbbell in her mouth while saying, "Salty, Fetch!" (By dumbbells here, I am referring to the canine version used in dog sports, which are made of wood or plastic and resemble the small dumbbells used for human weightlifting.)[43] Hearne then removes the dumbbell and praises Salty, repeating this practice a dozen times a day. While this activity is not initially religious for Hearne or Salty, through repetition and time, it becomes so: "There is now an object in our language, the dumbbell . . . when she does accept the dumbbell, I must respond with the awe that consists in honoring the details."[44] This ritual is part of the covenantal nature of the human-canine relationship that is solidified through language: When Salty accepts Hearne's command to hold the dumbbell, Hearne must respond with respect.

While retrieving in Hearne's account "makes possible a new sort of truth between Salty and [herself]," it also "makes new sorts of deception possible." Because Hearne's theology of training takes a fallen world as a given, disobedience and communication breakdowns are always risks. For instance, Hearne describes how Salty started sitting on top of the dumbbell she was supposed to retrieve and pretending that she didn't know where it was. In response to that act of dishonesty, Hearne "get[s] on [Salty's] ear and correct[s] her (by pinching her ear), and she screeches with the sting and the indignation of it. Suddenly she 'remembers' that it's under her chest and picks it up." Again, physical force and pain are part of Hearne's theology of training: If Salty is "dishonest," she is breaking a sacred contract, requiring Hearne to correct her. As she elaborates, when she says "Salty, Fetch!," she is saying "'I promise that something is going on here that is worth doing right, and I am deeply committed to getting it right, and I know it is appropriate for you to pick up the dumbbell when I command you to.'" As the language of promise and command indicate, Hearne has a responsibility to Salty: She is asking Salty to trust that she knows what is best for her and will reward or punish her as the situation dictates.[45]

Through this theology of training, which entails both pain and persistence, relational redemption eventually occurs between Hearne and Salty:

> One day I notice that the nature of her retrieving has changed. I can tell, by the knowing way she sails out, the purposefulness of her movements, the wholly gay seriousness with which she

scoops up the dumbbell, the addition to her performance of a degree of precision and fire I hadn't asked for since no one can ask for *this*, that it's Happened. She has walked, or galloped, into real retrieving. She is transformed, I am transformed and the world is transformed, for now I am able to mean all of *this* when I say, "Salty, Fetch!" Now there are all sorts of new ways our language can be projected. . . . I can, that is, use "Fetch" to name things, in somewhat the way we use "this" and "that" to name things."[46]

In Hearne's account, Salty's "precision and fire" is what relational redemption looks like from the outside. Between the two of them, relational redemption is transformative, marking the creation of a new language between an individual human and dog that radically changes the two of them, as well as the world around them. As Hearne explains, the command "Fetch!" has new meanings and possibilities, making room for Salty to innovate and expand the meaning of "Fetch!," leading Hearne to experience surprise and joy at Salty's creativity—another way that she makes herself present to Hearne as an individual dog.

In a 1991 article published in *Harper's*, Hearne further expands on the redemptive possibilities of training for dogs and humans.[47] For Hearne, dog training is not only about creating a shared language between a human and an animal but is about finding happiness together through the mutual work of training.[48] As Hearne explains, this is a form of happiness that "like the artist's, must come from something within the animal, something trainers call 'talent.' Hence it cannot be imposed on the animal. But it is also not something that does not come *ex nihilo*." Training is therefore the process of the trainer's recognizing an individual dog's particular talents—be that for obedience, agility, tracking, therapy work, and so on—and then working together with the dog to transform that raw talent into skills that can be actualized through human command and canine response. This process takes concerted effort on both parts, cannot be coerced (again, Hearne does not believe she coerced Salty), and should bring joy to both the human and the dog. "I bring up this idea of happiness as a form of work," Hearne states, "because I am an animal trainer, and work is the foundation of the happiness a trainer and an animal discover together."[49] Hearne's notion of training here is of a different order than training dogs to adhere to household rules—it is about seeing the dog's individual abilities and finding the best way to channel them into a shared activity with a human being. And yet, the kind of redemption made possible through dog training involves what some have called violence.

As Donna Haraway characterizes Hearne's philosophy of training, "This kind of happiness is about yearning for excellence and having the chance to try to reach it in terms recognizable to concrete beings, not to categorical abstractions. Not all animals are alike; their specificity—of kind and of individual—matters."[50] The kind of relational redemption that dog training enables for Hearne is therefore highly individualized, process based, and goal oriented; it also takes creativity, patience, and hard work. As the Salty examples show, the process of relational redemption as she practices it can be scary and painful for the dog and deeply frustrating for the human. But in the end, Hearne believes that the rewards for both the human and the dog are well worth the effort. It is only through moments of failed communication that relational redemption becomes possible; a central part of the work of training is the development of the relational quality. Until one knows one's dog, and vice versa, redemption is not possible; everything flows from the establishment of a reciprocal relationship between the person and the dog. Therefore, dog training for Hearne is covenantal, created through an interspecies language of command and response that restores the communication breakdown between humans and animals that resulted from the Fall. While this dynamic between person and dog may not be governed by equality, the restoration of this interspecies relationship is required to make the dog present.

"SHE ENRICHES MY IGNORANCE": DONNA HARAWAY'S MULTISPECIES NEGATIVE THEOLOGY OF TRAINING

Although Vicki Hearne and Donna Haraway agree that something mutually transformative is made possible through training, they have very different theologies; this leads to distinct versions of what relational redemption and canine presence look like.[51] While Haraway is also keenly aware that human-animal relations are damaged, Haraway primarily attributes the causes of this suffering to past and present scientific and economic realities, focusing on the intertwined role of domestication and capitalism in shaping human-animal relationships.[52] Haraway is therefore not interested in restoring something that was lost between humans and animals but instead in exploring new possibilities for understanding and experiencing human-animal relationships, especially through play.

Nonetheless, Haraway believes in redemption: a form of what the sociologist of religion Nancy Tatom Ammerman refers to as "a consciousness of transcendence, a recognition of a sacred dimension that goes beyond the ordinary."[53] Haraway's argument for the redemptive possibilities of training reveals two understudied aspects of her writing: the tendency to borrow from the language of Catholicism and to draw from more diffuse forms of religiosity that are not linked to a single religious tradition or institution. Training in Haraway's account has the possibility to show how the sacred can intercede in seemingly secular spaces. Like Hearne, Haraway is also interested in instances when redemption fails in training, when miscommunications interrupt communion. Such moments with dogs, according to Haraway, are important reminders of how hard it is to be in a relationship with another being, especially from a different species.[54] Yet she also sees these interspecies misunderstandings as opportunities to learn where things went wrong and to deepen the human-canine partnership.

Haraway's theology of training draws on and ultimately transcends her experiences growing up Catholic.[55] In *How Like a Leaf: An Interview with Thyrza Nichols Goodeve* (2000), Haraway speaks at length about being raised in a devout Irish Catholic home in Cold War–era America, growing up around intelligent and principled Catholic women like her mother and the nuns at the Catholic school she attended. Haraway repeatedly emphasizes that being Catholic "was a terribly important part of [her] intellectual and emotional life." After aligning herself with the Catholic left during the civil rights era, Haraway moved away from Catholicism's increasingly anticommunist Catholic worldview in college.[56] Although she no longer identifies as Catholic, Catholicism has an enduring importance in much of Haraway's thinking:

> My inability to separate the figural and the literal comes straight out of a Catholic relationship to the Eucharist. I told you I have a very Catholic sensibility as a theorist even though I am opposed to Catholicism and have lost my faith and developed this elaborate criticism. The fundamental sensibility about the literal

nature of metaphor and the physical quality of symbolization—all this comes from Catholicism. But the point is that this sensibility—the meaning of this menagerie I live with and in—gives me a menagerie where the literal and the figurative, the factual and the narrative, the scientific and the religious and the literary, are always imploded. Each of the pieces is not the same thing and requires its own working through, but all of them, as processes, have imploded as in a black hole.[57]

In her testimonial, Haraway locates a childhood steeped in Catholic doctrine and experience as being central to how she theorizes different forms of life. This insistence on infusing the spiritual within the material is consistent with how Robert A. Orsi characterizes Catholic practice in America. According to Orsi, "presence is central to the study of lived Catholic experience—the study of Catholicism in everyday life is about the mutual engagement of men, women, children, and holy figures present to each other."[58] Among other figures, Haraway would add the cyborg and the dog to these mutual entanglements.[59]

While her Catholic upbringing shapes Haraway's conception of human-canine relationships, she is also deeply attuned to the ways in which the interplay of domestication and capitalism have been deeply damaging for human-canine relationships. In the chapter from *When Species Meet* (2008) entitled "Training in the Contact Zone: Power, Play, and Invention in the Sport of Agility," Haraway first articulates this problem as follows:

> Taking themselves to be the only actors, people reduce other organisms to the lived status of being merely raw material or tools. The domestication of animals is, within this analysis, a

kind of original sin separating human beings from nature, ending in atrocities like the meat-industrial complex of transnational factory farming and the frivolities of pet animals as indulged but unfree fashion accessories in a boundless commodity culture. Or, if not fashion accessories, pets are taken to be living engines for churning out unconditional love—affectional slaves, in short. One being becomes means to the purposes of the other, and the human assumes rights in the instrument that the animal never has in "it"self. One can be somebody only if someone else is something. To be animal is exactly not to be human and vice versa.[60]

Whereas Adam and Eve's act of disobedience is the original sin for Hearne, Haraway suggests that this dominant account of human-animal relations frames domestication as humanity's original sin. In this interpretation—one that Haraway wants to complicate—domestication has led to an instrumentalist understanding of animals as passive objects of human exploitation, be it for financial profit, cultural capital, or emotional labor. While exploitation is part of the story of domestication, this interpretation is incomplete on its own.

Haraway's chapter on training is thus an attempt to challenge instrumentalist readings of domestication and instead to create new ways of living in a multispecies world that are not reliant on human dominance—the opposite of what someone like Cesar Millan endorses. In rethinking the legacy of domestication that accounts for animal agency, Haraway borrows from the work of the Belgian philosopher and psychologist Vinciane Despret, noting training's potential to be an "anthropo-zoo-genetic practice," a term that refers to the creation of historically situated relationships between people and animals. What is particularly useful for Haraway in Despret's thinking is its emphasis on the embodied quality of human-animal encounters, in which people and animals "become attuned to each other, in such a way that both parties become more interesting to each other, more open to surprises, smarter, more 'polite,' more inventive."[61] These encounters privilege a form of relationality that makes it possible for humans and animals to communicate in meaningful and inventive ways. These relations are "active" and "co-shaping" as opposed to possessive and unidirectional.[62] While all human-canine relationships rest on an uneven power dynamic, which Haraway acknowledges, the redemptive effects of training can only happen if the dog responds to the invitation to play.

Though "play" also happens between the person and the dog, it requires human attentiveness to what their dog is communicating to them. In explaining how training is a form of play, Haraway first presents the biologist and ethologist Marc Bekoff's research on canid play, which he and J. A. Byers define as "all motor activity performed postnatally that appears to be purposeless, in which motor patterns from other contexts may often be used in modified forms and altered temporal sequencing."[63] In other words, playing dogs exhibit behavioral changes that are predictable and often exaggerated (e.g., how young puppies leap and bounce), that start and stop (e.g., how a dog shakes a toy as though killing prey, but ideally the dog does not consume said toy). Play also involves side-to-side rather than forward movement and entails "self-handicapping," in which the faster or stronger dog mutes their response toward her play partner.[64]

Haraway builds on this definition, arguing that "purposelessness" can be understood as a form of "*joy* in the sheer doing."[65] The play Haraway is thinking about is an embodied language arising in the space between human and canine bodies; sometimes this involves verbal cues, but often it is about a person's physical posture and positioning. By way of example, she turns to her experiences "playing" the canine sport of agility with her dog Cayenne.[66] Agility requires that the human handler determine a plan for the person and the dog to move as quickly, accurately, and smoothly as possible through the course. While the dog does the jumping and navigating of the obstacles, the person has to follow the dog's path and be in the right place at the right time to give the dog the information he needs to know where to go next. Agility is thus a form of interspecies play, which "lures its apprentice stoics of both species back into the open of a vivid sensory present. That's why we do it. That's the answer to my question, Who are you, and so who are we?"[67] Relational redemption here is about both the person and the dog being radically present to one another—paying attention to no one and nothing else but their shared task at hand. As they acquire a shared language made possible through training, the dog and the person create something new together. Returning to Ammerman's account of the sacred, they transcend ordinary time.

While they have achieved success in the sport by achieving the Masters Agility Dog Title (titles are the primary forms of recognition), Haraway notes that "our championship eludes us; [Cayenne] enriches my ignorance."[68] While they have received the "Masters" title, they are not yet "champions." Training is thus a process of growth through failure and of coming to terms with how little one knows about the other, even when that other is their dearest canine companion. Because such frustrations are instructive, Haraway primarily focuses on instances when she and Cayenne fail to play agility together—with "together" being the operative word. As an example of the importance of learning from failure in training, Haraway describes a particular challenge she and her dog Cayenne faced: the inability to navigate an A-frame properly. (An A-frame is made up of two tall ramps that meet at the top to form an "A." The dog must run up to the top of the frame and then back down, being sure to touch "the contact zone" on both sides, which is the area closest to the ground that is painted yellow.)[69] Because Haraway was being "incoherent" in her communications about what Cayenne was supposed to do—a word also used by Hearne to describe failures in training—she kept leaping over the frame without touching the contact zone, disqualifying them from that run.[70] This may seem like a small problem, but it was holding Cayenne and Haraway back in their agility trials and reflecting a communication misfiring indicative of broader problems in their relationship.

Haraway takes personal responsibility for their training failures being "incoherent," which makes it impossible for Cayenne to understand what she is supposed to do. But Haraway's methods for fixing this problem are very different from Millan's and Hearne's punishment-based tactics. There is no room for dominance here—only cooperation. The first step is learning to trust one's dog: "A skilled human competitor in agility, not to mention a decent life companion, must learn to recognize when *trust* is what the human owes the dog. Dogs generally recognize very well when the human being has earned trust; the human beings I know, starting with myself, are less good at reciprocal trust."[71] As humans, it is easy to think that we know better than our dogs and to treat them like tiny children or mini versions of ourselves. But canine sports like agility demand interdependence; arguably, all human-canine relationships do.

The next step in their training relationship is for Haraway to stop "fantasizing that Cayenne was a native English speaker"—in other words, to honor the fact that Cayenne is a member of a different species.[72] In need of a canine translator, Haraway turns to her friend Pam, who is the guardian of Cayenne's littermate and a highly skilled agility competitor.[73] Haraway admits that at first she "was secretly critical of how relentlessly [Pam] worked with [her dog] Capp to fix his attention on her and hers on him in the activities of daily life." Haraway acknowledges that "Capp was aglow with pleasure in his doings, but I thought that Cayenne had greater animal happiness." At that time, Haraway viewed having a dog solely focused on their guardian as a sign of their limited freedom. And yet Pam and her dog Capp far surpassed Haraway and Cayenne's achievements in agility. This is where Pam needed to intervene, explaining that "Cayenne did not yet know her job because [Haraway] had not yet taught it."[74] In order to teach Cayenne her job, they had to return to the very basics of training—not simply for the sake of succeeding in agility but to improve their basic communication.

The close attention that Haraway initially saw as constraining was precisely what she and Cayenne needed to strengthen their relationship, as well as their performance. After lots of practice and patience (mainly granted by Cayenne), Haraway and Cayenne "retained each other," mastered the A-frame, and advanced in their competitions. What once was an obstacle became a source of joy. In a report to friends in the agility world, Haraway describes one competition as follows: "Cayenne sails through this performance [at an agility trial] with a gleam in her eye and pleasure written all over our coursing body. . . . reciprocal induction is the name of the game." Through playing agility—a sport that not only requires interdependence but the pleasure of play—Cayenne and Haraway transformed each other. This is not to say that everything was perfect in their relationship from then on, but that as Haraway describes, "the occasional breakdowns in that contact zone [in agility] that still happen are quickly fixed" because the two now speak the same language."[75] Redemption is possible for Haraway, but it requires mutual attention that transcends species boundaries and hierarchies. We humans have as much to learn from dogs as they do from us—perhaps more.

To understand what redemption means for Haraway, we first need to return to the refusal to separate the figural from the literal that Haraway attributes to her Catholic upbringing. Indeed, she insists that "the philosophic and literary conceit that all we have is representations and no access to what animals think and feel is wrong. Human beings do, or can, know more than we used to know, and the right to gauge that knowledge is rooted in historical, flawed, generative cross-species practices."[76] This raises the classic animal studies question of whether it is violent to reduce an animal to the figural.[77] But as Haraway's statement insists, both can be true at the same time. We are always moving back and forth between the dog as symbol and as "real" dog. Haraway's point is that we have an ethical responsibility to try as hard as possible to see the dog in front of us, rather than project our own desires onto the dog: "I suggest people must learn to meet dogs as strangers first in order to unlearn the crazy assumptions and stories we inherit about who dogs are. Respect for dogs demands at least that much."[78] So much of relational redemption for Haraway is not about recovering a lost past (like it is for Hearne) but unlearning the harmful stories we have inherited about dogs. But where do these harmful stories come from?

In part, Haraway argues that they come from Abrahamic religions—the very tradition in which she was raised. She concludes "Training in the Contact Zone" by offering a pointed critique of Genesis 1:

The sixth day of creation in Genesis 1:24–31 is when God, helpfully speaking English, said, "Let the earth bring forth living creatures according to their kinds . . . And God made the beasts of the earth according to their kinds and the cattle according to their kinds, and everything that creeps upon the ground according to its kind. And God saw that it was good." A little overfocused on keeping kinds distinct, God then got to making man (male and female) in his own image and giving them all too much dominion, as well as the command to multiply out of all bounds of sharing the earth. I think the sixth day is where the problem of joint mundane creaturely kinship versus human exceptionalism is sharply posed right in the first chapter of Jewish and Christian monotheism. Islam did no better on this point. We have plurals of kind, but singularity of relationship, namely human dominion under God's dominion. Everything is food for man; man is food only for himself and his God. In this feast, there are no companion species, no cross-category messmates at table. There is no salutary indigestion, only licensed cultivation and husbandry of all the earth as stock for human use. The posthumanities—I think this is another word for "after monotheism"—require another kind of open. Pay attention. It's about time.[79]

Like Hearne, Haraway turns to Genesis to make sense of where human-animal relationships went wrong. But her interpretation is quite different: The problem is not with the Fall of humankind severing the ability of humans and animals to communicate. Human exceptionalism, which Haraway critiques earlier in the book, is not the only issue. Instead, the problem lies in a creation narrative that endorses the Great Chain of Being, with humans sitting just below God and animals of all kinds beneath them. The fundamental theological problem, therefore, is the categorization and separation of species—that on the sixth day of creation, God made an error in joining living beings based on sameness. Since then, humans have been unable to think in nonhierarchical terms past our own kind, wreaking violence not only on companion species but on all forms of more-than-human life.

In her final turn, Haraway argues that we must move past monotheistic religions—that thinking beyond the human requires it. Given that redemption comes from the very traditions Haraway critiques, by implication, she is calling for new religious narratives for understanding human-canine relations that focus on play and joy rather than suffering and punishment.

TELLING NEW DOG TRAINING STORIES

What would Haraway's posthumanist, postmonotheistic vision look like? I do not have an answer, but I want to offer some examples that I think point us in the right direction. In Harlan Weaver's brilliant book *Bad Dog* (2021), he describes forms of human-canine relating that transcend conventional language and temporalities, what he calls "queerly affiliative bodyings." For Weaver, bodyings refer to the "affective travels and concomitant movements of bodies that emerge through human-dog relatings." This is another way of capturing the creation of a new interspecies language that develops in the process of human-canine relating—through interspecies body language grounded in canine ways of perceiving the world. "Affiliative," in Weaver's terms, reflects "a desire for contact and movement outward or together." Finally, these interspecies relatings are queer because they exist outside normative social structures, requiring a person to be as emotionally available to those outside their nuclear family as they would be to their spouse, children, or companion animals.[80]

Equally important for Weaver is the fact that training is predicated on a "deeply bodied practice" that "operates through a politics at the center of many feminist discussions: consent. The dog trainer Suzanne Dubnicka highlights how, in engaging R+ [rewards-based] training, her dog 'consents every time we work,' meaning 'she always has the choice to perform the behavior or not.' ... Through this choreography, what might seem like a hierarchical practice becomes, instead, a two-way conversation, one enacted entirely through bodyings."[81] Weaver's approach marks a rejection of the kinds of Abrahamic-based creation hierarchies that Haraway criticizes. This is also a radically different conception of human-canine relationships than the deeply masculinist "pack leader" model proposed by Cesar Millan, as well as the training methods reflected in Hearne's relationship with Salty. Consent-based training likely has less appeal than Millan's vision because it views training as an ongoing process through which the dog actively participates—to even suggest that a dog has the capacity to offer consent is a radical proposition for many. It forces humans to decenter ourselves and reject the allure of "pack leadership" and instead embrace a model of interspecies partnership. Consent is one way forward for thinking about more generative relationships between people and dogs.

Another way of thinking beyond redemption is reflected in what the philosopher Matthew Calarco calls the ideal of "*syntheōria*," or seeing with others. What is crucial here is that more-than-human animals themselves take part in this process of seeing and that we humans need to not only respect their unique ways of perceiving the world but try to respect and even inhabit them to the extent that this is possible. In doing so, we also recognize that Earth is not made for humans and that we should not have a special claim on it. When "seeing-with" other animals, humans get a chance to view the world "as glimpsed from an inhuman perspective, utterly lacking in divine or human telos but not, for all that, any less remarkable, meaningful, or valuable."[82] The point is not to reject religion outright but to approach human-animal (and in our case, canine) relationships from the perspective that humans are not the center of the universe—and that our cosmologies are not the only perspectives available to us. In short, we need to try to think alongside animals as co-creators of a world and to open ourselves up to new ways of approaching it that are not based in hierarchical relations and punishment-based theologies; therein lies the possibility of forms of redemption worth endorsing, those that are fundamentally relational.

4

TROUBLING REDEMPTION

On June 6, 2016, Bretagne, the last known surviving 9/11 search-and-rescue dog, died at the age of sixteen. In the immediate aftermath of the attack, Bretagne and her handler, Denise Corliss, were deployed with Texas Task Force 1 to take part in rescue efforts. While there were no survivors to be found, Bretagne worked twelve-hour shifts searching for human remains and comforting emergency responders.[1] Her death and memorialization received significant media coverage, including a viral video of more than a dozen first responders saluting the Golden Retriever as pallbearers from Bretagne's search-and-rescue unit escorted her body out of the clinic, her casket draped in the Texas state flag.[2] A statement released by the local fire department explained Bretagne's significance to them: "Some may say that the most a dog could be is a pet. However, to the over 400 members of the Cy-Fair Volunteer Fire Department, Bretagne was a civil servant, a hero and is family. We'll remember her fondly, and continue serving the community with her as inspiration."[3] As the 9/11 dogs grew old and eventually died, tales of their heroism and innocence became a way for people in the United States to tell feel-good stories about 9/11. These dogs demonstrate that even after such a tragic event and the highly divisive war in its wake, dogs are an outlet through which people in the United States can unite and reaffirm its central values. Put differently, stories about the 9/11 dogs are a form of US civil religion that uphold the fantasy of the United States as a "redeemer nation."[4]

In these 9/11 narratives, dogs symbolize an idealized vision of America: courageous, unified, resilient. As I discuss in this book's introduction and in the previous chapter, a central tenet of civil religion is the notion that moments of national crisis—what Robert N. Bellah refers to as "times of trial"—are occasions to test and revise the beliefs, symbols, and rituals people in the United States recognize as sacred.[5] Bellah cited three historical events that constituted times of trial and produced new national symbols, rituals, and values: the American Revolution, the Civil War, and the War in Vietnam. Following Bellah's logic, 9/11 can be understood as the fourth time of trial: a moment in which Americans were forced to reexamine their underlying principles as individuals and as a nation. If we understand dogs—or more specifically, what they signify—as being integral to American civil religion, then it makes sense that canine redemption narratives would appear in the aftermath of 9/11. Stories like Bretagne's are not only heartwarming; they do political work. These stories are so pervasive and compelling because they use the figure of the dog to represent the United States' redemptive goodness in the face of an amorphous, "evil" enemy.[6]

The multimedia artist Laurie Anderson's film *Heart of a Dog* (2015) and the queer feminist writer Eileen Myles's book *Afterglow (a dog memoir)* (2017) offer two avant-garde takes on the 9/11 dog narrative that employ some of the tropes of the canine redemption narrative only to subvert them. More specifically, both works offer a critique of the symbolic associations of dogs as unconditionally loyal and good in order to contest the myth of American innocence. Both works depend on the characteristics and functions of the 9/11 dog redemption narrative but allow for greater nuance and complexity in exploring the dynamics between "the dog" and the nation, as well as between individual dogs and people. These counternarratives are the kinds of canine stories that we can learn from. Specifically, these two stories show the danger of using dogs as a form of civil religion to justify American self-idolatry.[7] In the wake of the trauma of 9/11, Anderson and Myles show how easy it is to legitimize violence in the name of the vision of the United States as a "redeemer nation."[8] Anderson's and Myles's dogs are witnesses to US structural violence, and in the case of Myles's dog, a prophetic presence.

Heart of a Dog and *Afterglow* show how dogs can be used productively as symbolic forms of critique, but if we stop at the symbolic, then we miss an essential part of the story: the fact that dogs are, well, dogs, and to relate to them requires a subordination of our own human ways of encountering the world. This is easier said than done, but I think it is essential to try. The final part of this chapter focuses on a recurring problem built into the dog redemption narrative: the erasure of the dog in service of the human. As we have seen in the case of the Michael Vick dogs in chapter 1 and in the figure of the white dog in chapter 2, this genre depends on the dog's symbolic function. In contrast, a constant refrain in dog training, which I discussed in the previous chapter, is the demand that one *see the dog*.[9] Building on that concept, I will show how Anderson and Myles insist on narratively *making dogs present*.

The fact that this insistence on canine presence happens after the deaths of Anderson's and Myles's dogs is not a coincidence. When a loving guardian knows that their dog's time is limited, the contours of their relationship come into sharper focus, and we are forced to make difficult decisions about end-of-life care.[10] These choices are so challenging because dogs cannot tell us where they hurt—we can do our best to read their body language and draw on our lifetime of knowledge living with them, but this is a process with a lot of uncertainty. It is also a tremendous responsibility, terrifying and beautiful at the same time. Unlike the dog of the redemption narrative, these are not stories made meaningful through canine suffering but through facing the messiness of dying and death as realities that should not be sanitized; to do so diminishes the dignity of the relationship and the dog herself. Anderson and Myles dwell on their dogs' physical experiences of dying, showing how even as their dogs' bodies begin to fail, there are still opportunities to connect with them. Although Anderson and Myles draw from different religious traditions (Buddhism and Catholicism respectively), caring for their dying dogs becomes an act of religious devotion—the greatest final gift they can give to Lolabelle and Rosie.

THE 9/11 CANINE REDEMPTION NARRATIVE

Dogs play a central role in stories about 9/11—so much so that they can be considered a subgenre of the dog redemption narrative. While many of these stories about dogs and 9/11 made news headlines, a large number of their stories also appeared in the form of longer tributes geared toward a popular audience, spanning a variety of media, including illustrated children's books, photo essays, and documentaries.[11] Dogs are even included in the official 9/11 memorial website in the section on "Four-Legged 9/11 Heroes," cementing their redemptive role in this tragedy.¹² While the individual dogs matter in these stories, it is what they represent about everyday Americans and the nation that gives these narratives larger meaning. For instance, the tenth-anniversary edition of the first full-length book treatment of the search-and-rescue dogs present at Ground Zero (Nona Kilgore Bauer's book *Dog Heroes of September 11th*) includes a foreword by none other than New York City's mayor on 9/11: Rudy Giuliani. In reflecting on the importance of the 9/11 dogs, Giuliani states that "no American could be unmoved by the stories and images of these dogs and their handlers, who through their valiant efforts did their part to restore our great nation and to bring closure to thousands of grieving families [by returning their family members' remains to them]. Their journeys. . . . reinforce our resolve to persevere, rebuild, and keep our nation safe and strong."¹³ This statement is representative of the kinds of descriptions of the 9/11 dogs, whose qualities symbolize central US values and whose sacrificial actions are part of broader efforts to restore its status as a global power. This is just one example of the symbolic force of dogs to represent archetypal American ideals in the midst of a national crisis.

In addition to their centrality to US civil religion, some stories about the 9/11 dogs appeal directly to institutional religions, especially Protestant Christianity. Michael Hingson and Susy Flory's bestselling book, *Thunder Dog: The True Story of a Blind Man, His Guide Dog, and the Triumph of Trust at Ground Zero* (2012), is an explicitly Christian 9/11 dog redemption narrative.¹⁴ Hingson, a blind man, and his guide dog, Roselle, were in one of the Twin Towers the day of the attack. The memoir recounts how Roselle saved Hingson and many of his colleagues' lives that day by guiding them down dozens of stories of smoke-filled stairs. The book interprets this canine-driven act of salvation through a Christian providential lens. Hingson believes that God had a higher purpose for him and Roselle that required they survive the attack:

> I'm not sure why I lived. But I do know this: since I am alive, I must be here for a reason. I agree with Billy Graham, who spoke during the national prayer service at Washington National Cathedral on the Friday after the attacks. He said that we may never know why 9/11 happened, but we don't have to, because God is the sovereign One. He uses each of us in different ways, and I choose to trust that he used me that day. I know he used Roselle. The two of us interacted with so many others; some I remember and some I've forgotten. I don't know exactly what will come out of the part we played in September 11. I may never know. But I do know it's all about planting seeds, seeds of forgiveness, healing, teamwork, and trust.[15]

It is significant that Hingson references the famous Christian evangelist Billy Graham, also known as "America's Pastor," who stood alongside both Democratic and Republican US presidents to provide religious guidance in the name of unifying the country.[16] As Hingson interprets Graham's words, one cannot always understand why evil exists in the world, but instead, one must leave those questions to God. For his part, Hingson believes that God had a plan not only for him but also for his dog, Roselle—a divine instrument. In this interpretation of the event, Roselle's bravery is redemptive. She saved both Hingson and his coworkers from death and also gave him a new purpose in life: to share their uplifting story, which describes moments of heroism and hope during a tragic event.

In most 9/11 accounts, the dog operates as a symbol of forgiveness and healing on both the individual and national level. Although Roselle remains an individual dog with a particular relationship to her human companion, for the purposes of formulating a 9/11 dog redemption narrative, the text foregrounds Roselle's status as a symbol readily transportable into triumphalist narratives about US identity.[17] To be clear, I am not suggesting that the people who wrote these stories are insincere or that their dogs' heroism shouldn't be celebrated—of course they should be. At the same time, the fact that the qualities associated with these dogs symbolically transfer onto the nation warrants attention. As is so often the case in traditional canine redemption narratives, the stories are not actually about the dogs.

DECONSTRUCTING THE 9/11 CANINE REDEMPTION NARRATIVE

The Surveillance State in Heart of a Dog

Heart of a Dog is about storytelling—how we are unreliable narrators of our own experiences; how technologies like photographs, music, and film can imperfectly capture the past; and how narration is the primary mode for understanding loss. September 11 is such a central event in Laurie Anderson's film *Heart of a Dog* because it hastened the rise of the surveillance state, in which closed-circuit television (CCTV) is used to narratively reconstruct the past to understand the present. The problem, however, is that these surveillance apparatuses work imperfectly and only capture a minuscule moment in time, creating something akin to "fragmented conversations full of jump cuts and distortions."[18] These videos are like the visual equivalent of talking to someone on a cell phone with poor reception; we can only hear snippets of their sentences and have to try to make sense of what they're saying based on limited information. As Anderson explains, the reliance on video footage is also dangerous because "the data is put together and your story is constructed, backwards."[19] By its very nature, surveillance requires government actors to piece together video footage to construct a retrospective narrative that claims to explain how a given event occurred. Anderson is worried about the fact that surveillance is treated like objective data when it is subject to the same kinds of faulty interpretations that are the product of human memory. In the process, Anderson worries that this desire for a linear and coherent plot will create an oversimplified portrait of "what happened" that fails to take into account important context that cannot be captured on the screen.

The surveillance state as depicted in *Heart of a Dog* introduces a new sense of time akin to what Achille Mbembe refers to as "a combination of several temporalities."[20] Mbembe's argument helps parse the ways in which Anderson's film rejects traditional linear understandings of time in 9/11 narratives: "To think relevantly about *this time that is appearing*, this *passing time*, meant abandoning conventional views, for these only perceive time as a current that carries individuals and societies from a background to a foreground with the future emerging necessarily from the past and following that past, itself irreversible. . . . This time is not a series but an *interlocking* of presents, pasts, and futures that retain their depths of other presents, pasts, and futures, each age bearing, altering, and maintaining the previous ones."[21] In this respect, Mbembe critiques a teleological understanding of time because it presupposes that the past, present, and future are stable and objective categories. As a postcolonial theorist, Mbembe is quick to point out that an emphasis on a teleological conception of time also reveals the distinctly Western bias that privileges this kind of sequential temporal ordering.[22]

The cinematic techniques used in *Heart of a Dog* approximate a notion of time that is much closer to Mbembe's—the past, present, and future are always and sometimes literally overlapping through image, text, and sound. In the film, Anderson tells a story where the voice of the narrator (a version of Laurie Anderson) is the driving force, and the images Anderson creates tell a parallel story. *Heart of a Dog* is an example of what André Bazin, speaking of the French filmmaker Chris Marker's *Letter from Siberia* (1957), refers to as "an essay documented by film."[23] Like Marker's films—which Anderson cites as an influence—*Heart of a Dog* uses the device that Bazin called "horizontal montage," which "as opposed to traditional montage that plays with the sense of duration through the relationship of shot to shot. . . . a given image [in horizontal montage] doesn't refer to the one that preceded it or the one that will follow, but rather it refers laterally, in some way, to what is said."[24] *Heart of a Dog* brings together a variety of media that produce a multiplicity of stories: Anderson's digitally animated drawings, archival and personal footage shot by Anderson on everything from a drone to an iPhone, photographs, professionally produced performances that use doubles for Lolabelle and other characters in the story, as well as 8mm footage from Anderson's childhood. The effect of these cinematic techniques lends a fragmented quality to the film that literally prevents the viewer from ever seeing its subject clearly or for an extended period of time—whether it is Lolabelle, Anderson, or post-9/11 New York. This technique captures the disorientation experienced after 9/11 but refuses to provide a single overarching narrative to explain "what happened."

In contrast to the lifeless technologies just described, September 11 not only shifted Anderson's sense of space and time but also her sense of self, teaching her to occupy the perspective of an animal vulnerable to birds of prey. This is something Anderson did not fully understand until she experienced the world through Lolabelle, a tiny Rat Terrier. Seeking to escape the chaos of New York in the immediate aftermath, Anderson takes Lolabelle to California. But it turns out that the safety they felt there was an illusion: "One morning, suddenly . . . for no reason . . . [hawks] came swooping down right in front of me, dropping down through the air, their claws wide open, right on top of Lolabelle."[25] Instead of attacking Lolabelle, however, the hawks sweep back up into the sky and drop back down a few times before retreating, once they realized that Lolabelle was slightly too large to be suitable prey. As Anderson describes this moment, the video footage of the hawks plunging downward with their outstretched claws from above switches to a black-and-white photograph of Lolabelle's immobile body, her face tilted upward, her ears perked forward, her eyes focused. The image is captured from the hawks' point of view, but the shift to black-and-white recalls the kind of surveillance footage one might see from a drone, making Lolabelle a potentially innocent casualty to random and precise violence.

With the sound of a camera click, the lens of the drone camera zooms in closer and closer on Lolabelle's face. This moment profoundly affects Lolabelle, whom Anderson characterizes as having a "brand-new expression" on her face, born of "the realization that she was prey and that these birds had come to kill her. And second was a whole new thought. It was the realization that they could come from the air."[26] From that moment onward,

FIGURE 4.1. Lolabelle viewed from a drone.
Source: Screen grab.

Anderson says that Lolabelle assumes an increased level of vigilance on their hikes, keeping an eye out for threats from above and on the ground. By describing Lolabelle's new hypervigilance, Anderson captures the new awareness of time and space that many people living in the United States experienced after 9/11—a recognition of vulnerability that punctures triumphalist readings of the United States as impervious to external threats.

What may initially have seemed like a singular moment experienced by Anderson and Lolabelle quickly becomes a parable for American life after 9/11—moving from Lolabelle as dog to Lolabelle as a symbol for a broader experience:[27]

> And the rest of the time
> we were in the mountains,
> she just kept looking over her shoulder
> and trotting along
> with her head in the air,

her eyes scanning the thin sky
like there's something wrong
with the air.
And I thought,
where have I seen this look before?
And then I realized it was the same look
on the faces of my neighbors in New York
in the days right after 9/11,
when they suddenly realized,
first, that they could come
from the air.
And, second, that it would
be that way from now on.
And we had passed through a door,
and we would never be going
back.[28]

By telling a story about the near attack on Lolabelle, Anderson captures the consciousness of post-9/11 America. The sense of transformation that occurred after 9/11 is not only temporal ("we will never be going / back") but also spatial ("eyes scanning the thin sky," "there's something wrong with the air"). The repetition of the phrase "they could come from the air" also has a double meaning, potentially referring to the planes that struck the Twin Towers but also recalling the use of drone warfare. Lolabelle's—and by proxy all Americans'—new instinctive compulsion to look up reflects one of the ways that 9/11 changed the sense of space and time for those living in the United States. Even in an effort to escape the "mess" of New York City, at a time when Anderson's and Lolabelle's attempts to find a shared language were interrupted by the beauty around them, Anderson (via Lolabelle) was reminded that the state of terror brought on by 9/11 is enduring. Like Lolabelle, we humans are also prey, always vulnerable to technologies of random and impersonal killing.

The sense that 9/11 brought on a new form of attention to space and time recurs throughout the film. As Jasbir Puar notes, temporality and spatiality are central concerns for theorists of 9/11:

> The event-ness of September 11 refuses the binary of watershed moment and turning point of radical change, versus intensification of more of the same, tethered between its status as a "history-making moment" and a "history-vanishing moment." On behalf of his conceptualization of September 11 as a "snapshot"—a break and an explosion—Nilüfer Göle argues that "understanding September 11th requires building a narrative starting from the terrorist moment as an instance, that is an exemplary incident which, in one moment, allows different temporalities to emerge, and with them, a range of issues hitherto suppressed. For Göle, the snapshot encompasses the temporalities of the instant and the image, of fast-forwarding, rewinding, and shuttering, rather than being strictly anchored to the past, present and future."[29]

The specificity of Anderson's medium, which combines voiceover narration, drawings, 8mm film from Anderson's childhood, and more, allows for the kind of series of "snapshots" or illuminations that Puar describes. While the term "9/11" is shorthand for a rupture with a stable "before and after," the metaphor of the snapshot is a productive alternative to the teleological demand of redemption narratives. Instead of driving toward narrative resolution, the film illuminates these alternative times and experiences that were taking place, thinking about time as it overlaps rather than as it is contained in a stable past and present. There is no redemption in this account but instead a recognition that one can never fully anticipate or prepare for death, which is an ever-present threat—be it on the bustling streets of Manhattan or in the idyllic mountains of California.

I have been talking thus far about how Lolabelle and, by extension, everyone in the United States have been changed by 9/11. However, I want to emphasize a crucial difference that distinguishes Anderson's account from the kinds of 9/11 dog redemption narratives referenced earlier in this book. Although Anderson is changed by this moment, *Heart of a Dog* resists the neat categories of "good" and "evil" so often deployed in the wake of 9/11. As I have sought to show throughout this book, binary categories (good versus evil, sin versus salvation, and even human versus canine) are central to the structure of redemption narratives, demanding a transformation that is totalizing and complete. As a film that is not "about" a single event but draws on multiple stories and weaves them together, *Heart of a Dog* resists a linear understanding of time and a bounded sense of what it means to be human, instead introducing an ethics of discomfort that is incompatible with redemption.

The Canine Witness in Afterglow: *Rosie at Abu Ghraib*

Like *Heart of a Dog*, *Afterglow* merges genres—including memoir, a puppet show, a science fiction essay, and chapters written from Rosie the dog's perspective—as a way of demonstrating the representational challenges that are inherent to mourning both major events and the loss of individuals. *Afterglow* also refuses to settle on a single, linear narrative of 9/11 and its aftermath but instead revisits them from multiple perspectives. This rejection of linearity has the effect of requiring Rosie to be at one and the same time an individual dog with a particular connection to Myles and a symbol of Myles's broader political aims. Rosie is at once a singular dog with whom Myles is in relationship and a canine representative of a different kind of nation—one that is queer, feminist, and subversive.

As much as *Afterglow* plays with the question of whether it is a story about Myles or about Rosie, it also is a memoir about the nation. More specifically, it is a searing critique of US politics before and after 9/11. While Anderson focuses on the rise of the surveillance state, Myles forces the reader to contend with their complicity in US war crimes, specifically the use of torture at Abu Ghraib prison. Through fictional reconstructions that imagine Rosie as witness to the acts of torture at Abu Ghraib (referred to as "The Grave" in what follows), Myles recasts the state-sanctioned acts of torture from a canine perspective:

> Rosie had been to Abu Ghraib and ever-so-gently nudged the soldier who took the pictures—first to take them because he knew in his gut the way they were partying with the prisoners *was* wrong and later (nudge nudge) to send them home though his commander kept making it known that what happens in the Grave that was what they called the place what happens in the Grave stays in the Grave but he [the soldier] sent his pictures to his mother who worked at a local paper in a very small town in Gardener, Mass.[30]

As we now know based on reports and photographs from Abu Ghraib, there were in fact dogs present there to terrorize the prisoners. The prisoners were also treated like dogs, as depicted in the infamous photograph of a naked incarcerated man in the fetal position with a dog leash around his neck, held by a woman guard.[31] As Colleen Glenney Boggs states in her writings about the actual military dogs at Abu Ghraib, "images of bestiality and practices of bestialization lie at the crux of colonial violence and legal formation; they reveal the underlying 'pornography of the law' and inscribe animality at its founding."[32] But Rosie serves a very different purpose here: to act as the witness and conscience of the soldier present who knew he was witnessing and abetting war crimes. Myles's inclusion of Rosie in this scene revises the connection between dogs and the police state, instead endowing Rosie with a prophetic voice. In Myles's imagination, Rosie is the one who pushes the soldier with a conscience to take the photos and send them home to be disseminated.

This moment with Rosie is reminiscent of Bobby, the dog in Emmanuel Levinas's "The Name of a Dog, or Natural Rights" (1963). In this essay, Levinas describes his brief acquaintance with a "wandering dog" in a POW camp during World War II. The dog is named Bobby, "an exotic name, as one [gives] a cherished dog." What the prisoners valued the most about Bobby was his inability to recognize the social constructions engineered to dehumanize them. Instead, Bobby "would appear at morning assembly and was waiting for us as we returned, jumping up and down and barking delight. For him, there was no doubt that we were men."[33] Bobby makes Levinas and the other prisoners feel seen—he bears witness to their suffering by treating them as human beings. In a similar fashion, Myles positions Rosie at Abu Ghraib as not only a witness but an active presence who "nudges" the soldier who participated in these crimes to report them. This time, however, the dehumanizing agents are not the Nazis but the US military.

SEEING THE DOG

Making Lolabelle Present

At the same time that both *Heart of a Dog* and *Afterglow* deploy dogs as symbols of political critique, both Anderson and Myles also insist upon Lolabelle and Rosie as real dogs with whom they have specific relationships. A central thread in *Heart of a Dog* is the role of art in shaping Anderson and Lolabelle's relationship, particularly as Lolabelle grows older. As she goes blind and becomes terrified to move, unable to grasp her surroundings, Anderson enlists the help of Lolabelle's trainer, who teaches Lolabelle how to paint. Soon, Lolabelle is making several paintings a day, "bright red abstract works," as Anderson calls them.[34] The idea of a dog making art may sound absurd— and Anderson's voice does carry a bemused tone—but she also takes Lolabelle's needs seriously. Through making art, Lolabelle is given a task that is embodied—a form of "enrichment" highly specific to her relationship with Anderson.[35] Indeed, Anderson suggests that Lolabelle's artistic proclivities did not start with her blindness, as she was a co-creator in Anderson's other projects. "Lolabelle sat in the studio with me through lots of different record projects," Anderson recounts. "Rat terriers have really good hearing, especially in the upper registers. And they never seem to get bored. 'Hey, let's listen to that cello track for the 70th' time.' 'Great idea.'"[36] This is funny, yes, but by paying attention to Lolabelle's needs, Anderson is able to get Lolabelle past her blindness-induced paralysis, drawing her back into the world on terms highly specific to both of them. As Saige Walton describes it, "Anderson tasks us with the need to look beyond our own situated and human perspectives."[37] This is a moment of artistic co-creation between Anderson and

Lolabelle that allows Lolabelle to remain engaged with Anderson and the world.

This emphasis on decentering the human self also dictates how Anderson cares for Lolabelle as she grows increasingly ill. When Lolabelle starts to decline, Anderson describes spending a great deal of time at the veterinarian's office. There, the veterinarian would deliver the same speech to Anderson: "Of course you don't want her to be in pain. And so we just give her a shot and put her to sleep and then another shot, and she stops breathing."[38] Anderson is skeptical of this gentle imagining of Lolabelle's death, one that implies that veterinary euthanasia is the most ethical course of action. Often it is. It is our job as human guardians to mitigate suffering as much as possible, and it is indeed a kindness to end that suffering when there is no reasonable cure. But as anyone who has cared for a terminally ill dog knows, the ethical landscape can be quite murky; dying is not a linear process. While the standard consideration for determining when to euthanize a dog is based on pain, the bioethicist Jessica Pierce points out that there is a lot that scientists do not understand about animal pain.[39] Pierce argues that treating pain is not a simple process but one that involves a lot of trial and error, especially since dogs cannot tell us in human language where and how they are hurting.[40] Furthermore, it is not necessarily clear what "a good death" is.[41]

Unsure what to do, Anderson turns to her Buddhist teacher, intuitively rejecting the veterinarian's speech and the sterile environment of the veterinary clinic. The teacher tells Anderson to go to the veterinary hospital and bring Lolabelle home, explaining, "'animals are like people. They approach death, and then they back away. And it's a process, and you don't have the right to take that from them.'"[42] As this advice is narrated, the viewer sees filmed footage from what looks like an animal hospital—close-ups of dogs and cats with medical instruments like feeding tubes shoved in their nostrils and into their veins, implying that human intervention is unnatural and even violent. This is a very different approach to animal dying, but one that is intended to grant them the same dignity as humans. Within this religious framework, it is not Anderson's place to make the decision to end Lolabelle's life—to do so would be to rob her of her agency. She does, however, heed her teacher's recommendation to "get some good tranquilizers" and "good food," doing what she can to ameliorate Lolabelle's suffering.[43]

Instead of running away from Lolabelle and her death, Anderson keeps a vigil at her side, remaining radically available to Lolabelle, staying with her for three days as her breath slowed and ultimately stopped.[44] Unlike other scenes that visually or sonically distort the subject, Lolabelle's death is comparatively unmediated, with Anderson using photographs of dying Lolabelle instead of drawings. One standout image is a close-up photograph of Lolabelle's face. She is barely conscious, with her eyes rolled into the back of her head. It is a painful photo to confront, but the film demands that its viewer stay present with Lolabelle. After she dies, Anderson says that "we [Anderson and her partner, Lou Reed] had learned to love Lola as she loved us, with a tenderness we didn't know we had."[45] Instead of the dog being a site of projection, the human viewers are asked to decenter their own needs and remain present with Lolabelle. While Anderson uses narrative to make sense of Lolabelle's death, unlike the framework of redemption narratives, she does not attribute meaning to her suffering. It exists because it is part of life, but it is not elevated to a larger purpose with redemptive meaning. Instead, this part of the film focuses on the love that characterizes Anderson's relationship to Lolabelle and Lolabelle's relationship to Anderson—an experience with textures that words cannot capture, something that only the two of them can ever really understand.

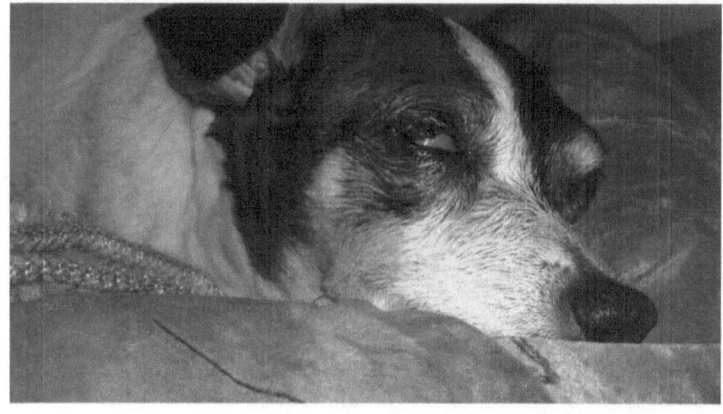

FIGURE 4.2. Lolabelle dying at home.
Source: Screen grab.

This emphasis on the relationship between death and love continues in the film, as Anderson grapples with her grief over Lolabelle's death. Again, Anderson turns to her Buddhist teacher, relaying his advice:

> When Lolabelle died, our teacher said,
> "Every time you think of her,
> give something away or do something kind."
> And I said,
> "Then I'd be giving things away nonstop."
> And he said,
> "So?"
> And it took me so long to figure it out,
> because death is so often about regrets
> or guilt.
> "Why didn't I call her
> Why didn't I say that?"

It's more about you
than the person who died.
But finally I saw it . . .
the connection between love and death
and that the purpose of death
is the release of love.⁴⁶

Earlier in the film, Anderson references the Zen Buddhist idea that one should not cry for the dead because it could confuse them. From this perspective, those who survived should be focused on the individual who died—and in mourning a death, one has the opportunity to honor their memory by releasing love back into the universe. As Anderson narrates this advice, one sees footage of the tips of trees shot from a moving car, rather than humans or even Lolabelle. Trees and the sky are recurrent images in this film, suggesting a nonanthropocentric vision of grief and mourning that connects Lolabelle to other living beings. This is not some kind of facile gesture but an opportunity to (in Buddhist terms) decenter oneself and memorialize the dead through generosity toward others.

In the end though, the film loops back to the same questions that open it: "Is it a pilgrimage? / Towards what?" It does not seek to provide answers to these questions, but through its use of various forms of media that shift from one story to the next, *Heart of a Dog* leaves the viewers with more questions than answers. There is no terminus to grief, but only questions that can be partially answered, at best. As Alice A. Kuzniar notes in *Melancholia's Dog* (2006), there is something uniquely devastating about the loss of a companion animal:

> In differentiating between mourning and melancholia Freud stipulated that, whereas the former moves toward a terminus in

the detachment from the lost object, the latter is ongoing because the indistinction between subject and object makes the acknowledgement of loss difficult to articulate. Applied to our relationship to pets, it is clear that the myriad ways in which our daily lives are intertwined with the constant presence and care of the pet cause the attachment to be inadvertently close. As a consequence, the final separation comes as a shock, the acuteness of which we tend to disavow.[47]

Because pets are part of our daily routines—we structure our lives around when they need to be fed, walked, let outside—their sudden absence is disorienting. This sense of bewilderment is compounded by feelings of shame that one could experience such profound grief for an animal. In her reading of Freud, Kuzniar argues that part of the challenge of grieving a pet is this notion that they are "just" pets and that therefore their lives, in Judith Butler's words, "do not qualify as 'grievable.'"[48] If we cannot fully mourn our animal companions, then, in Kuzniar's account of Freud, we remain melancholic, experiencing an ongoing sense of loss. There is no redemption of loss through representation in this work; grief does not end. Instead, *Heart of a Dog* embraces the inability to fully represent canine death, refusing the neat and tidy closure of canine redemption narratives referenced in previous chapters.

"My Dog/My God": The Profane Religiosity of Rosie's Decline and Death

By most appearances, *Afterglow* is an avowedly secular—if not even an antireligious—work. Throughout the text, Myles uses religion as a source of humor, be it through sardonic comments about Myles's stance on abortion or through playfully inverting the words "Dog" and "God" throughout the book.[49] I would like to suggest, however, that a more nuanced portrait of religion—one that has its roots in Myles's Catholic upbringing but is noninstitutional—emerges from the crudeness and comedy of these moments. This form of religion resembles the way that Donna Haraway talks about her religious experiences with her dog Cayenne, which were also shaped by her Catholic childhood.

Religion comes to the fore most clearly in *Afterglow* when Myles likens the process of caring for Rosie as her body begins to fail her as an act of religious devotion. While Anderson also sees giving Lolabelle the best care and attention until she dies as a religious act governed by her Buddhist principles, Myles's description carries Catholic resonances. In the second chapter of the book, entitled "Protect Me You," Myles writes a diary-like entry that details Rosie's slow and painful decline. Moving between observations about Rosie's physical deterioration and direct addresses to Rosie, Myles describes their relationship as "part discomfort & humiliation and part devotion."[50] Much like Haraway, Myles's relationship with Rosie is marked by a refusal to separate the body and the spirit. Throughout *Afterglow*, Myles emphasizes the physicality of their relationship with Rosie as she dies, presenting an unflinching portrait of the shit and piss and stench of death. Like Anderson, Myles refuses to sanitize the experience.

Even as it involves physical demands that can be grueling, the act of taking care of Rosie as she dies takes on the dimensions of a religious ritual for Myles. The first chapter of the book, entitled "My Dog/My God," references religion through the aphorism that "dog is God spelled backwards." While this is usually said with a degree of playfulness, Myles also wants us to take this claim seriously—to think about how caring for the dying is a sacred and beautiful act. At the same time, it's hard, painful, and even gross:

> My dog is dying. I kept saying it. I wash her ass and then I wash all the towels. One evening I was feeling a little extra naked after describing the ritual of mopping [Rosie's] piss [after she started having seizures] and I thought that's it. She's god. And I felt so calm. I've found god now. My God—My Dog. I chuckled. That's it. *Our Room. This is ecstasy & everything got bright.* She's dying & I'm watching her. I'm not *thinking* about it. Not that that makes any difference. I got this intention. This understanding. Did anyone ever say that suffering was about difference. It sops it all up. We are this picture of ourselves now, Rosie and I and we want to be seen.[51]

Through the profane act of cleaning up Rosie's urine, Myles realizes that their care has taken on a religious dimension, blurring the separation between Rosie and themself. Although Myles jokes about Rosie as a God who demands Myles's unconditional devotion, Myles also insists that they find something peaceful in the act of caring for Rosie—it requires a radical form of attention that forces Myles to stay present in the moment with their dog.

The life they created together became something holy; Myles describes the experience of Rosie's death as "having my religion torn from me."[52] Here, Colin Dayan's writing about dogs is useful in trying to disentangle what Myles means by "religion." As Dayan recounts, "Dogs live on the track between the mental and the physical and sometimes seem to tease out a near-mystical disintegration of the bounds between them. . . . We all experience our dogs' unprecedented and peculiar attentiveness. It comes across as an exuberance borne by a full heart."[53] As Dayan attests, it is so difficult to give language to the bond that we share with our dogs—but "attentiveness," which produces a radical disillusion of the boundaries between the body and the spirit, is an essential ingredient here. In another section of the book, Myles asks: "But who will I be without my dog?" echoing a question many dog guardians ask in the wake of such a stunning loss.[54] *Afterglow* can be read as a response to that question.

The act of writing about Rosie is a way of approximating but never fully capturing what it's like to be seen by a dog, and in turn, to look back at them. Myles can best capture this dynamic—the oscillation between flesh and the spirit—through writing. Like Anderson and Lolabelle, before Rosie's death, Myles wrote with and about Rosie. Once Myles realizes that Rosie's time is limited, their relationship to writing about her—and to Rosie herself—shifts. Here Myles's theological reckoning grows deeper. In a description of a book reading Myles did right before Rosie dies, they say: "I read for Rosie that night. Read every poem she was in. Dedicated it to her. Not that she needed it. She did not need poetry. She was it. Mainstay of my liturgy for sixteen point five almost seventeen years. She was observed. I was companioned, seen."[55] To be seen is to be companioned—and there is an interspecies reciprocity here, much like Donna Haraway's descriptions of her experiences training with her dog that I discuss in chapter 3. This witnessing also stands in stark juxtaposition with the role Rosie occupied in the earlier Abu Ghraib scene. In the description of her decline, Rosie is not the symbolic voice of conscience but instead the flesh-and-blood creature who shared nearly two decades of her life with her companion.

Unlike Anderson, who decides to have Lolabelle die at home without medical intervention, Myles eventually determines when it is time to bring Rosie to the vet and have her euthanized. Myles explains their reasoning as follows: "People said you'll know when I asked them how they knew it was time. When it was okay to take your dog's life. You'll know they said looking me right in the eye. And I did." Although Myles says that they knew when it was okay to euthanize Rosie, the moment is still filled with doubt. At the vet's office, Myles says, "Do you think I'm rushing her," to which the vet responds, "She's been ready for a while. It was you that was holding on. She didn't need to hang around all this time, did you Rose."[56] This moment suggests that it is an act of mercy to end Rosie's life since she has been suffering for a long time. After Rosie's heart stopped, Myles describes this moment as follows:

> The world was outside the door. It was Saturday morning. It was so generous. To just let us be in here now like this. Just us. She was a city dog, born on a sidewalk or a roof. There was always concrete and talk. The world out there now on the other side of the wall. In here, just us.
>
> How will I ever let go of you girl. The first one ever mine. I hugged her long body. Her mouth so still. Her eyes, closed I think. I don't know.
>
> I saw this movie about the jungle. The man died under a tree. His friends were leaving him. Travel well I said. All the seeds of you; and the dream of you, the rot.
>
> Then I stepped back into the world.[57]

In a way the texts in the previous chapters and the traditional 9/11 dog stories resist, Rosie is present *as Rosie*. This idea of "stepping back into the world" suggests that although Rosie died, Myles has to make a conscious choice to keep living. But to keep living is not to deny the meaningfulness of Rosie's life. Instead, through writing about Rosie's life—in all its fullness and complexity—Rosie lives on, though not in the same neat and tidy way dogs in traditional redemption narratives do. The process of continuing to reflect on Rosie's life requires Myles and the reader to experience the difficult and painful aspects of their relationship, as well as the heartwarming and beautiful ones. Suffering here does create connection and even transcendence of the self. But whatever redemptive element suffering produces is not symbolic of something greater, nor is it the defining element of Myles's and Rosie's relationship.

The final chapter of the book, "The Walk," makes this text's commitment to a nonredemptive reading of death particularly clear. In this scene, Myles transcribes a recording of the time they released Rosie's ashes into the water, accompanied by a friend, constituting the opposite of a baptism. The scene begins with Myles and switches between their statements and their friend's reply: "I think they're with us. / The man was taller than the woman. He smiled at her. / Do you. / Yes, you don't feel them. / Man huffs but without ill will. / I don't know what I feel. / Well this is a séance." By writing the final section as a poem, Myles makes it difficult to tell who is speaking to whom, creating a kind of interspecies conversation. Myles continues, pondering the ethics of recording these final moments with Rosie's ashes: "Do you think it's gross that I'm recording this. / You're an artist. You have to do it. / I could turn it off."[58] This discomfort with recording the final moments that Myles and Rosie are physically together reflects a broader discomfort with using Rosie in service of their art, but at the same time, their art is also written in service of Rosie, even if she cannot understand the words. In the end, Myles scatters Rosie's ashes in the water:

C'mon swim baby.
It's just us.

> She dumps more and more of the powder into the water. There aren't any clumps. Maybe this isn't even her. Bullshit . . .
> No it's nice.
> They stand there for a moment . . . Bye Rosie. *And the foghorn blows.*
> They look at each other and laugh.
> They snort.
> *Our dogs.*
> *Our dogs.*[59]

This moment is marked by the question of whether or not Rosie is really Rosie, as Myles faces the humbling recognition that all they have left of the physical manifestation of their dog is dust. Or that the total lack of physical materiality makes it difficult to discern that this was ever Rosie—there is no evidence of her specificity. The moment also contains humor, captured by the melodramatic eruption of the foghorn and the laughter that follows. But as the repetition of "our dogs" suggests, Myles has not lost Rosie; they are irrevocably bound together. This scene reflects Myles's ethics throughout the book: a coexisting of the profane and the sacred that refuses a single interpretation. *Afterglow* is invested in subjecting readers to a kind of discomfort that requires being immersed in an uneasiness with the complexity of reality that cannot be contained in redemption narratives. Instead, for Myles an ethics of discomfort—which requires recognizing the messiness of our relationships with our dogs and with other human beings—is the most moral path forward.

CONCLUSION

Laurie Anderson and Eileen Myles present an alternative relationship between dogs and the nation. Unlike Bretagne, Rosie and Lolabelle are decoupled from US nationalism. But this does not mean that the dogs are exempt from being used as symbols. In both texts, Rosie and Lolabelle operate as voices of critique of US policy or expressions of vulnerability in the wake of the 9/11 attacks and patriotic narratives of redemption. While Bretagne's actions were undeniably heroic and reflect dogs' incredible scenting capacities, stories about her also involve a great deal of projection about who Americans wanted to be in the wake of 9/11: strong and loyal. Lolabelle and Rosie arguably possess those traits, but Anderson and Myles are worried about projecting their personal feelings and desires onto the dogs. Even when wielded for social critique, Lolabelle and Rosie remain stubbornly canine, relentless in their individual presence.

CODA

Dogs Save makes a case for how and why the canine redemption narrative has become the dominant genre for understanding the relationships between people and dogs in the United States. Drawing from Christian roots and sometimes explicitly invoking them, these narratives are about a total transformation from bad to good, sin to salvation. On the one hand, they are highly individualistic, and in the case of people, redemption narratives depend on personal confessions followed by punishment.[1] On the other hand, canine redemption narratives are so effective because they invoke what Robert N. Bellah famously called "American civil religion" to describe the central values, rituals, and symbols that all people in the United States identify as holding transcendent value.[2] Civil religion appears outside of traditionally religious spaces—in football stadiums, in presidential inauguration addresses, and, as I have shown in this book, with dogs in animal shelters, prisons, training facilities, and homes. However, as many critics have rightly pointed out, American civil religion is aspirational in character, meaning that these rituals, symbols, and values are often more fantasy than reality, serving to uphold dominant power structures rather than to deconstruct them.[3]

As prime sites of projection about who the people living in the United States want to be, canine redemption narratives reveal contested parts of American civil religion, laying bare instances of exclusion as much as inclusion, fragmentation as well as consensus.[4]

Because the canine redemption narrative is a genre about identity formation in the United States, it is impossible to talk about redemption without also talking about white supremacy. Ernest Lee Tuveson's *Redeemer Nation* (1968)—the first in-depth exploration of the rhetoric of redemption in US religious and political history—begins by defining the elements of what he calls "the redeemer nation": "a chosen race, chosen nation, millennial-utopian destiny for mankind, a continuing war between good (progress) and evil (reaction) in which the United States is to play a starring role as world redeemer."[5] Racist hierarchies, binaries of good and evil, and grandiose fantasies about the United States' preordained role in the world recur throughout the canine redemption narratives analyzed in this book. As Tuveson demonstrates, in the context of the United States, redemption's theological grounding became (and is still used as) a form of justification for political violence at home and abroad.

As outlined in the introduction, the original etymology of the word "redemption" is central to understanding the power of the canine redemption narrative. In its original Latin, redemption refers to the act of repurchasing an enslaved person from bondage. This linguistic inheritance is important because it recalls the centrality of enslavement, as well as the rhetoric of payment and indebtedness, to stories of redemption in the United States. People on both sides of the debate over slavery would mobilize the language of redemption. After Reconstruction in the nineteenth century, "The Redemption" referred to the self-proclaimed movement by southern whites to reclaim their state governments from federal control, which "represented a powerful and lasting narrative about the role of violence in American politics."[6] As this history demonstrates, redemption is bound up in white supremacy—violence that, as I show in chapter 2, is not contained to the South but is a national project.

Drawing on this context, *Dogs Save* traces the ways in which redemption is essential to the work of animal rescue in the contemporary United States. Like prisons, animal shelters also rely on rituals of discipline and punishment in order to make redemption possible—biopolitical processes that Katja M. Guenther refers to as the interrelated constellation of "helping/policing/killing."[7] When an owner reclaims a lost animal, shelters call this a "redemption." In order to redeem a dog, the person must provide proof of ownership, since animals are legally considered property; they usually also pay a fee to the shelter for the costs of housing and feeding. At the same time that animal rescue involves an economic dimension, the act of redeeming a dog from the shelter resembles Christian prison conversion narratives, in which, after a period of incarceration and economic restitution, a dog is saved from death and "born again."[8] As I show throughout the book, animal shelters do important and life-saving work, but as Harlan Weaver reminds us, their historic (and often continued) connection to law enforcement also means they share similarities to carceral systems for human beings.[9] *Pit Bulls & Parolees*—the paradigmatic canine redemption narrative that I use to open this book—makes this connection explicit by pairing a maligned and racialized dog breed ("pit bulls") with marginalized and racialized people ("parolees"). Even as these are important sites to critique dominant power structures, animal shelters also involve moments of genuine interspecies connection.

The first part of the book introduces the genre of the canine redemption narrative, showing both its possibilities and limitations. In chapter 1, I introduce the central literary conventions of the canine redemption narrative by analyzing two books about the Michael Vick dogfighting case—one written by Vick (*Finally Free*, 2012), the other about the dogs and authored by a sports journalist (*The Lost Dogs*, 2010). In reading these texts together, I show how in their classic form, canine redemption narratives reduce systemic problems to personal failings. In my analysis of *Finally Free*, I argue that Vick must focus on his individual choices, confess his guilt, and affirm that his imprisonment was required for his redemption because it brought him back to Christianity. While individual accountability is important, in redemption narratives like Vick's, the logic of redemption requires personal confession and punishment at the expense of exploring the broader social context that shaped him (namely, growing up in a predominantly Black and poor neighborhood where dogfighting was pervasive). In my analysis of *The Lost Dogs*, I argue that the case for the innocence of "the Vick dogs" depends on graphic depictions of their suffering, as we saw in the horrific passages about the "little red dog" murdered on Vick's property. By forever linking them to their abusive pasts, these narratives imply that only traumatized dogs deserve redemption. Both narratives reflect the perilous implications of the genre—that redemption is predicated on suffering and punishment.

As I argue in my reading of the film *White Dog* (1982) in chapter 2, efforts to represent anti-Black racism through canine redemption narratives are bound to fail because the genre simply cannot accommodate complexity at a systemic level. The film's title refers to the historic use of dogs to track and kill enslaved Black people, and its plot centers on a white woman who inadvertently rescues a white dog and enlists a Black trainer determined to train the racism out of the dog. While the white dog is meant to serve as a symbol of the possibility of changing hearts and minds through antiracist education, it once again locates the site for transformation in the individual rather than the system. Further, the redemption framework in the film suggests that someone is either racist or not, comparing racism to a disease that can be cured. Ultimately, the film places the burden on its Black characters to not only educate an imagined white audience but to protect white people from facing our culpability in the broader systems that led to the creation of a "white dog" in the first place.

If the first part of the book is about how canine redemption narratives use dogs as symbols of broader white social anxieties around race that make real dogs absent, the second part explores the possibility of canine presence in redemption narratives through stories about individual people and dogs. Chapter 3 focuses on dog training as a religious ritual—what I call "relational redemption"—that occurs outside traditionally religious contexts, even when Christianity is the primary referent. I first analyze the celebrity dog trainer Cesar Millan's popular TV shows as classic canine redemption narratives, in which training is the tool to restore domestic harmony and to keep the dog in a home (animal shelters or euthanasia are ever-present threats on the show). However, as canine redemption narratives, they also involve punishment and suffering, which I show through Millan's widely criticized use of aversive training techniques. In contrast, Vicki Hearne and Donna Haraway strive to reckon with the dogs in front of them in all their complexity. In its ideal form, training for Hearne and Haraway allows for the individual person and dog to create a new reality together through an interspecies language. While imperfect and, in the case of Hearne, reliant on some problematic aversive training techniques too, both texts work to make the dogs present as dogs rather than symbols of human social problems.

Chapter 4, "Troubling Redemption," analyzes the work of avant-garde artists and writers, namely, Laurie Anderson and Eileen Myles, to explore what it looks like to subvert the canine redemption narrative. As artists living in New York City during 9/11, both Anderson and Myles deploy dogs as figures of critique of the rising surveillance state and the use of torture at the Abu Ghraib prison. This chapter most directly confronts the dangers of the theopolitical inheritance of the United States as a "redeemer nation." At the same time as these works are about national concerns, they are also very much about Anderson's and Myles's individual dogs, Lolabelle and Rosie, respectively. Created in the wake of their dogs' deaths, Anderson's Buddhist framework and Myles's anarchist-Catholic approach both offer an ethics of discomfort that requires confronting questions of scale and responsibility akin to those raised by *White Dog*. This time, however, dogs are not symbols of anti-Black racism but of US war crimes. Both texts explore what it means to mourn dogs, both of whom lived rich, long lives, in the midst of unrelenting human violence and loss. Unlike *White Dog*, in which the dog is more symbol than individual, these works insist on the specificity of their relationships to Lolabelle and Rosie.

I want to conclude by way of exploring Mary Oliver's poem "Percy Wakes Me (Fourteen) Today" from 2010. This poem represents a mode of living with, loving, and being loved by dogs that is not redemptive in nature. It is much smaller in scale than the stories I've analyzed thus far—both in terms of genre (it is a poem) and scope (it is about an individual relationship between a person and a dog). And yet it is these precise features that make "Percy Wakes Me" a prime example of a literary work that makes dogs present:

> Percy wakes me and I am not ready.
> He has slept all night under the covers.
> Now he's eager for action: a walk, then breakfast.
> So I hasten up. He is sitting on the kitchen counter
> Where he is not supposed to be.
> How wonderful you are, I say. How clever, if you needed me,
> to wake me.
> He thought he would hear a lecture and deeply
> his eyes begin to shine.
> He tumbles onto the couch for more compliments.
> He squirms and squeals; he has done something
> that he needed
> and now he hears that it is okay.
> I scratch his ears, I turn him over
> and touch him everywhere. He is
> wild with the okayness of it. Then we walk, then
> he has breakfast, and he is happy.
> This is a poem about Percy.
> This is a poem about more than Percy.
> Think about it.[10]

In "Percy Wakes Me," Oliver describes an all-too-familiar experience for those of us who share our lives with dogs: being jarred out of sleep by a canine companion insistent on starting the day. When we fail to heed their call or to pay attention, we often find our dogs in places where they are "not supposed to be": on counters, tables, and other pieces of furniture traditionally reserved for people. Instead of growing angry or frustrated, however, the speaker compliments Percy on his ingenuity, and in turn, he "squirms and squeals" when she praises and pets him. This canine joy derives from the fact that "[Percy] has done something / that he needed / and now he hears that it is okay." The person understands what Percy is asking and listens, placing his needs over her own. Rising out of bed, she takes him for a walk and then feeds him breakfast. The result is that "he is happy," and the implication is that the speaker is too. The poem concludes with these enigmatic three lines: "This is a poem about Percy / This is a poem about more than Percy / Think about it." On the one hand, the speaker is describing a highly specific experience involving Percy—the name of one of Mary Oliver's dogs in real life.[11] On the other hand, the fact that the speaker does not have a name and the poem is written in the first person suggests that she could be any one of us. In doing so, the poem asks its readers to imagine how we would respond in a similar situation. Written in the imperative, "think about it" demands that we humans consider the world from a canine perspective instead of prioritizing our own.

This poem is a striking example of what I have been describing as "making dogs present"—and in this instance, it is a wholly nonredemptive framework. There is no transformation, people and dogs are not confined to binaries of "good" and "evil," and punishment is not part of the picture.[12] Instead, there is connection, delight, and attention—what the speaker initially calls "disobedience" ultimately becomes "cleverness" once she interprets Percy on his own terms. Percy's joy comes from not being yelled at or punished, which is what he anticipated, but instead from being seen and loved for who he is. This is a poem about allowing Percy to revel in the "okayness" of being himself in companionship with the speaker.

Based on this reading, the central verb in the title, "to awaken," holds two meanings. In a literal sense, Percy wakes the speaker from her slumber. And at the metaphorical level, Percy allows for a deeper kind of awakening—one that nudges the speaker to look beyond herself and to be radically present, pulling her outside of her internal monologue and into the moment with the dog in front of her. At one and the same time, Percy is the creature who is the speaker's dog and also a symbol of interspecies communication and connection. In the stories we tell about dogs, we are constantly shifting registers from the literal to the figural. But the "dogness" of Percy remains a constant throughout these shifts. In other words, even as a symbol, he is all dog.

Of course, not every morning will be like that one. And as Percy teaches us, that is okay too. We all fail our dogs sometimes, and other times, they disappoint us. A perfect relationship—human or canine—does not exist. Similarly, I also do not mean to offer this poem as an easy solution for the problems raised by the dog redemption narrative. While expert at capturing the intricacies in this interspecies moment, this poem does not reckon with the systemic factors that shape human-canine relationships: race, class, gender, and, of course, religion. It is also not trying to offer such a solution. What this poem does provide, however, is one example of what it looks like to tell stories that make dogs present by understanding what they are communicating to us and responding in kind. What if, instead of reading redemption narratives, which are necessarily written by humans, we started reading our dogs by learning about canine forms of communication?[13]

We cannot tell different stories about dogs until we actually try to understand them from their perspective. As Alexandra Horowitz writes in *Inside of a Dog* (2009), "the dog uses his body expressively: communication writ through movement."[14] Instead of assuming that all dogs are happy to meet us, perhaps we need to try to see what individuals are telling us when we encounter them. This is possible through attention to the movement of their tails, ears, eyes—in other words, by learning canine communication cues that signal what they want. Contrary to dominant representations of them in US culture, in which dogs exist solely to meet human needs, dogs do not owe us their loyalty and trust, especially if we have not worked to earn it.

In a book about dogs, and in a section arguing for the importance of reading canine body language, it is therefore fitting to conclude with a coda, which comes from the Latin word *cauda*, meaning tail.[15] This delights me not only because tails naturally remind me of dogs but because the tail is such a powerful canine communication tool—a way of providing humans with information about what our dogs are telling us, of allowing us to be present with them.[16] Understanding what a dog is signaling by her tail can be the difference between a friendly greeting or a bite. While dogs may not speak the same language as us and therefore cannot narrate their own stories, if we pause and pay attention, we will fail our dogs less often. Dogs are capable of what Alexandra Horowitz refers to as the "absence of linguistic noise."[17] My hope for this book is that it opens more avenues for dogs to be dogs, for us to read what they communicate, and to hold close to what they have to offer beyond redemption—complexity, relation, and presence.

ACKNOWLEDGMENTS

Writing does not happen in isolation, and it is my great privilege to thank the family members, friends, editors, colleagues, teachers, students, behaviorists, veterinarians, dogs, and cats who have supported me over the duration of this project.

I have been fortunate to learn from gifted teachers whose interventions at key moments in my life shaped who I am today. Thank you to my high school English teachers Michael Wolf and Linda Weatherby, for teaching me the joys of close reading and for encouraging me to keep writing. My life was changed for the better in college when I took my first literature course with Carla A. Arnell, a professor, mentor, and friend who has indelibly shaped me as a reader, writer, and teacher. Carla, thank you for your steadfast support for over two decades; if I can be half the teacher you are, then I will be happy. I am also deeply grateful to the faculty at Lake Forest College, who showed me what it looks like to take courses with people who love to teach. Thank you to Robert Archambeau, Judy Dozier, Benjamin Goluboff, Dan LeMahieu, Richard Mallette, Siobhan Moroney, Ahmad Sadri, and Davis Schneiderman. I was a lot better at the academic than social part of the whole college thing, and I am grateful that I met Stephanie Hicks in our English senior seminar. To my college bestie of nearly twenty years: Thank you for being my roommate even after I brought home a (shall we say, "sassy?") calico cat named Stella, for recommending everything from scholarly sources to hilariously vile television, and for our conversations about academia, dogs, whiteness, friendship, teaching, love, and Chicago.

Dogs Save was not the book I had originally petitioned to write, and I am so grateful to Richard A. Rosengarten for being flexible and trusting that the dogs and I were on to something. Rick, thank you for believing in my work and encouraging me to use my voice. Thank you for teaching me how to read (and now teach!) theory and for your feedback on this project at various stages along the way. To Heather Keenleyside: This project simply would not have happened without you. Thank you for catching me at a critical moment, for sharpening my thinking and writing, and for stepping up when you absolutely did not have to do so. I was also fortunate to know Wendy Doniger and James T. Robinson. Wendy, thank you for inviting me over for talks about dogs (with Kimberly, of course). Jim, thank you for teaching me that intellectual rigor and empathy are not mutually exclusive—my gratitude for you is immeasurable. Thank you also to Angela Jaffrey for her encouragement, reading suggestions, and for providing feline therapy (much love to Falak, Avi, and Mimi). I benefited from the teaching and mentorship of many other Chicago faculty, including Catherine A. Brekus, Ryan Coyne, Sarah Hammerschlag, and Paul Mendes-Flohr (z"l).

I found a supportive and vibrant intellectual community through the Animal Studies Workshop, advised by Heather Keenleyside and Mark Payne. I could not have worked with a better co-coordinator than Bill Hutchison, a person who met me with generosity and patience when I was feeling quite lost. Thank you to my other Animal Studies workshop comrades: Les Beldo, Hannah Chazin, Ashley Drake, Zoe Hughes, Hannah Frank, Joela M. Jacobs, Jacob Leveton, Agnes Malinowska, Nell Pach, and Jessica Robinson. Thank you also to my dear R&L community for reading multiple drafts of this work in its earliest stages: Mandy Burton, Brett Colasacco, David Gregg, M. Cooper Harriss, Alison Davis Ricketts, and R. L. Watson. Thank you also to other UChicago friends, especially Katherine Alexander, Samuel Hayim Brody, Kristel Clayville, Mary Emily Briehl Duba, Allison Gray, Sarah Imhoff, Sarah Kunjummen, Ekaterina Lomperis, Willa and Jacob Swenson-Lengyel, Michael Mols, Alex Perry, and Sarah Yardney. As a Junior Fellow with the Martin E. Marty Center, I was fortunate to receive both funding and a community of brilliant interlocutors. Last but not least, thank you to Cass Turner for their incredible mind, for their ability to zoom out and see the big picture, for reading drafts and brainstorming together for over a decade, for gifting me the book title, and of course, for their friendship.

Thank you to the Chicago dog and cat people who informed this book in countless ways by teaching me how to live and work with animals: Cynthia Bathurst, Kathleen Budrean, Keri Burchfield, Anita Denes-Meador, Ann and Joan Goliak, Mollie Green, Susan Keller, Christine and Nabi Lee, Andrea Juracek, Hyosub and Willie Kim, Robin Roseth, Aimee Schneider, Amy Teister, Angela Tomasino, Janice Triptow, Amy Ujiki. I also want to recognize my dear friend Darvis R. Dennis, who tragically did not live to see this book in print. Darvis's conversations, care, insight, and intelligence changed my life, and this book for the better; he will be missed but his legacy lives on in these pages.

I was so lucky to find a rich community during my time working at Whitman College and living in Walla Walla, Washington. Thank you to Lauren E. Osborne and Peter Shultz for being like family to us (four cat minimum forever). Major thank you to other members of our group chat—Jackie Woodfork and Michelle Jenkins—who have provided life-sustaining friendship over the past eight years. Thank you to the other members of the religion department for providing instrumental guidance as I learned how to teach full-time: Courtney Fitzsimmons, Dan Kent, Daniel Schultz, Jon Walters, and Xiobo Yuan. Special thanks to Rebecca Hanrahan and Lisa Uddin for helping me navigate the academic job market. Thank you also to my new faculty cohort (Lauren Berger, Miles Canaday, Elizabeth Danka, Emily K. Harrison, Mark Hendricks, and Rosie Mueller) and other amazing humans I met along the way (Nancy Day, Adam Gordon, Russ Gordon, Laurel Hendricks, Michelle Janning, Emily Jones, Helen Kim, Marina Ptukhina, Em Sibley, Monica Streifer, Kisha Lewellyn Schlegel, Lindsay Szramek, and Stan Thayne). A huge thank you to my Whitman students, especially those who took the Animals, Religion, and Ethics courses with me. Thank you to the folks at Animal Clinic East, including Dr. Susan Fazarri and Dr. Brooke Cox, and to the vet techs and support staff who kept our animals alive and helped us manage Stella's decline and Zoe's cancer diagnosis. Thank you to Brooke and Dan Davey for being the most welcoming next-door neighbors I've ever had—for shoveling the sidewalk when I was injured, for offering much-needed reminders to take breaks, and for reminding me of the importance of community.

I also wish to acknowledge the wider group of scholars who offered feedback, friendship, and support along the way. Thank you to Danielle Alesi, Kirsty Jones, Karen Griffin, Kathryn

Kirkpatrick, Pollyanna Rhee, Juno Salazar Parreñas, Limor Hemed Petel, and Drew Winter.

There have been so many animal studies people who have supported this work. First, I must thank my colleagues and friends in the AAR Animals and Religion Unit: Dave Aftandilian, Barbara Ambros, Geoffrey Barstow, Christopher Carter, Andrea Dara Cooper, Dorothy Dean, Jonathan Dickstein, Aaron Gross, Adrienne Krone, Eric Daryl Meyer, and Jeania Ree Moore. Thank you for your insight and feedback over the development of this book.

Thank you to Jane Desmond and Kim Marra for organizing the Human-Animal Studies Summer Institute at the University of Illinois at Urbana-Champaign and for providing a space for me to receive smart feedback on this book and find more of my people. Special thanks to Cara and Turf Miller for embodying what genuine canine-human partnership looks like—I love you both, always and forever.

I am proud to call Western Carolina University my home institution and to work in a department committed to strong teaching, research, and community. Thank you to my philosophy and religion colleagues, past and present: Andréa Daventry, Daryl Hale, David Henderson, Christopher Hoyt, Myron Jackson, Robert Jones, Jason LeCureux, Thomas Daventry Shea, Jonathan LaTourelle, Amy McKenzie, James McLachlan, Michelle Sorensen, John F. Whitmire Jr., and Jeffrey Vickery. I am especially grateful to David Henderson for his leadership as department head, John Whitmire for his mentorship, and Amy McKenzie for her support and friendship (and patience with me constantly locking myself out of my office). Andréa and Thomas, thank you for lending your philosophical thinking to this project and for all the Saturday night movie hangouts. I am so grateful to the Heidi Buchanan and Sarah Steiner, the philosophy and religion subject librarians whom I consider friends and without whom I would not be able to do my work. Thank you to my broader community of Western folks (past and present): Lisa Bloom, Alleyne Broomell, Nora Doyle (thank you for all the garden bounty and supportive texts/coffee chats!), Kristy Doss, Sara Duncan, Betty Farmer, Jessica Hayden, Hal Herzog, Candy Noltensmeyer, Travis Rountree, Vincent Russell, Katerina Spasovska, Tonya Vickery, and Claire Wofford. I owe Laura Wright a special thank you for welcoming and grounding me when I started here, for our biannual road trip (mis)adventures, for understanding my work, for loving animals as much as I do, and last but not least, for designing the stunning cover of this book. I am so incredibly honored to know you. To Freddie and Scottie Kapel: Thank you for becoming our family away from home. There's no one Kevin and I would rather survive a hurricane with than you two. Scottie, thank you for your instrumental support as I wrapped up this project, for your wry sense of humor, your intuitive understanding of my neuroses, for welcoming me into a workout community, and for becoming a trusted confidante and dear friend.

I would be remiss if I did not thank all the WCU students who enriched my life (and listened to me drone on about this book for the past five years). If I had space to thank all of you personally, I would. I want to send a special shout-out to folks from the Animals and Religion course and to those of you who have helped me think about this project more deeply, including Rosalie Alff, Jackson Bedenbaugh, Jeremy Browning, Ashbury Haight, Marcus Ibarra, Jordan McCoy-Bruce, Madelin McEuen, Nathan Travis, Matthew Miyagi Tuten, Jared Ross, and Amaranth Schmoyer.

The "Anti-Burnout Collective" (ABCs) was there every step of the way as I worked on this book. To Rebecca McWilliams

Ojala Ballard, Lauren Herold, Rebecca Oh, Allison Page, and Nicole Morse: Thank you for reading every single chapter of this book multiple times, for your incisive and insightful feedback, for talking me down more times than I can remember, and for being a feminist writing community when I needed it the most. I love you all so much.

It turns out that writing a book is hard. I owe a huge thank you to developmental editor extraordinaire Laura Helper for teaching me the difference between genres, for the photos of Frederick and Angel, for holding all my anxiety throughout this process, and for reminding me to make space for joyful dog stories.

Kate Schechter has been an instrumental presence in my life for over a decade. Kate, thank you for helping me find my voice and teaching me how to use it. I wouldn't be the person I am today without you, and so much of this book comes from our rich conversations over the years. For that, I am eternally grateful.

There are three people who have supported this project from the beginning and who have taught me what feminist mentorship looks like. Thank you to Colin Dayan for your support, wisdom, and luminous prose, which continue to nourish and inspire me. Thank you to Kathryn Lofton for her steadfast support and belief that a book like this one might offer something to scholars of religion in the United States. Finally, I am so grateful to Harlan Weaver for not only responding when I cold emailed him out of the blue but for teaching me that academic precarity demands to be met with generosity and solidarity. The influence of Harlan's work on dogs, gender, and race is present across this book, and I thank him for all the years of mentorship and conversation.

This book would not exist without Wendy Lochner at Columbia University Press, to whom I thank for her steadfast support at all stages of this project. Thank you to Wendy for being this book's biggest advocate, for working with me in the midst of so much chaos, and for our conversations about cats. I am so grateful for everything you have and continue to do for me. I also want to thank the anonymous peer reviewers whose incisive and generous feedback made this a much stronger book. Any remaining faults are certainly my own. Thank you also to Emily Elizabeth Simon for her generous patience with all my questions and for her assistance preparing the book for copyediting and production. Thank you to Milenda Nan Ok Lee for the gorgeous cover design. I am also grateful to Rob Fellman for his meticulous copy edits and to Paula and Oreo Durbin-Westby for thoughtfully indexing the book.

My original three feline and canine companions—Stella, Freddie, and Zoe—were present as I wrote most of this book, both physically and intellectually. Freddie sat on my lap from my qualifying exams up to my drafting of this manuscript in March 2024. Stella taught me to love the cat you meet, not the one you want. Zoe is what animal rescue people call my "heart dog," my canine soulmate who inspired this entire project and brought me into the dog world of Chicago.

Kevin and I have been fortunate to bring other more-than-human animals into our lives, including Jake and Elwood (our darling Blues Brothers), Joni Mitchell (the soulful dog/excellent cuddler), and Frankie (seventy-five pounds of enthusiasm who was a rambunctious puppy who constantly woke me as I was revising, testing my capacity for attention and presence).

Thank to the animal people I've been able to meet in Western NC, including April Kormenac, Tina Manning, Windy McKinney, Caitlin Morrow, everyone at the Animal Hospital of Waynesville, Sarge's Animal Rescue Foundation, and Dr. Monica Tschosik at Upstate Vet for keeping Freddie alive for so long. Special shout out to my family veterinarians—my brother Kevin Pflaum and sister-in-law Amelia Tabor—who will always remain our Asheville family: Thank you for all your support with my book, the move, and our animals. We miss you.

To my parents, Julie Rand and Steven Pflaum, thank you for instilling a love of reading and writing in me. Mom, thank you for raising me surrounded by dogs and books, for teaching me about empathy, for your chocolate chip oatmeal cookies, and for sending me *The Lost Dogs*, the book that began this journey. Dad, thank you for all hours spent teaching me how to read and write, for your dad jokes, your patience, and unconditional support. To Matthew Pflaum and Alyssa Beer, Brian and Jodie Pflaum, thank you for making me an auntie and for always remembering holidays and birthdays when I was in the writing cave. Thank you to Karen Robertson, Krista LeRay, and Kimberlee Mott for bringing more family and love into my life. A big thank you to Marc Magliari for your intelligence, honesty, humor, and for always picking me up at the airport. Thank you to Shirley Pflaum, Pamela and Tom Davies, Elizabeth Schindler, Andrew Davies, and my other dear aunts, uncles, and cousins for being a huge presence in my life. I am so lucky to have all of you. Thank you to Steve and Lynn Mershon for their encouragement, for allowing us to bring our wild beasts into their house, and for understanding why I was always working. I am also grateful that David and Julie Mershon, Jim, Dori, and Valerie Decker, as well as Norma Schiller, are part of my family.

When my great-grandfather Abraham Yellin came to this country in hopes of finding safety and stability, he wanted to go to college to become a journalist. Grandpa Abe was a writer at heart but supported his family by opening a deli on the West Side of Chicago. This book is the fruit of his and many other family members' sacrifices—you are all part of this book. I was fortunate to grow up with grandparents who were a constant loving presence in my life and who instilled in me a deep love of education: Al and Florence Rand and Sharon and Donald Pflaum. I want to send a special thank you to Grandma Sharon for her material and emotional support over the years: We are lucky to have you as our matriarch.

Thank you to my childhood friends (you know who you are!). Sending special shout outs to my oldest friend, Kristin Aardsma-Kosokoff, an accomplished and gorgeous writer in her own right, and to Caroline Manley, a force of nature whose determination inspires me daily.

To Joela Jacobs, meine Schwesternfreundin, for whom we needed to invent a German word to capture our relationship: Thank you for showing me how to make things happen; for holding me accountable all of these years with your loving but firm honesty (we know I needed it); for your comments on this manuscript at all stages; for our Chicago walks; for your unmatched generosity, humor, and love; for your last-minute assist with the coda; and for talking to me about teaching, writing, and life every single day for over a decade.

Thank you to Kevin Mershon, my partner of twenty years, for supporting my prolonged graduate study, for moving to remote locales in different parts of the country for my job, for making career sacrifices that have allowed me to continue doing what I love, for cooking so much delicious food, for greeting the new litter of kittens I would bring home with bemusement, and for being my best friend. This book is for you.

NOTES

INTRODUCTION: REDEMPTION AND THE "AMERICAN DOG"

1. *Pit Bulls & Parolees*, season 9, episode 2, "Redeemed," featuring Tia Torres and Earl Moffett, aired November 12, 2016, on Animal Planet (22:56). Because terms like "parolee" are dehumanizing, I try to avoid using them except when directly referencing the show.
2. VRC originally was located in California, but they moved to New Orleans in the show's development, recognizing the underresourced state of animal shelters in the South. They now are located in Assumption Parish, Louisiana. Villalobos Rescue Center, "FAQs," https://www.vrcpitbull.com/about/faq/.
3. The show was canceled because Animal Planet was sold to Warner Bros. Warner Bros. Discovery, "Combination of Discovery and WarnerMedia Creates Warner Bros. Discovery, Global Leader in Entertainment and Streaming," press release, April 8, 2022. For *Pit Bulls and Parolees*' Facebook announcement, see https://www.facebook.com/VillalobosRescueCenter/photos/pb.100044332334480.-2207520000./10158644223986143/?type=3.
4. "Dysfunctional" is the word Torres uses to describe her childhood. As she recounts in her memoir, animals were the most steadfast presence in her life populated by unreliable humans. Tia Torres, *My Life Among the Underdogs: A Memoir* (William Morrow, 2019), 2.
5. Twin brothers Kanani and Keli'i [Moe] were legally adopted by Torres as young teenagers when they were all living in California. For

more on their story, see Discovery, "Tia Torres," https://www.discovery.com/profiles/tia-torres.

6. Moffett's popularity is reflected by the fact that the show features at least three episodes centered on his story ("Redeemed," season 9, episode 2; "Fall from Grace," season 16, episode 6; "Earl's Path," season 17, episode 4). He has 44,000 followers on his Facebook page. https://www.facebook.com/profile.php?id=100066650380722.
7. *Pit Bulls & Parolees*, season 9, episode 2, "Redeemed" (3:48).
8. *Pit Bulls & Parolees*, season 9, episode 2, "Redeemed." I tried to find information about how much Moffett and other workers at the shelter were paid by Animal Planet, but I hit a dead end. Torres has stated that she donates all earnings back to the shelter. See https://www.facebook.com/VillalobosRescueCenter/photos/a.172848176142/10153466444556143/?type=3.
9. This language comes from the show's opening credits. *Pit Bulls & Parolees*, season 8, episode 19, "Second Savior," featuring Tia Torres and Earl Moffett, aired February 20, 2016, on Animal Planet.
10. I will address the complexity of the "pit bull" in chapter 1. "Pit bull" also refers to several purebred dogs, including the American Pit Bull Terrier, the American Staffordshire Terrier, the American Bull Terrier, and the American Bully. I am highlighting their physical characteristics over their heredity because their appearance determines how they are labeled in rescue. For more, see chapter 1 and Bronwen Dickey, *Pit Bull: The Battle Over an American Icon* (Knopf, 2016).
11. Dickey, *Pit Bull*, esp. chap. 7.
12. The fact that Bullet was a Katrina dog is also significant because it revived a powerful trope in Black commentary on American racism—that, as Kanye West famously said, white Americans care more about dogs than Black people. To read an analysis of that moment, see Claire Jean Kim, *Dangerous Crossings: Race, Species, Nature in a Multicultural Age* (Cambridge University Press, 2015), esp. 284–87. See also Bénédicte Boisseron, *Afro-Dog: Blackness and the Animal Question* (Columbia University Press, 2018). Boisseron specifically addresses West's comments on xv and 204n9.
13. *Pit Bulls & Parolees*, season 8, episode 19, "Second Savior," featuring Tia Torres and Earl Moffett, aired February 20, 2016, on Animal Planet, 6:30, 40:39.

14. While these stories appear in more media than literature, I want to hold on to the term "literary" because this is fundamentally a narrative form. For a groundbreaking study of the central role of narrative in understanding the complex entanglement between human and more-than-human forms of life, see Susan McHugh, *Animal Stories: Narrating Across Species Lines* (University of Minnesota Press, 2011).
15. Think of the ubiquitous bumper magnets on cars asking "Who Rescued Who?" There are numerous dog rescues bearing that name, but it is not unique to dog rescue. There are countless social media posts, popular articles, films, and books about people who have experienced trauma finding solace in a dog's unconditional love. For a tiny sampling, see the website "The Dodo—for Animal People," https://www.thedodo.com/topics/dog-rescue; Victoria Schade, *Who Rescued Who* (Penguin, 2020). Look at social media posts about dogs, and you'll find this trope everywhere.
16. Robert N. Bellah, "Civil Religion in America," *Daedalus* 96, no. 1 (1967): 1–21.
17. Here I am referencing Harlan Weaver's *Bad Dog*, which builds on the work of queer and feminist theorists like Eve Sedgwick and Cathy Cohen to describe how ideas about "a good home" in dog rescue rely on the white, heterosexual, nuclear, patriarchal family as the ideal. I will talk about this more in chapter 1. Harlan Weaver, *Bad Dog: Pit Bull Politics and Multispecies Justice* (University of Washington Press, 2021).
18. Ernest Lee Tuveson, *Redeemer Nation: The Idea of America's Millennial Role* (University of Chicago Press, 1968), vii–viii, ix–x, 18–19; emphasis in original.
19. Tuveson, *Redeemer Nation*, x. Later Tuveson writes about the responsibility that comes with the notion of Americans as the new chosen people. He says that "for Americans there was always the awful and baffling question, what is the chosen people to *do*? The prophecies might point to them, but were silent, to a large extent, about their exact functions. This problem has constantly been in the background and often in the foreground of the great political debates of our history. In the controversies over expansion, isolation, colonies, entry into foreign wars, abolition, even prohibition—again and again it has been at least implied. We must behave, not just as a prudent and well-meaning nation but as a 'peculiar people'" (158–59).

20. *Oxford English Dictionary*, s.v. "Redemption."
21. To see an example of how animal shelters describe animal redemption, see Chicago Animal Care and Control's website, http://www.cityofchicago.org/city/en/depts/cacc/provdrs/care/svcs/lost_pet_recovery.html. The site states that "to redeem a lost pet from Chicago Animal Care & Control, a valid photo ID is required to sign in at the facility and proof of animal ownership (veterinary records, purchase receipt, or pictures of the pet) must be provided." Animal redemption therefore hinges on proof of ownership. In this formulation, dogs who were not previously owned cannot be redeemed.
22. As an example of what this policy looks like in practice, a local Animal Control regulations state the following under a section called "redemption by owner": "As a condition of redemption . . . the owner shall be issued a fifty [sic] ($50.00) citation for failure to maintain the required form of identification on the dog or cat. This citation may be waived upon proof of micro chip or collar with identification within three (3) business days." Haywood County General Regulations, chapter 91, "Animal Services," amended July 18, 2022, 15.
23. For a discussion of these factors, see the website of Maddie's Fund, a nonprofit leader in progressive animal sheltering in the United States. Sheila Segurson D'Arpino, "Behavioral Assessment in Animal Shelters," Maddie's Fund, 2007, https://www.maddiesfund.org/behavioral-assessment-in-animal-shelters.htm.
24. Weaver, *Bad Dog*, 159, 42. In his field work, Weaver quotes a volunteer who says that "only 'solid' dogs should be going out [of the shelter,] 'not the—you know, not because . . . it has one more day before it's gonna be euthanized!' Like [another volunteer], Sara pushes for a timing of adoptions based on accountability to a larger public, rather than saving dogs from imminent euthanasia. In both their accounts, safety trumps salvation as the central concern or care needed in this type of work" (42).
25. Rebecca F. Wisch and Ashley Dillingham, "Table of State Holding Laws," Animal Legal & Historical Center, 2017, https://www.animallaw.info/topic/state-holding-period-laws-impounded-animals.
26. To be clear, I am not blaming individual people who work at animal shelters. I am pointing to the general logic/rhetoric used to justify violence against dogs. I am also not advocating for warehousing dogs

for years on end. This is a long debate that is outside the scope of this project.

27. In *Afro-Dog*, Boisseron states: "The image of dogs attacking blacks haunts American collective consciousness, as it reveals a compulsion, in the history of the black diaspora of the Americas, to represent (make present again) this image.... In other words, one no longer needs to see the black man next to the dog's fangs or the white man holding the leash in order to know that the attack dog *means* racism." Bénédicte Boisseron, *Afro-Dog: Blackness and the Animal Question* (Columbia University Press, 2018), 78–79.

28. For a gorgeous exploration of more generative ways of thinking about the relationships between Black people and dogs, see Joshua Bennett, *Being Property Once Myself: Blackness and the End of Man* (Harvard University Press, 2020).

29. Carole Emberton, *Beyond Redemption: Race, Violence, and the American South After the Civil War* (University of Chicago Press, 2013), 2–3. The Radical Republicans had their roots in the antebellum abolitionist movement and were led by Charles Sumner, Benjamin Wade, and Zachariah Chandler in the Senate and Henry Winter Davis, Thaddeus Stevens, George Sewall Boutwell in the House. While they weren't a cohesive group, they all shared a commitment to emancipation and racial justice. Their most significant efforts were the Reconstruction Acts of 1867 and 1868, which placed southern states under military government and required universal suffrage for men. For a primer on the Reconstruction period, see Eric Foner, *A Short History of Reconstruction: 1863–1877*, updated ed. (Harper Perennial, 2015). For a classic work on the subject, see W. E. B. Du Bois, *Black Reconstruction in America* (Harcourt, Brace, and Company, 1935).

30. Emberton, *Beyond Redemption*, 4–5. It's also important to avoid placing all the moral blame on the South, which even today symbolically represents the site of the nation's sins, particularly related to racial violence. By making racist violence a regional issue, we risk missing the fact that it was systemic. Emberton notes that scholars should "think critically about the ways that violence structures not just Southern culture but American culture" (214).

31. Drew Faust, *This Republic of Suffering: Death and the American Civil War* (Knopf, 2008), xiii.

32. Emberton, *Beyond Redemption*, 6–8.
33. Joshua Dubler and Vincent W. Lloyd, *Break Every Yoke: Religion, Justice, and the Abolition of Prisons* (Oxford University Press, 2019); Aaron Griffith, *God's Law and Order: The Politics of Punishment in Evangelical America* (Harvard University Press, 2020), 4. The label "evangelical" is complex and contested within the field of American religious history. I am not interested in wading into those waters. For the sake of clarity, I follow Griffith's characterization of evangelicals as follows: being concerned with "biblical Christian doctrine" against the secular world, being focused on conversion as a central marker of one's faith, being disinterested in denominational labels, as well as being white and politically conservative. Griffith, *God's Law and Order*, 8–9.
34. Griffith, *God's Law and Order*, 56, 83–85, 4, 90.
35. Marjorie Spiegel, *The Dreaded Comparison: Human and Animal Slavery* (Mirror, 1996); Charles Patterson, *Eternal Treblinka: Our Treatment of Animals and the Holocaust* (Lantern, 2002).
36. Neel Ahuja, "Postcolonial Critique in a Multispecies World," *PMLA* 124, no. 2 (2009): 557–58.
37. Boisseron, *Afro-Dog*, xx; emphasis in the original.
38. Weaver, *Bad Dog*, 13.
39. Barbara R. Ambros, *Bones of Contention: Animals and Religion in Contemporary Japan* (University of Hawaii Press, 2012); Eric Daryl Meyer, *Inner Animalities: Theology and the End of the Human* (Fordham University Press, 2018); Aaron S. Gross, *The Question of the Animal and Religion: Theoretical Stakes, Practical Implications* (Columbia University Press, 2015); Laura Hopgood-Oster, *Holy Dogs and Asses: Animals in the Christian Tradition* (University of Illinois Press, 2008); Donovan Schaefer, *Animal Affects: Animality, Evolution, and Power* (Duke University Press, 2015).
40. J. L. Austin, *How to Do Things with Words* (Harvard University Press, 1975).
41. Zakiyyah Iman Jackson, *Becoming Human: Matter and Meaning in an Antiblack World* (New York University Press, 2020); Boisseron, *Afro-Dog*; Kim, *Dangerous Crossings*; Weaver, *Bad Dog*.

1. THE CLASSIC CANINE REDEMPTION NARRATIVE

1. Indictment, *United States v. Vick*, Criminal No. 3:07CR (E.D. Va. filed July 17, 2007).

1. THE CLASSIC CANINE REDEMPTION NARRATIVE ❧ 179

2. The dogs would be held at a government-owned shelter without the chance to leave their cages as the cases made their way through the courts. After the decision was made, the dogs were euthanized. Emily Giambalvo, "A Second Chance," *Washington Post*, September 18, 2019.
3. There are numerous scientific studies that dispute the argument that pit bulls are inherently aggressive toward humans. See Karen Delise, *The Pit Bull Placebo: The Media, Myths, and Politics of Canine Aggression* (Anubis, 2007); and Janice Bradley, "Dog Bites: Problems and Solutions" (Animals and Society Institute, 2014).
4. The Canine Good Citizen Test is a program facilitated by the American Kennel Club. The test involves ten elements (e.g., sitting politely for petting, walking on a loose lead, etc.). The test also includes a "responsible dog owner's pledge," in which the dog's owner pledges to be responsible for their dog's physical health (routine veterinary care, daily exercise, and regular bathing), mental health (giving their dog attention, playtime, and providing basic training), and the protection of the wider community's health (picking up waste, supervising their dog with children, etc.). For more, see http://www.akc.org/cgc-pledge/.
5. This terminology is widely used among supporters of the Vick dogs. Upon being seized, nineteen of the fifty-one Vick pit bulls went to the Sussex County Animal Shelter; the rest were distributed among five other facilities. Jim Gorant, *The Lost Dogs: Michael Vick's Dogs and Their Tale of Rescue and Redemption* (Gotham Books, 2010), 41. To see a detailed account of what happened to each Vick dog, see the "Where Are They Now?" section of Gorant, *The Lost Dogs*, 252–72. Since the time of the book's publication, all the Vick dogs have died. Emily Giambalvo, "Frodo, the Last Surviving Dog Rescued from Michael Vick, Dies Surrounded by Loved Ones," *Washington Post*, December 21, 2021.
6. For more on the racist response to Vick's case, see Claire Jean Kim, *Dangerous Crossings: Race, Species, and Nature in a Multicultural Age* (Cambridge University Press, 2015), 269, 264.
7. The book is technically cowritten with Brett Honeycutt and Stephen Copeland, evangelical Christians themselves. However, Vick is the primary author, and I am going to treat him as such here.
8. *The Lost Dogs* is a continuation of Gorant's 2008 *Sports Illustrated* cover story on the dogs, in which he noted that the publication of the *Sports Illustrated* piece "generated a massive response, with the

magazine receiving almost 500 emails and letters about the story and the dog pictured on the cover—the most we got in response to any issue for that entire year." Gorant, *The Lost Dogs*, ix.

9. I am using the Christian language of "sin" here intentionally to stay faithful to the way Vick describes his own story.
10. Vick, *Finally Free*, 5.
11. Vick, *Finally Free*, 6.
12. A 2010 census report from Newport News, Virginia, lists the Black population at 39.7 percent. The southeast end, where Vick lived, was 88.6 percent Black. "Newport News Through the Years (Statistical Profiles) | Newport News, VA—Official Website," https://www.nnva.gov/1811/Statistical-Profile-Reports.
13. As the sociologist Reuben Jonathan Miller stated in 2021, "Today, 19.6 million people live with a felony record. . . . Almost all of these people lived in dire poverty before they entered a cage, and they return to these same conditions on the day of their release. One-third are black; one in three currently living black American men have felony records." Reuben Jonathan Miller, *Halfway Home, Race, Punishment, and the Afterlife of Mass Incarceration* (Little, Brown, 2021), 8. Here Miller is drawing on Wendy Sawyer and Peter Wagner, "Mass Incarceration: The Whole Pie 2019," *Prison Policy Initiative* 19 (2019). See also Ta-Nehisi Coates, "The Case for Reparations," *The Atlantic*, May 22, 2014.
14. Vick, *Finally Free*, 13–15.
15. Vick, *Finally Free*, 15–18.
16. Vick, *Finally Free*, 58.
17. Daniel Buffington, "Contesting Race on Sundays: Making Meaning Out of the Rise in the Number of Black Quarterbacks," *Sociology of Sport Journal* 22 1, no. 12 (2005): 19–37. In this piece, Buffington describes how "the quarterback position in the NFL has been reserved for white men, who are stereotypically harder workers, team-oriented, and more mentally astute" (20). In contrast, Black male athletes were seen as having "natural" talent with "superior physical skills" (20). See also Kim, *Dangerous Crossings*, 264–66.
18. In another section, for instance, he expresses the desire to win a game that would give him the opportunity to become the third Black quarterback to start in the Super Bowl. Vick, *Finally Free*, 67.

1. THE CLASSIC CANINE REDEMPTION NARRATIVE ◌ 181

19. Vick characterizes his descent into immoral behavior as "slow, but steady." Vick, *Finally Free*, 85.
20. Vick, *Finally Free*, 72, 74, 99.
21. For examples of the kind of coverage Vick received related to scandals before dogfighting, see "Falcons QB Vick Settles Lawsuit with Woman," New England Patriots, https://www.patriots.com/news/falcons-qb-vick-settles-lawsuit-with-woman-95226; "Vick Water Bottle Confiscated by Miami Airport Security," ESPN, https://www.espn.com/nfl/news/story?id=2735061. In contrast, for example, Tucker Carlson suggested that Vick should be "executed" for killing dogs. "Tucker Carlson Backs Off 'Execution' Comments About Michael Vick; Host 'Overspoke' Last Week (VIDEO)," *New York Daily News*, January 4, 2011, https://www.nydailynews.com/2011/01/04/tucker-carlson-backs-off-execution-comments-about-michael-vick-host-overspoke-last-week-video/.
22. Vick had a large team of PR people who were working to rehabilitate his image, including Judy Smith, the woman the primetime TV show *Scandal* is based on. For more, see Judith Newman, "Another Client for Ms. Fix-It," *New York Times*, November 16, 2012, sec. Fashion, https://www.nytimes.com/2012/11/18/fashion/judy-smith-enters-the-petraeus-spotlight.html. And as mentioned earlier, the book had ghostwriters.
23. Vick, *Finally Free*, 96.
24. Vick, *Finally Free*, 96.
25. Vick, *Finally Free*, 97.
26. Vick, *Finally Free*, 97.
27. Vick, *Finally Free*, 101.
28. Vick, *Finally Free*, 103–4; emphasis in original.
29. See, for example, "Michael Vick Dogfighting Case Opens Racial Divide," NFL.com, August 3, 2007. For a detailed academic analysis of the role of race in Vick's case, see Kim, *Dangerous Crossings*; and Harlan Weaver, *Bad Dog: Pit Bull Politics and Multispecies Justice* (University of Washington Press, 2021).
30. Vick, *Finally Free*, 104.
31. Vick, *Finally Free*, 113.
32. Peter Brooks, *Troubling Confessions: Speaking Guilt in Law and Literature* (University of Chicago Press, 2001), 3.

33. There are numerous studies of American evangelicalism's heart-centered focus, which shifts the weight of authority about whether or not an individual has been converted to that person themself. See Catherine A. Brekus, *Sarah Osborne's World* (Yale University Press, 2013), which analyzes the anxiety around discerning tangible "evidence" of an individual's conversion. See also Grant Wacker, *Heaven Below: Early Pentecostals and American Culture* (Harvard University Press, 2001).
34. Brooks, *Troubling Confessions*, 6.
35. Vick, *Finally Free*, 114.
36. Daniel A. Grano, "Michael Vick's 'Genuine Remorse' and Problems of Public Forgiveness," *Quarterly Journal of Speech* 100, no. 1 (January 2, 2014): 95.
37. Bryan Curtis, "The NFL's Spiritual Guru," *Daily Beast*, February 3, 2010, https://www.thedailybeast.com/the-nfls-spiritual-guru.
38. There are numerous examples, but see Vick, *Finally Free*, 154–58, 208, 228, 259.
39. Grano, "Michael Vick's 'Genuine Remorse' and Problems of Public Forgiveness," 88.
40. Vick, *Finally Free*, xiv.
41. Vick, *Finally Free*, 192.
42. Vick, *Finally Free*, 235.
43. Tom Junod, "The State of the American Dog," *Esquire*, July 14, 2014, http://www.esquire.com/news-politics/a23731/american-dog-0814/.
44. For more on the connection between human and animal violence, see Keri Burchfield, "The Sociology of Animal Crime: An Examination of the Incidents and Arrests in Chicago," *Deviant Behavior* 37 (2016): 1–17.
45. Delice, *The Pit Bull Placebo*, 95.
46. Bronwen Dickey, *Pit Bull: The Battle Over an American Icon* (Knopf, 2016), 127.
47. Delise, *The Pit Bull Placebo*, 97. In contrast, between 1966 and 1975, there is only one documented case of a fatal dog attack in the United States by a pit bull–type dog (95).
48. Delise, *The Pit Bull Placebo*, 97.
49. Vicki Hearne, *Bandit: Dossier of a Dangerous Dog* (1991; Alkadine, 2002), 114.

1. THE CLASSIC CANINE REDEMPTION NARRATIVE ∞ 183

50. Two of the common tropes of the anti–pit bull articles are to associate pit bulls with rapists and to allege that they are child killers. See, for example, E. M. Swift, "The Pit Bull Friend and Killer," *Sports Illustrated*, July 27, 1987, http://www.si.com/vault/1987/07/27/115813/the-pit-bull-friend-and-killer-is-the-pit-bull-a-fine-animal-as-its-admirers-claim-or-is-it-a-vicious-dog-unfit-for-society.
51. Harlan Weaver, "'Becoming in Kind': Race, Class, Gender, and Nation in Cultures of Dog Rescue and Dogfighting," *American Quarterly* 65, no. 3 (September 2013): 694.
52. Christian Red, "Trained to Be Killers, Vick's Pit Bulls Now on Death Row," *New York Daily News*, August 30, 2007, http://www.nydailynews.com/sports/football/trained-killers-vick-pit-bulls-death-row-article-1.241194.
53. Red, "Trained to Be Killers, Vick's Pit Bulls Now on Death Row."
54. See "Inappropriate Chewing and Destructive Behavior," SSPCA, http://www.sspca.org/PDFs/Dog-Behavior/Chewing%20and%20Destructive%20Behavior.pdf.
55. There are numerous scientific studies that dispute the argument that pit bulls are inherently aggressive toward humans. See Delise, *The Pit Bull Placebo*; Janice Bradley, "Dog Bites: Problems and Solutions" (Ann Arbor, MI: Animals and Society Institute, 2014), https://www.nationalcanineresearchcouncil.com/uploaded_files/publications/541422429_Dog%20Bites%20Problems%20and%20Solutions%202nd%20Edition.pdf.
56. Even leading members of animal welfare organizations believed the Vick dogs were too dangerous to be kept alive, including Wayne Pacelle, the president and chief executive of the Humane Society of the United States at the time, who called the dogs "some of the most aggressively trained pit bulls in the country." For more, see Michael S. Schmidt, "In the Case Against Vick, Dogs Are Held as Evidence," *New York Times*, August 1, 2007. PETA also issued a statement stating that "these dogs are a ticking time bomb . . . rehabilitating fighting dogs is not in the cards. It's widely accepted that euthanasia is the most humane thing for them." Quoted in Gorant, *The Lost Dogs*, 91.
57. Michael S. Schmidt, "Menacing Dogs from Vick Case Await Their Fate," *New York Times*, September 1, 2007, http://www.nytimes.com/2007/09/01/sports/football/01vick.html; Juliet Macur, "Given

Reprieve, N.F.L. Star's Dogs Find Kindness," *New York Times*, February 2, 2008, http://www.nytimes.com/2008/02/02/sports/football/02vickdogs.html.
58. Gorant, *The Lost Dogs*, 4, 6.
59. Gorant, *The Lost Dogs*, 20.
60. Gorant, *The Lost Dogs*, 93.
61. The idea that "all dogs are individuals" has become a common refrain in dog rescue, and is even the Animal Farm Foundation's slogan. On their website, the non-profit organization justifies this slogan as follows: "**All dogs are individuals means:** We owe it to all dogs to see them for who they really are, free of prejudice, stereotypes, and assumptions that are based on a known pedigree, a breed label guess, physical appearance, or their past history." Bold in original. https://animalfarmfoundation.wordpress.com/2012/11/29/all-dogs-are-individuals/.
62. Gorant, *The Lost Dogs*, 126, 138.
63. Bénédicte Boisseron, *Afro-Dog: Blackness and the Animal Question* (Columbia University Press, 2018), 46.
64. Colin Dayan, *With Dogs at the Edge of Life* (Columbia University Press, 2015), 80.
65. Gorant, *The Lost Dogs*, 120–21.
66. Gorant, *The Lost Dogs*, 213–14.
67. Gorant, *The Lost Dogs*, 247.
68. To read about the central role anti-Blackness played in the adjudication of Michael Vick's case, see Boisseron, *Afro-Dog*; Dayan, *With Dogs at the Edge of Life*; Megan H. Glick, "Animal Instincts: Race, Criminality, and the Reversal of the 'Human,'" *American Quarterly* 65, no. 3 (2013): 639–59; Kim, *Dangerous Crossings*; Kathy Rudy, "Michael Vick, Dog Fighting, and Race," *Duke Today*, August 29, 2007, https://today.duke.edu/2007/08/vick_oped.html; Weaver, "'Becoming in Kind'"; Weaver, *Bad Dog*.
69. Joshua Dubler and Vincent W. Lloyd, *Break Every Yoke: Religion, Justice, and the Abolition of Prisons* (Oxford University Press, 2020), 174.
70. Steve Wyche, "Colin Kaepernick Explains Why He Sat Down During the National Anthem," NFL.com, August 28, 2016, http://www.nfl.com/news/story/0ap3000000691077/article/colin-kaepernick-explains-protest-of-national-anthem.

2. FAILURES OF THE CANINE REDEMPTION NARRATIVE ○R 185

71. For a brilliant reading of how whiteness structures American civil religion, see Korie Little Edwards, "Seeing Bellah's Civil Religion Through a Black Feminist Lens," in *Civil Religion Today: Religion and the American Nation in the Twenty-First Century*, ed. Rhys H. Williams, Raymond Haberski Jr., and Philip Goff (New York University Press, 2021), 118–36. Special thanks to Amaranth Schmoyer for bringing this chapter to my attention.
72. Gorant, *The Lost Dogs*, 249.

2. THE FAILURES OF THE CANINE REDEMPTION NARRATIVE

1. See, for example, *Where the North Begins*, dir. Chester M. Franklin (Warner Bros., 1923, 1 hour); *Lassie Come Home*, dir. Fred M. Wilcox (Metro-Goldwyn-Mayer [MGM], 1943, 1 hour 29 minutes); *Old Yeller*, dir. Robert Stevenson (Walt Disney Productions, 1957, 1 hour 23 minutes); *Beethoven*, dir. Brian Levant (Universal Pictures and Northern Lights Entertainment, 1992, 1 hour 27 minutes); *Homeward Bound*, dir. Duwayne Dunham (Touchwood Pacific Partners 1 and Walt Disney Pictures, 1993, 1 hour 24 minutes); *101 Dalmatians*, dir. Stephen Herek (Walt Disney Pictures, Wizzer Productions, and Great Oaks Entertainment, 1996, 1 hour 43 minutes); *Air Bud*, dir. Charles Martin Smith (Air Bud Entertainment and Walt Disney Pictures, 1997, 1 hour 38 minutes); *Marley & Me*, dir. David Frankel (Fox 2000 Pictures, Regency Enterprises, Sunswept Entertainment, and made in association with Dune Entertainment III, 1998, 1 hour 55 minutes); *Hachi: A Dog's Tale*, dir. Lasse Hallström (Stage 6 Films, 2011); *A Dog's Purpose*, dir. Lasse Hallström (Amblin Entertainment, Pariah Entertainment Group, Reliance Entertainment, and Walden Media, 2017, 1 hour 40 minutes). These films represent just a fraction of the genre of the Hollywood dog film.
2. For more, see David Kelsey's description of "extra-Christian" uses of redemption in *Imagining Redemption* (Westminster John Knox, 2005), 6.
3. Dogs in particular have long held an important role in cinema, from its inception to the present. Two qualities distinguish dogs from other animals that make them particularly attractive to film directors: their

close affinity with human beings, which often led to them being brought to sets, as well as their ability to be easily trained. Pao-chen Tang, "Of Dogs and Distractions in Early Cinema," *Early Visual Popular Culture* 15, no. 1 (2017): 44. Such examples include the Vitagraph Studios' dog Jean (the first animal star of the silent film era), Cecil Hepworth's family dog Blair (better known as Rover in Lewin Fitzhamon's *Rescued by Rover* [1905]), and Warner Bros.' Rin-Tin-Tin. Tang, "Of Dogs and Distractions," 45. These qualities made dogs into well-known film stars, from classic figures like Rin-Tin-Tin and Lassie to Uggie, the Jack Russell Terrier from *The Artist* (2011). As the film studies scholar Claire Molloy argues: "The production of the star image was a process that reshaped animals—things of nature—into culturally accessible humanized commodities. This process of commodifying animals meant that only very rarely did Hollywood reveal the *animality* of animal stars, preferring instead to represent the animal star in human terms." Claire Molloy, *Popular Media and Animals* (Palgrave MacMillan, 2011), 46. This claim holds true for classic canine redemption narratives, which tend to anthropomorphize dogs as childlike or to make them symbols of stock values like loyalty and unconditional love.

4. Take, for example, *A Dog's Purpose* (2017), which is about the heartwarming relationship between a boy named Ethan and a dog named Bailey. After Bailey dies, he is reincarnated into different dogs (without Ethan's knowledge). They are eventually reunited at the end of the film, when Ethan is an adult and needs Bailey the most. The film concludes with Bailey the dog providing this lesson: "So, in all my lives as a dog, here's what I've learned: Have fun, obviously. Whenever possible, find someone to save and save them. Lick the ones you love. Don't get all sad-faced about what happened and scrunchy-faced about what could. Just be here now. Be. Here. Now. That's a Dog's Purpose." Through this mixture of comedy, sentimentality, and old-fashioned wisdom, *A Dog's Purpose* recapitulates many of the redemptive themes present in classic Hollywood dog films, demonstrating the prevalence and persistence of this genre, which celebrates the ability of dogs to heal human beings, to save their lives, to restore their families, and to remind them to release the past and to live in the present. *A Dog's Purpose*, dir. Lasse Hallström (Amblin Entertainment,

2. FAILURES OF THE CANINE REDEMPTION NARRATIVE ⟡ 187

Pariah Entertainment Group, Reliance Entertainment, and Walden Media, 2017, 1 hour 40 minutes).

5. *White Dog*, dir. Samuel Fuller and Curtis Hanson (Paramount Pictures Corporation, 1982, 1 hour 24 minutes).
6. Tyler D. Parry and Charlton W. Yingling, "Slave Hounds and Abolition in the Americas," *Past & Present* 246, no. 1 (February 2020), 75.
7. For more on the history of the weaponization of dogs to capture enslaved people running to freedom, as well as prisoners, see Bénédicte Boisseron, *Afro-Dog: Blackness and the Animal Question* (Columbia University Press, 2018), esp. chap. 2, "Blacks and Dogs in the Americas," 37–80. See also Colin Dayan, *The Law Is a White Dog* (Princeton University Press, 2011), in which Dayan describes the use of dogs to attack incarcerated people, as well as the ways in which Black and canine ontologies are co-constituted in the law. See also Marion Schwartz, *A History of Dogs in the Early Americas* (Yale University Press, 2011). As the memory of the deployment of police dogs at the Birmingham, Alabama, civil rights demonstrations in 1963 and the more recent use of dogs against the Native Americans at Standing Rock attest, the deployment of dogs as weapons against people of color continues in America up to the present day. See, for example, Audie Cornish, "How the Civil Rights Movement Was Covered in Birmingham," *All Things Considered*, June 18, 2013; "Guards Accused of Unleashing Dogs, Pepper Spraying Oil Pipeline Protestors," *CBS News*, September 5, 2016.
8. Hanson and Fuller, *White Dog*.
9. Romain Gary, "White Dog," *Life*, October 9, 1970, 57–74. This was later turned into a novel by Gary entitled *Chien blanc* (Gallimard, 1972). In 2022, a French film version of *Chien blanc* was released. It more faithfully adheres to Gary's original script. Anaïs Barbeau-Lavalette et al., *Chien blanc* (Sphere Films, 2022, 1 hour 36 minutes).
10. Lisa Dombrowski, *The Films of Samuel Fuller: If You Die, I'll Kill You!* (Wesleyan University Press, 2008), 191–92; emphasis in original.
11. Dombrowski, *The Films of Samuel Fuller*, 193; emphasis in original.
12. I am breaking convention and referring to Julie Sawyer by her first name because that is how she is addressed in the film, and her femininity is essential to my argument.
13. The dog is only referred to with a name twice—once as the "Hound of Baskervilles," referencing Arthur Conan Doyle's gothic crime

novel about the legend of a diabolical dog, and once as "Mr. Hyde," alluding to Robert Louis Stevenson's gothic horror novella. As these chilling literary references suggest, something is dangerously awry with the dog. Susanne Schwertfeger, "Re-Education as Exorcism: How a White Dog Challenges the Strategies for Dealing with Racism," in *Animal Horror Cinema: Genre, History, and Criticism*, ed. by Katarina Gregersdotter, Johan Höglund, and Nicklas Hållén (Palgrave MacMillan, 2015), 130.

14. Dombrowski, *The Films of Samuel Fuller*, 191–92.
15. Quoted in Dombrowski, *The Films of Samuel Fuller*, 195.
16. Dombrowski, *The Films of Samuel Fuller*, 195.
17. Dombrowski, *The Films of Samuel Fuller*, 194, 196.
18. "Critics Honor White Dog Release," Criterion Collection, https://www.criterion.com/current/posts/999-critics-honor-white-dog-release.
19. I have not been able to find commentary from Fuller about why he made the rapist white—something the screenplay specifies. Samuel Fuller and Curtis Hanson, *Screenplay*, 1981. Bénédicte Boisseron argues that the fact that the dog serves as Julie's protector against sexual predators of any race, combined with the dog's status as a white dog, "functions as a historical trigger, recalling the plantation-based connection between dog attacks, rape, and blackness. The storyline in Fuller's movie changes the course of history, as it justifies the use of canine weaponry against the black, who is subliminally portrayed as a racist." Boisseron, *Afro-Dog*, 151.
20. Dombrowski, *The Films of Samuel Fuller*, 194.
21. Samuel Fuller, "The White Dog Talks," *Framework*, January 1, 1982, 25.
22. Samuel Fuller, quoted in Dombrowski, *The Films of Samuel Fuller*, 12.
23. Tears are perhaps the most common trope associated with sentimental works from the eighteenth century onward. For a collection of works that explore the role of the body in representations of race, gender, and sexuality in America, see Lauren Berlant, *The Female Complaint: The Unfinished Business of Sentimentality in American Culture* (Duke University Press, 2008); Shirley Samuels, *The Culture of Sentiment: Race, Gender, and Sentimentality in Nineteenth-Century America* (Oxford University Press, 1992); and Linda Williams, *Playing the Race*

2. FAILURES OF THE CANINE REDEMPTION NARRATIVE ⚭ 189

Card: Melodramas of Black and White from Uncle Tom to O.J. Simpson (Princeton University Press, 2002).

24. I will talk about dog training in greater depth in the next chapter, but the fact that the dog attacked Julie's coworker (Molly) unprovoked should have been cause for concern. Most dogs give warning signs before they bite; this dog did no such thing. For an instructive read on dog bites, see American Veterinary Medical Association (AMVA), "Preventing Dog Bites," https://www.avma.org/resources-tools/pet-owners/dog-bite-prevention.

25. Robin DiAngelo, *White Fragility: Why It's So Hard for White People to Talk About Racism* (Beacon, 2018), 2.

26. It seems strange that Joe's response is to call the police, given the fact that white dogs have been used against Black people by law enforcement in the past. However, the film is not that invested in the nuances of systemic critique.

27. Joshua Bennett, *Being Property Myself: Blackness and the End of Man* (Harvard University Press, 2020), 140–41.

28. See Tyler D. Parry and Charlton W. Yingling, "Slave Hounds and Abolition in the Americas," *Past & Present* 246, no. 1 (February 2020): 75; Larry H. Spruill, "Slave Patrols, 'Packs of Negro Dogs,' and Policing Black Communities," *Phylon* 3 no. 1 (2016): 42–66; Tyler Wall, "'For the Very Existence of Civilization': The Police Dog and Racial Terror," *American Quarterly* 68, no. 4 (2016): 861–82.

29. Schwertfeger, "Re-Education as Exorcism," 137. The quotation from Toni Morrison comes from Toni Morrison, "Black Matters," in *Playing in the Dark: Whiteness and the Literary Imagination* (Harvard University Press, 1992), 9–10.

30. Williams, *Playing the Race Card*, 37. *White Dog* falls within Williams's overall definition of the racial melodrama, but it is outside the scope of this project to delve into the relationship between the two genres.

31. Madison's letters are cited in Richard Newton, "The African American Bible: Bound in a Christian Nation," *Journal of Biblical Literature* 136, no. 1 (2017): 221. For an opinion piece tracking how US politicians describe slavery as "America's original sin," see James Goodman, "It's Time to Stop Calling Slavery America's 'Original Sin,'" CNN.com, February 16, 2021, https://edition.cnn.com/2021/02/16/opinions/dont-call-slavery-americas-original-sin-goodman.

32. See G. H. Jacobs, "Evolution of Color Vision and Its Reflections in Contemporary Mammals," in *Handbook of Color Psychology*, ed. A. J. Elliot, M. D. Fairchild, and A. Franklin (Cambridge University Press, 2015), 110–30.
33. For a rich discussion of this conception of racialization, see Williams, *Playing the Race Card*. Thank you to Allison Page for this insight.
34. Boisseron, *Afro-Dog*, 67.
35. Schwertfeger, "Re-Education as Exorcism," 133.
36. Thank you to Nicole Erin Morse for this important insight.
37. Schwertfeger, "Re-Education as Exorcism," 132.
38. J. Hoberman, "*White Dog*: Sam Fuller Unmuzzled," Criterion Collection, November 27, 2008, https://www.criterion.com/current/posts/847-white-dog-sam-fuller-unmuzzled.
39. Noel Simsolo, "Fuller Without a Script," *La Revue du Cinéma* 375 (September 1982): 56–62; this interview was reprinted in *Samuel Fuller: Interviews*, ed. Gerald Peary, (University Press of Mississippi, 2012), 90.
40. I borrow this phrase from Donna J. Haraway's wonderful book *Staying with the Trouble: Making Kin in the Chthulucene* (Duke University Press, 2016).
41. Boisseron, *Afro-Dog*, 65.
42. I am deliberately using heart-centered language because it is a characteristic of the Christian conversion narratives to which dog redemption narratives are indebted. For more on this topic, see Aaron Griffith, *God's Law and Order: The Politics of Punishment in Evangelical America* (Harvard University Press, 2020).

3. RELATIONAL REDEMPTION

1. Millan was also there to promote his show, *Cesar Millan: Better Human, Better Dog* (National Geographic, 2021–present). One can apply to become an "Empire State Building Lighting Partner" to promote a cause or business. In the actual ceremony, the significance of the colors is not explained. A profile on Millan that mentions the event explains that the colors symbolize Millan's life: "yellow for his National Geographic's success; orange for his love for mother nature, and blue for training." Andrea Huspeni, "Cesar Millan Just

Celebrated 20 Years on TV. Not Everyone Is Happy About It," *This Dog's Life*, June 3, 2024, https://www.thisdogslife.co/cesar-millan-just-celebrated-20-years-on-tv-not-everyone-is-happy-about-it/.

2. "Cesar Millan Lights Up The Empire State Building!," Empire State Building YouTube Channel, 2024, https://www.youtube.com/watch?v=GHuSNvy5fAo. Millan gained US citizenship in 2009. For more on his journey, see "Cesar Millan's Long Walk to Becoming the 'Dog Whisperer,'" *All Things Considered*, NPR, March 30, 2014.

3. At the time of writing, there have been sweeping ICE raids across the nation. See, for example: Rebekah Riess and Bill Kirkos, "37 People Arrested and American Kids Separated from Parents After ICE Raid at Chicago Apartments," CNN, October 3, 2025. Kayla Epstein, "Trump Has Long Called for Using the Military to Quash Protests. Los Angeles Gave Him an Opening," BBC, June 13, 2025. Here are just a few examples of Trump's language and its effects, written before his election: Jillian McKoy, "Trump's Anti-Immigrant Rhetoric, Policies, Contributed to Decline in Preventive Healthcare Visits among Children of Immigrants," Boston University School of Public Health, September 15, 2023, https://www.bu.edu/sph/news/articles/2023/trumps-anti-immigrant-rhetoric-policies-contributed-to-decline-in-healthcare-among-children-of-immigrants/; Nathan Layne, "Trump Repeats 'Poisoning the Blood' Anti-Immigrant Remark," Reuters, December 16, 2023.

4. Robert N. Bellah, "Civil Religion in America." *Daedalus* 96, no. 1 (1967): 1–21.

5. For an insightful reading and critique of Bellah's work on American civil religion, see Korie Little Edwards, "Seeing Bellah's Civil Religion Through a Black Feminist Lens," in *Civil Religion Today: Religion and the American Nation in the Twenty-First Century*, ed. Rhys H. Williams, Raymond Haberski Jr., and Philip Goff (New York University Press, 2021), 95–117. In this essay, Edwards argues that "even after outlining how America repeatedly failed to live out his American civil religion in *The Broken Covenant* [Bellah's book-length expansion on his essay], Bellah remained steadfastly committed to a belief in the reality and, if practiced righteously, its redemptive power. He simply would not, perhaps he could not, given his standpoint, entertain the notion that America's stubborn incapacity to live up to

its ideals of equality and inclusivity was because those ideals were not what America truly aspired to be" (112). In other words, while Bellah's conceptualization of civil religion reveals forms of inequality, it does not interrogate the fundamentally racist underpinnings of American civil religion itself. Thanks to Amaranth Schmoyer for alerting me to this collection.

6. See my short article that argues against apolitical readings of dogs: Katharine Mershon, "Are Dogs Part of American Civil Religion?," *American Religion: Sources*, 2021, https://www.american-religion.org/provocations/dogs. The ubiquity of pet ownership in the United States may be why people view it as an apolitical phenomenon; it just seems normal. According to the American Pet Products Association's 2025 "National Pet Owners Survey Stats," 68 million US households own pets. https://americanpetproducts.org/industry-trends-and-stats. The American Veterinary Medical Association 2024 survey states that 45.5 percent of US households own dogs, which is 59.8 million people. https://www.avma.org/resources-tools/reports-statistics/us-pet-ownership-statistics. For a recent account of the relationship between dog training and politics, see Alicia P. Q. Wittmeyer, "My Year of Being Very Online About Dogs," *New York Times*, December 20, 2023.

7. In 2004, *The Dog Whisperer* premiered on the National Geographic TV channel (also called Nat Geo), airing for nine seasons and becoming the network's most-watched show for six. Each episode of Millan's TV show focuses on redeeming a dangerous dog from death and restoring harmony to a family. Huspeni, "Cesar Millan Just Celebrated 20 Years on TV."

8. Clive D. Wynne, "The Indispensable Dog," *Frontiers of Psychology* 12 (July 2021).

9. John W. S. Bradshaw, Emily J. Blackwell, and Rachel A. Casey, "Dominance in Domestic Dogs—Useful Construct or Bad Habit?," *Journal of Veterinary Behavior* 4, no. 3 (May 1, 2009): 135–44.

10. For a detailed account of Millan's rise to fame and the backlash he received, see Jeninne Lee-St. John, "Dog Training and the Myth of Alpha-Male Dominance," *Time*, July 30, 2010, https://time.com/archive/6934564/dog-training-and-the-myth-of-alpha-male-dominance/.

3. RELATIONAL REDEMPTION ⊗ 193

11. Indeed, the newspaper profile that spurred Millan's success was titled "Redeeming Rover," reflecting how redemption narratives are central to dog training. BettiJane Levine, "Redeeming Rover," *Los Angeles Times*, September 25, 2002.
12. Huspeni, "Cesar Millan Just Celebrated 20 Years on TV."
13. After a particularly upsetting episode of *Cesar 911*, the American Society for Veterinary Behavior issued a position statement on Cesar Millan: "Cesar Millan Response," American Society for Veterinary Behavior, 2016, https://avsab.org/wp-content/uploads/2019/01/Cesar_Millan_Response-download.pdf.
14. I am not suggesting that Millan is intentionally cruel. As with Michael Vick, we cannot know what is truly in his heart. All we can do is assess his behavior.
15. The same point stands for Vicki Hearne. I am not interested in litigating Hearne's "goodness" or "badness," but instead want to take her work seriously by assessing its theological implications.
16. We will see how Hearne's philosophy and her training methods are at odds with one another. Regardless, based on her extensive writings, I maintain that her goals are the same as Haraway's.
17. Thank you to Laura Helper for this language.
18. This is a sampling of scholars in animal studies whose work engages with Hearne's thinking: Colin Dayan, *With Dogs at the Edge of Life* (Columbia University Press, 2016); Alice A. Kuzniar, *Melancholia's Dog: Reflections on our Animal Kinship* (University of Chicago Press, 2006); Susan McHugh, *Dog* (Reaktion, 2004); Kathy Rudy, *Loving Animals: Toward a New Animal Advocacy* (University of Minnesota Press, 2011); Kari Weil, *Thinking Animals: Why Animal Studies Now?* (Columbia University Press, 2012); Cary Wolfe, *Animal Rites: American Culture, The Discourse of Species, and Posthumanist Theory* (University of Chicago Press, 2003).
19. Hearne also was a horse trainer and writes about horse training in *Adam's Task* as well. To read her writings on horse training, see chapters 4, 5, and 6 (77–165). For the purposes of this book, I am going to focus on her writings about dogs.
20. Hearne, *Adam's Task*, 4–8.
21. Hearne, *Adam's Task*, 43, 47–48. Thank you to Marshall Cunningham for pointing out that Hearne conflates Genesis 1 and 2 and also places

an emphasis on human-animal relationality that is not present in the original text. In this way, she recasts the creation story to fit her own theology of training.

22. Hearne, *Adam's Task*, 48.
23. Hearne, *Adam's Task*, 169-70.
24. See Derrida's *animot* in *The Animal That Therefore I Am*. In this lecture, later translated into English and published in *Critical Inquiry*, Derrida speaks about the tension between "the animals" as a concept versus animals as individuals. He emphasizes this point by creating a neologism, *animot*, a term that combines the plural of animals (*animaux*) with the French word for word (*mot*), which sound indistinguishable when pronounced aloud but is grammatically incorrect when used in the singular. The purpose of such a word emphasizes how the individual animal is often erased in the way we speak about them and how the line between the words about and the presence of animals is unstable. Jacques Derrida, Marie-Louise Mallet, and American Council of Learned Societies, *The Animal That Therefore I Am*, ed. Marie-Louise Mallet (Fordham University Press, 2008).
25. Hearne reiterates this point throughout the passage, describing how the shelter manager "gestured at the dogs, most of them doomed, in the runs at the shelter and said, 'Goddamit! [*sic*] Most of them wouldn't be here if only they knew their names!'" Hearne, *Adam's Task*, 168. When a dog doesn't have a name that binds them to a human being but instead has a label, the dogs living in the shelter are destined to die. Of course, this is not the dog's fault; it is the result of broader failures that landed the dog in the shelter in the first place.
26. In the canine sport of tracking, a dog is taught not only to follow a scent but also to retrieve objects dropped by the person who laid the track. Hearne, *Adam's Task*, 13. It is officially recognized by the American Kennel Club, which describes tracking as follows: "KC Tracking is a canine sport that demonstrates a dog's natural ability to recognize and follow a scent and is the foundation of canine search and rescue work. In tracking the dog is completely in charge, because only he knows how to use his nose to find and follow the track. For many, the greatest pleasure of tracking are the hours spent outside, training and interacting with their dogs." For more, see American Kennel Club, http://www.akc.org/events/tracking/. Canine nosework is a relatively

new sport founded by trainers in law enforcement seeking to find engaging activities for their retired police and military dogs. In nosework, dogs are trained to identify and locate designated odors in a variety of conditions and with a firm time limit. To learn more, see National Association of Canine Scent Work, https://www.nacsw.net/.
27. Hearne, *Adam's Task*, 30. The language of covenant is mine, not Hearne's, but I use it because it best characterizes how she talks about the redemptive potential of dog training.
28. See Exodus 24:1–11 and Deut. 5:4–20. The translation of the Hebrew word for covenant (בְּרִית, b'rit) comes from its Latin rendering as *foedus/pactum* in Hieronymus's *Vulgata*. The meaning of the term "covenant" depends on the particular context in which it is used: Two partners with equal rights mutually bind themselves (1 Kings 5:26, 15:19), a stronger partner imposes unilateral claims upon a weaker one, or the stronger partner voluntarily binds himself without any claims toward someone else (1 Kings 20:34; Hos. 12:2; Ezek. 17:13). Again: While Hearne does not use the term "covenant," I believe this concept captures the religious dimensions of her theology of dog training, which draws from the Hebrew Bible. For more on the idea of covenant, see Eckart Otto, "Covenant," in *Encyclopedia of Religion*, ed. Lindsay Jones, 2nd ed. (Macmillan Reference USA, 2005), 3:2047–51.
29. Hearne does not directly address the question of whether non–dog owners (or those who do not live with or like animals) can attain redemption. While I do not think anything in Hearne's corpus indicates that she would go so far as to argue that non–dog owners are doomed to hell, I would argue that she believes that those who do not live and work with animals live significantly impoverished religious and intellectual lives.
30. Hearne, *Adam's Task*, 60–65.
31. While I am not supporting the use of aversive training methods, I am also not advocating for absolute equality between humans and dogs. This is a phenomenon that I believe would be untenable and irresponsible; such a vision also does not take into account how humans and dogs coevolved together. For more on the subject, see Raymond Coppinger and Lorna Coppinger, *What Is a Dog?* (University of Chicago Press, 2016).

32. Hearne, *Adam's Task*, 43, 67.
33. Hearne, *Adam's Task*, 67; emphasis in original. For more on the reasons why dogs have accidents in the house, see Jean Donaldson, *Oh Behave! Dogs from Pavlov to Premack to Pinker* (Dogwise, 2008), section 3, "Behavior Problems," 109–53.
34. For more, see: "How to Get Your Dog to Stop Digging," *The Humane Society of the United States*, https://www.humanesociety.org/resources/stop-dogs-digging; Grant Piper, "Why Do Dogs Dig? 6 Vet-Reviewed Reasons & Solutions," *Dogster*, August 9, 2024. https://www.dogster.com/lifestyle/why-do-dogs-dig.
35. Hearne, *Adam's Task*, 67.
36. Hearne, *Adam's Task*, 67.
37. Hearne, *Adam's Task*, 68.
38. Suzanne Clothier, *Bones Would Rain from the Sky* (Grand Central, 2002), 222.
39. Hearne, *Adam's Task*, 68; emphasis in original.
40. Hearne, *Adam's Task*, 68–69.
41. Hearne, *Adam's Task*, 68–69.
42. For more information, see Jim Barry, "Dog Field Sports: How to Hunt Without Killing Anything," Karen Pryor Clicker Training, April 1, 2007, http://www.clickertraining.com/node/1134.
43. For an example of what dumbbells look like, see https://www.jjdog.com/obedience-equipment/dog-dumbbells. In contrast to the image of a person throwing a ball and having a dog retrieve it, the kind of retrieving Hearne is teaching Salty is a rigorous dog field sport sponsored by different kennel clubs that allows dogs bred or predisposed to retrieving game to exercise this skill in partnership with a human handler.
44. Hearne, *Adam's Task*, 69–70.
45. Hearne, *Adam's Task*, 72.
46. Hearne, *Adam's Task*, 74.
47. Vicki Hearne, "What's Wrong with Animal Rights: Of Hounds, Horses, and Jeffersonian Happiness," *Harper's*, September 1991, 59–64. For more on Hearne's writings about animal happiness, see Vicki Hearne, *Animal Happiness* (HarperCollins, 1994).
48. For an extended analysis of the role of Wittgenstein, Stanley Cavell, and philosophy of language in Hearne's thought, see Wolfe, *Animal Rites*, 44–96; and Kuzniar, *Melancholia's Dog*, esp. 25–36.

49. Hearne, *Adam's Task*, 60. In her 1994 book *Animal Happiness*, Vicki Hearne says: "The great animal trainer who has dealings with the profane world, the world created in, say the Fall or the Tower of Babel, when the animals and our words were torn from each other so that we actually have to teach a dog to come when called, must occasionally learn Job's lesson. The significance of domestic animals.... is that through respect for them, through a discipline of admiration, one of whose names is training, we can come, momentarily, perhaps in spiritual danger or perhaps not, to a higher happiness than that allotted to our species. Acceptance of that knowledge entails acceptance of one's own limitations.... The hawk trainer does not complain at how God has made the hawk but learns to fly her.... And then and only then do the sacred and the ordinary transcend the artificial boundaries given to them by the idea—the very idea!—of the profane and the secular. Then and only then does happiness as a creature sharing the planet with other creatures become knowing her own business and uttering it with the promptness that such a knowledge gives" (236).
50. Donna J. Haraway, *The Companion Species Manifesto* (Prickly Paradigm, 2003), 52–53.
51. Haraway has engaged with Hearne's writings about dog training throughout her work on companion species, seeking to recuperate aspects of Hearne's thinking while also raising objections to her particular training methods. In the *Companion Species Manifesto*, Haraway first explains why Hearne is problematic for her and others, using the language of conversion to characterize Hearne's refusal to embrace evidence-based force-free and reward-based training techniques: "Hearne, who died in 2001, remains a sharp thorn in the paw for the adherents of positive training methods. To the horror of many professional trainers and ordinary dog folk, including myself, who have undergone a near-religious conversion from the military-style Koehler dog-training methods.... to the joys of rapidly delivering liver cookies under the approving eye of behaviorist learning theorists, Hearne did not turn from the old path and embrace the new" (48). While Haraway and others have been "converted" to the school of positive reinforcement, Hearne remained unapologetically resolute in her faith in the rightness of her own training methods. Yet Haraway insists that Hearne and the behaviorists she so vociferously

maligned remain "blood sisters under the skin." Donna Haraway, *When Species Meet* (University of Minnesota Press, 2008), 343–44.
52. Haraway, *When Species Meet*, 245.
53. Nancy Tatom Ammerman, *Sacred Stories, Spiritual Tribes: Finding Religion in Everyday Life* (Oxford University Press, 2014), 293. As Ammerman notes, the recognition of the sacred in these spiritual narratives "need not be embodied in a deity, although it very often is. It need not be systematized into a set of doctrines, although centuries of work by legions of theologians have provided ample resources. It need not be organized into legally recognized institutions, although the modern world has tended to try. It need not even have a name, although some forms of commonly used language seem inevitable in each society and time. When sociologists study religion, it is this sacred consciousness that is at the heart of our enterprise. Recognizing a wider range of variation will allow us more powerful explanatory models" (293).
54. Haraway, *When Species Meet*, 208.
55. Haraway has talked extensively about her Catholic upbringing in interviews and throughout her work, and it is central to understanding both how Haraway thinks about companion species in general and dog training in particular. The feminist theologian Zandra Wagoner sheds some light on why Haraway's Catholic upbringing might have been overlooked in most feminist work to date. As Wagoner explains, there is a "pervasive trend within feminist theory that places feminist work in religion, particularly theology, outside the bounds of acceptable feminism." Zandra Wagoner, "Kinship Figures, Polluted Legacy, and Recycling: Pragmatic Considerations for Feminist God-Talk," *American Journal of Theology and Philosophy* 28, no. 2 (2017): 251–70. Whereas Wagoner's primary goal is to bring together Haraway with the feminist theologian Catherine Keller in order to create a space for productive engagement between theology and feminist theory, I want first to highlight how Haraway speaks about her Catholicism and then to explain why Haraway's Catholic upbringing is central to her theology of dog training.
56. Donna J. Haraway, *How Like a Leaf: An Interview with Thyrza Nichols Goodeve* (Routledge, 2000), 8–10, 13. In reflecting on her childhood, Haraway says: "Yes, in hindsight it's quite an image. There I was reading St. Thomas Aquinas, just entering into high school,

surrounded by Catholic patriarchy, the Cold War, and the results of McCarthyism. And it's important to highlight that I experienced McCarthyism from the point of view of an Irish Catholic family that was anti-Communist and convinced by Cold War ideology. It was a very thoughtful family but nonetheless very much a part of middle America and a white middle-class formation" (11).

57. Haraway, *How Like a Leaf*, 141.
58. Robert A. Orsi, *Between Heaven and Earth: The Religious Worlds People Make and the Scholars Who Study Them* (Princeton University Press, 2005), 73.
59. Colin Dayan also uses the language of flesh and spirit throughout her book *With Dogs at the Edge of Life*. For instance, she says, "Dogs bear the burden of revelation. With them and succumbing to their gaze, as unintelligible as that of Cousteau's dog, I try to narrow the gap between the body and mind, human and nonhuman, matter and spirit" (xiii). Dayan also locates the ineffable in her everyday encounters with dogs. In another section of her book, she uses even more explicitly Christian language, stating that "to have the dog in you is to have Christ in your heart. . . . Dogs take their breath at the limits of the mental and the physical. They live out their lives suspended between themselves and their humans. Their knowing has everything to do with perception, an unprecedented attentiveness to the sensual world" (98).
60. Haraway, *When Species Meet*, 206. As suggested by the first chapter on the Vick dogs, dogfighting is part of these exploitative practices that bring together domestication and capitalism.
61. Haraway, *When Species Meet*, 207. For more on Despret's work, see Vinciane Despret, "The Body We Care For: Figures of Anthropo-zoo-genesis," *Body & Society* 10, no. 2–3 (2004): 111–34; Vinciane Despret, *What Would Animals Say If We Asked the Right Questions?* (University of Minnesota Press, 2016). In this book, Despret poses twenty-six questions—from "do animals have a sense of humor?" to "Do animals form same-sex relations?"—all of which are meant to argue that the behaviors that are most commonly defined as separating humans from animals do not belong exclusively to humans.
62. Haraway, *When Species Meet*, 208.
63. Haraway, *When Species Meet*, 240. For the original study, see Marc Bekoff and J. A. Byers, "A Critical Reanalysis of the Ontogeny of

Mammalian Social and Locomotor Play: An Ethological Hornet's Nest," in *Behavioural Development: The Bielefeld Interdisciplinary Project*, ed. K. Immelmann, G. W. Barlow, L. Petrinovich, and M. Main (Cambridge University Press, 1981), 296–337.

64. The animal behaviorist Patricia B. McConnell deciphers this quotation in her article "The Pause That Refreshes: Play or Warming Up for a Fight—How to Tell the Difference," *Bark*, 2009, https://www.patriciamcconnell.com/wp-content/uploads/2012/05/Bark-2009-Nov-Dec-The-Pause-that-Refreshes.pdf. The term "handicapping" is ableist, but I am not familiar with the use of an alternative.

65. Haraway, *When Species Meet*, 240; emphasis in original.

66. Haraway, *When Species Meet*, 232. To "play" at agility is a common way that practitioners talk about the sport. For people unfamiliar with agility, Haraway describes the canine sport as follows: "Picture a grassy field or dirt-covered horse arena about one hundred by one hundred feet square. Fill it with fifteen to twenty obstacles arranged in patterns according to a judge's plan. The sequence of the obstacles and difficulty of the patterns depend on the level of play from novice to masters. Obstacles include single, double, or triple bar jumps. . . . weave poles, consisting of six to twelve in-line poles through which the dog slaloms. . . . A frames (between 5.5 and 6.5 feet high, depending on the organization), and dog walks. These last are called contact obstacles because the dog must put at least a toenail in a painted zone at the up and down ends of the obstacle. Leaping over the contact zone earns a 'failure to perform' the obstacle, which is a high point penalty" (208–9). Reward-based training methods are the dominant approaches used in agility, and there is a stigma against using negative methods. In agility, the human handler is responsible for knowing the sequence of obstacles and for determining a plan for the human and dog to move quickly, accurately, and smoothly through the course. The dog does the actual jumping, but the human has to be in the right position at the right time to give the dog good information (209).

67. Haraway, *When Species Meet*, 209, 240.

68. Haraway, *When Species Meet*, 208.

69. For an example of what this looks like, see: Travis Agility Group, "About Agility," https://www.austintag.org/about-agility.html.

70. Haraway, *When Species Meet*, 240.
71. Haraway, *When Species Meet*, 224; emphasis in original. This is also the case in nosework, where the common mantra is "trust your dog." On the National Association of Canine Scent Work's website, it states, "Your K9 Nose Work® experience, at workshops or in class, should always be one which puts the dog first, creating an environment where your dog is free to express his natural scenting talents and learn scenting skills through problem solving and self-reward, and where your relationship with your dog deepens as you learn to trust in and support your dog's newly developed talents." "From Intro to First Trial: Getting Started," National Association of Canine Scent Work, https://www.nacsw.net/ort-trial-information/trial-information/intro-first-trial-getting-started. As this dog-centered language suggests, it is important and difficult for human handlers to let go of their attachment to being in control and to put their full trust in their dog's superior scent abilities.
72. Haraway, *When Species Meet*, 227.
73. I am using the word "guardian" instead of "owner," but I still think it's an imperfect approximation of the relationship.
74. Haraway, *When Species Meet*, 227.
75. Haraway, *When Species Meet*, 227–28.
76. Haraway, *When Species Meet*, 229.
77. Jacques Derrida, *The Animal That Therefore I Am*, ed. Marie-Louise Mallet (Fordham University Press, 2008).
78. Haraway, *When Species Meet*, 232.
79. Haraway, *When Species Meet*, 245.
80. Harlan Weaver, *Bad Dog: Pit Bull Politics and Multispecies Justice* (University of Washington Press, 2021), 149, 151–52.
81. Harlan Weaver, *Bad Dog*, 150–51.
82. Matthew Calarco, *The Three Ethologies: A Positive Vision for Rebuilding Human-Animal Relationships* (University of Chicago Press, 2024), 108, 120, 115.

4. TROUBLING REDEMPTION

1. Daniel Victor, "Mourning Bretagne, a Search Dog and Symbol of 9/11 Heroism," *New York Times*, June 7, 2016.

2. Peter Slattery, "Last Living 9/11 Rescue Dog Given a Funeral Fit for a Hero," *Daily Beast*, June 7, 2016. For more coverage, see Andrew Kragie, "Last Known 9/11 Search Dog Euthanized in Houston Area," *Chron*, June 6, 2016; Krishnadev Calamur, "Remembering Bretagne, the Last Known 9/11 Rescue Dog," *The Atlantic*, June 7, 2017; Saeed Ahmed and Thomas Patterson, "Last Known 9/11 Search and Rescue Dog Laid to Rest," CNN, June 7, 2016. To see the video of Bretagne walking into the clinic surrounded by those honoring her, see "Exit of the Final 9/11 Search and Rescue Dog," Cy Fair, TX Fire Department, June 6, 2016, https://www.youtube.com/watch?v=U_pU9YDqQzk.

3. Katie Mettler, "Firefighters Gave a Final, Farewell Salute to This Old Golden Retriever, the Last 9/11 Rescue Dog," *Washington Post*, June 7, 2016. This is just one example of the many social media tributes that poured in from across the country, including one from Texas's governor Greg Abbott, who stated, "The last living 9/11 rescue dog has passed away. Texas & America are forever grateful for Bretagne's service. Victor, "Mourning Bretagne."

4. See my discussion of Ernest Lee Tuveson, *Redeemer Nation: The Idea of America's Millennial Role* (University of Chicago Press, 1968), in the introduction. In his chapter on images of national identity, Rhys H. Williams provides helpful context for understanding the United States as a redeemer nation. "There is very little documentation for *a* civil religion in the way Bellah and many of those following him applied," Williams argues. "However, there is 'civil religious discourse' in American political culture and depictions of national identity. That is, there are ways of talking about American national history, identity, and destiny that link the nation to a sense of the sacred, and those representations imbue the nation with a special status in the world and often require special responsibilities as well. These are what many have called the 'legitimating myths' of the American nation; indeed, Bellah himself claimed that understanding America's sacred legitimating myths was his true interest in 1967, not the naming of another 'religion' per se." Rhys H. Williams, "Uncle Sam, the Statue of Liberty, and Images of National Identity," in *Civil Religion Today: Religion and the American Nation in the Twenty-First Century*, ed. Rhys H. Williams, Raymond Haberski Jr., and Philip Goff (New York University Press, 2021), 139.

5. Robert N. Bellah, "Civil Religion in America." *Daedalus* 96, no. 1 (1967): 1–21.
6. The use of binary categories of good and evil appeared as early as George W. Bush's initial address to the nation on the evening of September 11, 2001. For more, see "Statement by the President in Address to the Nation," White House, September 11, 2001, https://georgewbush-whitehouse.archives.gov/news/releases/2001/09/20010911-16.html.
7. This was a risk that Bellah was very much attuned to. He was misread as endorsing a kind of national self-idolatry, which was the opposite of what he wanted. At the beginning of a 1991 reprint of this essay, Bellah wrote: "This chapter was written for a Dædalus conference on American Religion in May 1966. It was reprinted with comments and a rejoinder in *The Religious Situation: 1968*, where I defend myself against the accusation of supporting an idolatrous worship of the American nation. I think it should be clear from the text that I conceive of the central tradition of the American civil religion not as a form of national self-worship but as the subordination of the nation to ethical principles that transcend it in terms of which it should be judged. I am convinced that every nation and every people come to some form of religious self-understanding whether the critics like it or not. Rather than simply denounce what seems in any case inevitable, it seems more responsible to seek within the civil religious tradition for those critical principles which undercut the everpresent danger of national self-idolization." Robert N. Bellah, *Beyond Belief: Essays on Religion in a Post-Traditionalist World* (University of California Press, 1991), 168.
8. See the introduction for a discussion of the lineage of the United States as a redeemer nation. Tuveson, *Redeemer Nation*.
9. While this is a mantra I have heard from numerous dog trainers I've worked with, Suzanne Clothier explicitly invokes this concept as integral to what she calls "relationship-centered dog training." See Suzanne Clothier, *Relationship Centered Training: Living the Connection* (Flying Dog, 2025), 14–15.
10. I recognize that the ability to care for one's dog as one wishes is a privilege that involves financial resources and time. I do not mean to cast blame on people for whom this is not a possibility—quite the contrary. All one can do is their best. I do think we owe it to dogs and

people to make veterinary care more accessible. For more on how affordable veterinary care is a social justice issue, see the final chapter of Harlan Weaver, *Bad Dog: Pit Bull Politics and Multispecies Justice* (University of Washington Press, 2021).

11. See, for example: Nona Kilgore Bauer, *Dog Heroes of September 11th: A Tribute to America's Search and Rescue Dogs* (Kennel Club Books, 2011); Ron Burns, *The Dogs of Ron Burns—a Tribute to the Dogs of 9/11* (Burns Studio Publishing, 2014); Charlotte Dumas, *Retrieved* (Ice Plant Publishing, 2011); Isabel George, *The 9/11 Dogs: The Heroes Who Searched for Survivors at Ground Zero* (HarperCollins, 2015); Meish Goldish, *Ground Zero Dogs (Dog Heroes)* (Bearport Pub. Co., 2013).

12. "Four-Legged 9/11 Heroes," National September 11 Memorial & Museum, https://www.911memorial.org/connect/blog/four-legged-911-heroes.

13. Kilgore Bauer, *Dog Heroes of September 11th*, 9.

14. Michael Hingson and Susy Flory, *Thunder Dog: The True Story of a Blind Man, His Guide Dog, and the Triumph of Trust* (Thomas Nelson, 2012).

15. Hingson and Flory, *Thunder Dog*, 162.

16. Grant Wacker, *America's Pastor: Billy Graham and the Shaping of a Nation* (Harvard University Press, 2014).

17. This is also the case for other dogs deployed to Ground Zero, including Bretagne, Nike, Sirius, and more. To see an example of this phenomenon, I recommend this short documentary: Kenn Bell, Tanya Kelen, and Nadine Pequeneza, *Hero Dogs of 9/11* (Kelencontent, 2013).

18. There is a large (and growing) body of literature in the field known as "surveillance studies." See David Lyon, *Surveillance Studies: An Overview* (Polity, 2007); Kirstie Ball, Kevin D. Haggerty, and David Lyon, eds., *Routledge Handbook of Surveillance Studies* (Routledge, 2012).

19. Laurie Anderson, *Heart of a Dog* (Abramorama/HBO Documentary Films, 2015, 75 minutes).

20. Anderson, *Heart of a Dog*.

21. Achille Mbembe, *On the Postcolony* (University of California Press, 2001), 16; emphasis in original.

22. In contrast to teleological models of time, Mbembe explains that "African social formations are not necessarily converging toward a

single point, trend, or cycle. They harbor the possibility of a variety of trajectories neither convergent nor divergent but interlocked, paradoxical. More philosophically, it may be supposed that the present as experience of a time is precisely the moment when different forms of absence become mixed together: absence of those presences that are no longer so that no one remembers (the past), and the absence of those others that are yet to come and are anticipated (the future)." Mbembe, *On the Postcolony*, 16. While I am not going to focus on the surge of discourse after 9/11 that pitted "the West" against the "the East" in this chapter, it is notable that this critique of dangerous binaries comes from the perspective of a postcolonialist scholar whose insights have revealed the Protestant-based assumptions grounding the academic study of religion. Cf. Tomoko Masuzawa, *The Invention of World Religions* (University of Chicago Press, 2005). For a canonical account of the kinds of Orientalist discourse that surged in the wake of 9/11, see Lila Abu-Lughod, "Do Muslim Women Really Need Saving? Anthropological Reflections on Cultural Relativism and Its Others," *American Anthropologist* 104, no. 3 (2002): 783–90.

23. Michelle Orange, "Dog-Seeing Eye: The Cinematic Work of Laurie Anderson," *Virginia Quarterly Review*, Winter 2016, 193–96. André Bazin, "Lettre de Sibérie" (1958), in *Le cinéma français de la Libération à la nouvelle vague* (Cahiers du Cinéma, 1983); for an English translation, see "André Bazin on Chris Marker," trans. David Kehr, *Film Comment*, 2003.

24. Anderson talks about Marker's influence in a conversation with *Heart of a Dog*'s co-producer, Jake Perlin, in the DVD's special edition features. The quotation comes from Kehr, "André Bazin on Chris Marker."

25. Anderson, *Heart of a Dog*.

26. Anderson, *Heart of a Dog*.

27. I am rendering Anderson's words in stanza form to reflect Anderson's description of *Heart of a Dog* as a "cinematic tone poem." There is an accompanying album with lyrics by Laurie Anderson: https://laurieanderson.com/?portfolio=heart-of-a-dog.

28. Anderson, *Heart of a Dog*.

29. Jasbir Puar, *Terrorist Assemblages: Homonationalism in Queer Times* (Duke University Press, 2007), xxvi. See also Nilüfer Göle, "Close

Encounters: Islam, Modernity, and Violence," in *Understanding September 11*, ed. Craig Calhoun, Paul Price, and Ashley Timmer (Norton, 2002), 332–44; David Kazanjian, *The Colonizing Trick: National Culture and Imperial Citizenship in Early America* (University of Minnesota Press, 2003), 27.

30. Myles, *Afterglow*, 73. Underline in original.
31. Colleen Glenney Boggs, *Animalia Americana* (Columbia University Press, 2013), 41–42.
32. Boggs, *Animalia Americana*, 68. The quotation within this quotation comes from Kalpana Shesadri-Crooks, "Being Human: Bestiality, Anthropology, and Law," *Umbr(a)* 3, no. 1 (2003): 97–114.
33. Emmanuel Levinas, *Difficult Freedom: Essays on Judaism*, trans. Seán Hand (Johns Hopkins University Press, 1997), 153.
34. Anderson, *Heart of a Dog*. Lolabelle also learned how to make small sculptures by pressing her paw into lumps of plasticine.
35. Here I am using "enrichment" in the dog training sense, which refers to providing mental, social, environmental, and physical stimulation.
36. Anderson, *Heart of a Dog*.
37. Saige Walton, "Other Sides: Loving and Grieving with *Heart of a Dog* and Merleau-Ponty's Depth," *Projections* 13, no. 2 (June 2019): 46.
38. Anderson, *Heart of a Dog*.
39. Jessica Pierce, *The Last Walk: Reflections on Our Pets at the End of Their Lives* (University of Chicago Press), 10.
40. Pierce, *The Last Walk*, chap. 4, esp. 100–3.
41. The literal translation of euthanasia comes from the Greek *eu*, "good, well," and *thanatos*, "death." Pierce, *The Last Walk*, 165.
42. Anderson, *Heart of a Dog*. Throughout this section, I am going to discuss Buddhism as Anderson approaches it. Because it is outside the scope of this project, I am not going to discuss these Buddhist teachings in detail here. For a brilliant text on Buddhist approaches to the deaths of companion animals through the lens of pet ownership in contemporary Japan, see Barbara R. Ambros, *Bones of Contention* (University of Hawai'i Press, 2012).
43. It is becoming increasingly common to allow animals to die at home in a familiar setting, surrounded by loved ones. There is also a growing animal palliative care and hospice movement, in which the goal is

to "help animals die without pain and suffering and to help human companions figure out when an animal's quality of life shifts from acceptable to unacceptable." Pierce, *The Last Walk*, 134.

44. Anderson, *Heart of a Dog*. The "we" here refers to Anderson and her husband, Lou Reed. He's another ghost in this film. He plays the character of a doctor at one point, and then the film is dedicated to him at the end. (He died while Anderson was working on it.)
45. Anderson, *Heart of a Dog*.
46. Anderson, *Heart of a Dog*. Because Anderson describes the film as a "cinematic tone poem," the quotations are written in stanza form.
47. Alice A. Kuzniar, *Melancholia's Dog: Reflections on Our Animal Kinship* (University of Chicago Press, 2006), 138.
48. Judith Butler, *Precarious Life: The Powers of Mourning and Violence* (Verso, 2004), 32. I am referring here to the objections that non-pet-lovers make that the dog does not understand its death, and so lacks the sadness of a dying human, or that dogs do not "matter" as much as humans because they do not possess the same cognitive faculties and therefore not as much is lost when a dog dies.
49. In a chapter called "The Rape of Rosie," Myles talks about how they left the TV on during a failed attempt at mating Rosie with another dog, and there happened to be a religious program on the air: "There was a priest on from Operation Rescue. He was going on a long theological explanation of the Catholic Church's deeply thought out position. Rosie's for life, laughed Doug [the owner of the other dog] and I didn't know where I stood." Myles, *Afterglow*, 63–64.
50. Myles, *Afterglow*, 4.
51. Myles, *Afterglow*, 11–12. Emphasis in original.
52. Myles, *Afterglow*, 22.
53. Colin Dayan, *With Dogs at the Edge of Life* (Columbia University Press), 10.
54. Myles, *Afterglow*, 24.
55. Myles, *Afterglow*, 22.
56. Myles, *Afterglow*, 11, 26.
57. Myles, *Afterglow*, 27.
58. Myles, *Afterglow*, 198.
59. Myles, *Afterglow*, 206–7.

CODA

1. Peter Brooks, *Troubling Confessions: Speaking Guilt in Law and Literature* (University of Chicago Press, 2001).
2. Robert N. Bellah, "Civil Religion in America," *Daedalus* 96, no. 1 (1967): 1–21.
3. For a sampling, see Rhys H. Williams, Raymond Haberski Jr., and Philip Goff, eds., *Civil Religion Today: Religion and the American Nation in the Twenty-First Century* (New York University Press, 2021); Nichole R. Phillips, *Patriotism Black and White: The Color of American Exceptionalism* (Baylor University Press, 2018).
4. Katharine Mershon, "Are Dogs Part of American Civil Religion?," *American Religion: Provocations*, 2021, https://www.american-religion.org/provocations/dogs.
5. Ernest Lee Tuveson, *Redeemer Nation: The Idea of America's Millennial Role* (University of Chicago Press, 1968), vii–viii.
6. Carole Emberton, *Beyond Redemption: Race, Violence, and the American South After the Civil War* (Chicago: University of Chicago Press, 2013), 3–4.
7. Michel Foucault's work on the rise of the modern prison inevitably informs my thinking here. Michel Foucault, *Discipline and Punish: The Birth of the Prison*, ed. Alan Sheridan (Pantheon, 1977). For more on this connection in animal shelters, see Katja M. Guenther, *The Lives and Deaths of Shelter Animals* (Stanford University Press, 2020), esp. chap. 2, "Helping/Policing/Killing."
8. See Aaron Griffith, *God's Law and Order* (Harvard University Press, 2020), for a close analysis of prison conversion narratives.
9. Harlan Weaver, *Bad Dog: Pit Bull Politics and Multispecies Justice* (University of Washington Press, 2021), esp. 177–78.
10. Mary Oliver, "Percy Wakes Me (Fourteen) Today," in *Swan: Prose and Poems* (Beacon, 2010). Reprinted by the permission of The Charlotte Sheedy Literary Agency as agent for the author. Copyright © 2010, 2013 by Mary Oliver with permission of Bill Reichblum.
11. For a story about Mary Oliver and her relationship to Percy, see Dana Jennings, "Scratching a Muse's Ears," *New York Times*, October 3, 2013.
12. I am also not arguing for total canine anarchy; clarity and structure are incredibly important in dogs' lives. As the beings with more power in

the relationship, we owe dogs clear communication, respect, and consistency. Suzanne Clothier, *Relationship-Centered Training: Living the Connection* (Flying Dog, 2025). For more, see Suzanne Clothier, *Bones Would Rain from the Sky* (Grand Central, 2005). I also highly recommend Patricia B. McConnell, *The Other End of the Leash* (Ballantine, 2003)

13. This is an example of what Kári Driscoll and Eva Hoffmann refer to as "zoopoetics," which identifies "a certain affinity between 'poetic thinking' and 'animal thinking.'" Kári Driscoll and Eva Hoffmann, *What Is Zoopoetics?* (Palgrave Macmillan, 2018), 2. As Driscoll and Hoffmann argue, zoopoetics "involves not only seeing but also . . . attentive listening—a practice of 'listening otherwise' (cf. Driscoll 2017)—to the animal in order to recover something that has been forgotten or repressed" (3). "Percy Wakes Me" is one such example. The full citation of the 2017 piece referenced in the quotation is Kári Driscoll, "An Unheard, Inhuman Music: Narrative Voice and the Question of the Animal in Kafka's 'Josephine, the Singer or the Mouse Folk,'" *Humanities* 6, no. 2 (2017): article no. 26, https://www.mdpi.com/2076-0787/6/2/26. For a rich account of the relationship between human and canine figuration, see Joela M. Jacobs, *Animal, Vegetal, Marginal* (Indiana University Press, 2025).

14. Alexandra Horowitz, *Inside of a Dog: What Dogs See, Smell, and Know* (Scribner 2010), 112.

15. "Coda," *Oxford English Dictionary*, July 2023, https://doi.org/10.1093/OED/1748588647.

16. Horowitz, *Inside of a Dog*, 112.

17. The passage from which I pulled that quotation is worth including in full. Horowitz writes: "Imagining that dogs' thoughts are but cruder forms of human discourse does the dog a disservice. And despite their marvelous range and extent of communication, it is the very fact that they do not use language that makes me especially treasure dogs. Their silence can be one of their most endearing traits. Not muteness: absence of linguistic noise. There is no awkwardness in a shared silent moment with a dog: a gaze on the other side of the room; lying sleepily alongside each other. It is when language stops that we connect most fully." Horowitz, *Inside a Dog*, 119. Here I do not take Horowitz to be arguing that dogs do not have language but that the space between their ways of communicating and humans is a site of possibility for connection.

BIBLIOGRAPHY

Ahmed, Sarah, and Thomas Patterson. "Last Known 9/11 Search and Rescue Dog Laid to Rest." CNN. June 7, 2016.
Ahuja, Neel. "Postcolonial Critique in a Multispecies World." *PMLA* 124, no. 2 (2009).
Alsup, Dave. "Michael Vick Cancels Book Tour After Threats." CNN. March 12, 2013.
Ambros, Barbara R. *Bones of Contention: Animals and Religion in Contemporary Japan*. University of Hawai'i Press, 2012.
American Kennel Club. "Canine Good Citizen Test." http://www.akc.org/cgc-pledge/.
American Veterinary Society of Animal Behavior. "Cesar Millan Response." 2016. https://avsab.org/wp-content/uploads/2019/01/Cesar_Millan_Response-download.pdf.
Ammerman, Nancy Tatom, ed. *Everyday Religion: Observing Religious Lives*. Oxford University Press, 2006.
———. *Sacred Stories, Spiritual Tribes: Finding Religion in Everyday Life*. Oxford University Press, 2014.
Anderson, Laurie. *Heart of a Dog*. Abramorama/HBO Documentary Films. 75 minutes. 2015.
Austin, J. L. *How to Do Things with Words*. Harvard University Press, 1975.
Badano, Solange E., Steven J. Burgermeister, Sidney Henne, Sean T. Murphy, and Benjamin M. Cole. "Legitimacy Concerns in Animal Advocacy Organizations During the Michael Vick Dogfighting Scandal." *Society & Animals* 22, no. 2 (2014): 111–34.

Bauer, Nona Kilgore. *Dog Heroes of September 11th: A Tribute to America's Search and Rescue Dogs.* Kennel Club Books. 2011.

Bazin, André. "Lettre de Sibérie" (1958). In *Le cinéma français de la libération à la nouvelle vague.* Cahiers du cinéma, 1983.

———. "André Bazin on Chris Marker." Trans. Dave Kehr. *Film Comment* (2003).

Bekoff, Marc. *The Emotional Lives of Animals.* New World Library, 2008.

Bell, Kenn, Tanya Kelen, and Nadine Pequeneza. *Hero Dogs of 9/11.* Kelencontent, 2013.

Bellah, Robert N. "Civil Religion in America." *Daedalus* 96, no. 1 (1967): 1–21.

Bennett, Joshua. *Being Property Once Myself.* Harvard University Press, 2020.

Berger, John. *Why Look at Animals?* Penguin, 2009.

Berlant, Lauren. *The Female Complaint: The Unfinished Business of Sentimentality in American Culture.* Duke University Press, 2008.

———. *The Queen of America Goes to Washington City: Essays on Sex and Citizenship.* Duke University Press, 2007.

Berlin, Adele, ed. "Redemption." In *The Oxford Dictionary of the Jewish Religion.* Oxford University Press, 2011.

Bersani, Leo. *The Culture of Redemption.* Harvard University Press, 1990.

Bird, Diana. "The Problem with the 'Pack Leadership' Mentality." *Positively.* October 13, 2015. https://positively.com/dog-training/post/pack-theory-the-problem-with-the-pack-leadership-mentality.

Boggs, Colleen Glenney. *Animalia Americana: Animal Representations and Biopolitical Subjectivity.* Columbia University Press, 2013.

Boisseron, Bénédicte. *Afro-Dog: Blackness and the Animal Question.* Columbia University Press, 2018.

Bradshaw, John W. S., Emily J. Blackwell, and Rachel A. Casey. "Dominance in Domestic Dogs—Useful Construct or Bad Habit?" *Journal of Veterinary Behavior* 4, no. 3 (2009): 135–44.

Brekus, Catherine A. *Sarah Osborne's World.* Yale University Press, 2013.

Brockes, Emma. "Punk Poet Eileen Myles, on Their Dog Memoir: 'We Were Regarded as an Unruly Pair.'" *The Guardian*, February 16, 2018.

Brooks, Peter. *Troubling Confessions: Speaking Guilt in Law and Literature.* University of Chicago Press, 2001.

Brown, Bill. "The Dark Wood of Postmodernity (Space, Faith, Allegory)." *PMLA* 120, no. 3 (2005): 734–50.
Brown, Royal S. "White Dog." *Cinéaste* 34, no. 3 (Summer 2009): 54–55.
Buffington, Daniel. "Contesting Race on Sundays: Making Meaning Out of the Rise in the Number of Black Quarterbacks." *Sociology of Sport Journal* 22, no. 1 (2005): 19–37.
Bulanda, Susan. "A Personal History of Dog Training." *IAABC Foundation Journal*, May 2019.
Burchfield, Keri. "The Sociology of Animal Crime: An Examination of the Incidents and Arrests in Chicago." *Deviant Behavior* (2016): 1–17.
Burns, Ron. *The Dogs of Ron Burns—a Tribute to the Dogs of 9/11*. Burns Studio Publishing, 2014.
Burton, Johanna. "Laurie Anderson." *Artforum International* (2005).
Butler, Judith. *Precarious Life: The Powers of Mourning and Violence*. Verso, 2004.
Byosiere, Sarah-Elizabeth, Philippe A. Chouinard, Tiffani J. Howell, and Pauleen C. Bennett. "The Effects of Physical Luminance on Colour Discrimination in Dogs: A Cautionary Tale." *Applied Animal Behaviour Science* 212 (2019): 58–65.
Calamur, Krishnadev. "Remembering Bretagne, the Last Known 9/11 Rescue Dog," *The Atlantic*. June 7, 2017.
Calloway, Jamall A. "Religion, Animals, and Black Theology: The Spiritual Praxis of Sparing." *Religions* 13, no. 5 (2022): 383.
Cameron, Bruce. *A Dog's Purpose: A Novel for Humans*. Forge, 2011.
Cannon, Eoin F. *The Saloon and the Mission: Addiction, Conversion, and the Politics of Redemption in American Culture*. University of Massachusetts Press, 2013.
Cavell, Stanley. *Must We Mean What We Say? A Book of Essays*. Cambridge University Press, 2002.
"Cesar Millan's Long Walk to Becoming the 'Dog Whisperer.'" NPR. March 30, 2014.
Chen, Mel Y. *Animacies: Biopolitics, Racial Mattering, and Queer Affect*. Duke University Press, 2013.
Clothier, Suzanne. *Bones Would Rain from the Sky*. Grand Central, 2002.
Coffey, Laura T. "Last 9/11 Search Dog's Legacy Lives On in Rescue Work—and in a Furry Kid Sister." *Today.com*. September 7, 2021.

Cohen, Judy, and John Richardson. "Pit Bull Panic." *Journal of Popular Culture* 36, no. 2 (2002): 285–317.

Collier, Stephen. "The Pit Bull Terrier: A Dangerous or a Defamed Breed?" *Journal of Veterinary Behavior* (2006): 17–22. http://dapbt.org/collier.html.

Cornish, Audie. "How the Civil Rights Movement Was Covered in Birmingham." *All Things Considered*, June 18, 2013.

Crane, Jonathan K., ed. *Beastly Morality: Animals as Ethical Agents*. Columbia University Press, 2016.

Crenshaw, Kimberlé. "Mapping the Margins: Intersectionality, Identity Politics, and Violence Against Women of Color." *Stanford Law Review* 43, no. 6 (1991): 1243–44.

Criterion Collection. "Critics Honor *White Dog* Release." January 5, 2009. https://www.criterion.com/current/posts/999-critics-honor-white-dog-release.

Croce, F. F. "*White Dog*: Film Review." *Slant Magazine*, December 12, 2008. http://www.slantmagazine.com/film/review/white-dog.

Crous, Marius. "All Dogs Go to Heaven." *The Conversation*, May 29, 2017. http://theconversation.com/all-dogs-go-to-heaven-78272.

Curtis, Bryan. "The NFL's Spiritual Guru." *The Daily Beast*, February 3, 2010.

Daston, Lorraine, and Gregg Mitman, eds. *Thinking with Animals: New Perspectives on Anthropomorphism*. Columbia University Press, 2005.

Dayan, Colin. "Exterminate the Brutes: Your Pit Bull Is Too Violent to Live—Even If It Isn't." *Boston Review*, May 8, 2012. http://bostonreview.net/colin-dayan-exterminate-the-brutes-pit-bulls.

——. "Dogs Are Not People." *Boston Review*, January 23, 2014. http://bostonreview.net/books-ideas/colin-dayan-dogs-are-not-people-humanity

——. *The Law Is a White Dog: How Legal Rituals Make and Unmake Persons*. Princeton University Press, 2011.

——. *With Dogs at the Edge of Life*. Columbia University Press, 2015.

Delise, Karen. *The Pit Bull Placebo: The Media, Myths, and Politics of Canine Aggression*. Anubis, 2007.

DeMello, Marge. *Animals and Society: An Introduction to Human-Animal Studies*. Columbia University Press, 2012.

Dennett, Darcy, dir. *The Champions*. Firefly Filmworks. 90 minutes. http://www.championsdocumentary.com/. 2015.

Derrida, Jacques. *The Animal That Therefore I Am*. Trans. David Wills. Fordham University Press, 2008.

Despret, Vinciane. "The Body We Care For: Figures of Anthropo-zoo-genesis." *Body & Society* 10, no. 2–3 (2004): 111–34.

———. *What Would Animals Say If We Asked the Right Questions?* University of Minnesota Press, 2016.

Driscoll, Kári, and Eva Hoffman, eds. *What Is Zoopoetics?* Palgrave Macmillan, 2018.

———. "An Unheard, Inhuman Music: Narrative Voice and the Question of the Animal in Kafka's 'Josephine, the Singer or the Mouse Folk.'" *Humanities* 6, no. 2, article no. 26 (2017). https://doi.org/10.3390/h6020026.

Dickey, Bronwen. *Pit Bull: The Battle Over an American Icon*. Knopf, 2016.

DiValerio, David M. "Buddhism and Hinduism." *The Oxford Encyclopedia of American Cultural and Intellectual History*. Oxford University Press, 2013.

Dombrowski, Lisa. *The Films of Samuel Fuller: If You Die, I'll Kill You!* Wesleyan University Press, 2008.

———. "Me and Sam Fuller." Criterion Collection. December 29, 2008. https://www.criterion.com/current/posts/980-me-and-sam-fuller.

Donaldson, Jean. *The Culture Clash: A Revolutionary New Way of Understanding the Relationship Between Humans and Dogs*. Dogwise, 1996.

———. *Oh Behave! Dogs from Pavlov to Premack to Pinker*. Dogwise, 2008.

Doniger, Wendy. *The Implied Spider: Politics and Theology in Myth*. Rev. ed. Columbia University Press, 2010.

Doty, Mark. *Dog Years: A Memoir*. HarperCollins, 2007.

Dubino, Jeanne, Ziba Rashidian, and Andrew Smyth, eds. *Representing the Modern Animal in Culture*. Palgrave Macmillan, 2014.

Dubler, Joshua, and Vincent Lloyd. *Break Every Yoke: Religion, Justice, and the Abolition of Prisons*. Oxford University Press, 2019.

Du Bois, W. E. B. *Black Reconstruction in America: An Essay Toward a History of the Part Which Black Folk Played in the Attempt to Reconstruct Democracy in America, 1860–1880*. Harcourt, Brace, 1935.

Edwards, Anna. "The Last 9/11 Rescue Dogs: Portraits of the Last Surviving Animals Who Scoured Ground Zero One Decade On." *Daily Mail*, September 5, 2011.

Elder, Glen, Jennifer Wolch, and Jody Emel. "Race, Place, and the Bounds of Humanity." *Society and Animals* 6, no. 2 (1998): 183–202.

Emberton, Carole. *Beyond Redemption: Race, Violence, and the American South After the Civil War.* University of Chicago Press, 2013.

Empire State Building. "Cesar Millan Lights Up the Empire State Building." April 10, 2024. https://www.youtube.com/watch?v=GHuSNvy5fAo.

Faust, Drew. *This Republic of Suffering: Death and the American Civil War.* Knopf, 2008.

Fessenden, Tracy. *Culture and Redemption: Religion, the Secular, and American Literature.* Princeton University Press, 2006.

Festa, Lynn. *Sentimental Figures of Empire in Eighteenth-Century Britain and France.* Johns Hopkins University Press, 2006.

Foner, Eric. *A Short History of Reconstruction: 1863–1877.* Updated ed. Harper, 2015.

Fraiman, Susan. "Pussy Panic Versus Liking Animals: Tracking Gender in Animal Studies." *Critical Inquiry* 39 (Autumn 2012): 89–115.

Franke, Katherine. *Repair: Redeeming The Promise of Abolition.* Haymarket, 2019.

Franklin, Chester M., dir. *Where the North Begins.* Warner Bros. 1 hour. 1923.

Freccero, Carla. "Carnivorous Virility, or Becoming-Dog." *Social Text* 29, no. 1 (2011): 177–95.

——. "Figural Historiography: Dogs, Humans, and Cynathropic Becomings." In *Comparatively Queer: Interrogating Identities Across Time and Cultures*, ed. Jarrod Hayes, Margaret R. Higonnet, and William J. Spurlin, 45–68. Palgrave Macmillan, 2010.

Fuller, Samuel, dir. *White Dog.* DVD. 90 minutes. 1982.

——. "The White Dog Speaks—to Sam Fuller." *Framework* 19 (1982). https://www.criterion.com/current/posts/2372-the-white-dog-speaks-to-sam-fuller.

Fuller, Samuel, and Curtis Hanson. *White Dog.* Screenplay. 1981.

Garnham, Nicholas. *Samuel Fuller.* Viking, 1971.

Gary, Romain. *Chien blanc.* Gallimard, 1970.

——. "White Dog." *Life*, October 9, 1970, 57–74.

——. *White Dog.* New American Library, 1970.

George, Isabel. *The 9/11 Dogs: The Heroes Who Searched for Survivors at Ground Zero.* HarperCollins, 2015.

Glick, Megan L. "Animal Instincts: Race, Criminality, and the Reversal of the 'Human.'" *American Quarterly* 65, no. 3 (2013): 639–59.

Goldish, Meish. *Ground Zero Dogs (Dog Heroes)*. Bearport, 2013.
Gorant, Jim. *The Lost Dogs: Michael Vick's Dogs and Their Tale of Rescue and Redemption*. Gotham Books, 2010.
Gladwell, Malcolm. "Troublemakers." *New Yorker*, January 29, 2006.
Grano, Daniel A. "Michael Vick's 'Genuine Remorse' and Problems of Public Forgiveness." *Quarterly Journal of Speech* 100, no. 1 (January 2, 2014): 81–104.
Gregersdotter, Katarina, Johan Höglund, and Nicklas Hållén. *Animal Horror Cinema: Genre, History, and Criticism*. Springer, 2016.
Griffith, Aaron. *God's Law and Order: The Politics of Punishment in Evangelical America*. Harvard University Press, 2020.
Gross, Aaron. *The Question of the Animal and Religion: Theoretical Stakes, Practical Implications*. Columbia University Press, 2015.
Gross, Aaron, and Anne Vallely, eds. *Animals and the Human Imagination*. Columbia University Press, 2012.
Gross, Terri. "Laurie Anderson Reflects on Life and Loss in 'Heart of a Dog.'" NPR. November 19, 2015.
Gruen, Lori. *Entangled Empathy*. Lantern, 2015.
Guenther, Katja M. *The Lives and Deaths of Shelter Animals*. Stanford University Press, 2020.
Guenther, Katja M., and Julian Paul Keenan, eds. *When Animals Die: Examining Justifications and Envisioning Justice*. New York University Press, 2024.
Haraway, Donna J. *The Companion Species Manifesto: Dogs, People, and Significant Otherness*. Prickly Paradigm Press, 2003.
——. "enlightenment@science_wars.com: A Personal Reflection on Love and War." *Social Text* 50 (Spring 1997): 123–29.
——. *How Like a Leaf: An Interview with Thyrza Nichols Goodeve*. Routledge, 2000.
——. *Modest_Witness@Second_Millennium.FemaleMan_Meets_OncoMouse: Feminism and Technoscience*. Routledge, 1997.
——. "Situated Knowledges: The Science Question in Feminism and the Privilege of Partial Perspective." *Feminist Studies* 14, no. 3 (Autumn 1988): 575–99.
——. *Staying with the Trouble: Making Kin in the Chthulucene*. Duke University Press, 2016.
——. *When Species Meet*. University of Minnesota Press, 2008.

Hardy, Phil. *Samuel Fuller*. Praeger, 1970.
Hearne, Vicki. *Adam's Task: Calling Animals by Name*. Skyhorse, 1986.
——. *Animal Happiness*. HarperCollins, 1994.
——. *Bandit: Dossier of a Dangerous Dog*. HarperCollins, 1991.
——. "What's Wrong with Animal Rights: Of Hounds, Horses, and Jeffersonian Happiness." *Harper's*, September 1991, 59–64.
"Heart of a Dog, with Laurie Anderson." *New Sounds with WNYC Public Radio*. May 12, 2018. https://www.wnyc.org/story/3790-heart-dog-laurie-anderson-encore/.
Hingson, Michael, and Susy Flory. *Thunder Dog: The True Story of a Blind Man, His Guide Dog, and the Triumph of Trust*. Thomas Nelson, 2012.
Hoberman, J. *The Magic Hour: Film at Fin de Siècle*. Temple University Press, 2003.
——. "*White Dog*: Sam Fuller Unmuzzled." Criterion Collection. November 27, 2008.
Holdener, Mark, and James Kauffman. "Getting Out of the Doghouse: The Image Repair Strategies of Michael Vick." *Public Relations Review* 40, no. 1 (2014): 92–99.
Hallström, Lasse. Dir. *A Dog's Purpose*. Amblin Entertainment, Pariah Entertainment Group, Reliance Entertainment, and Walden Media. 1 hour 40 minutes. 2017.
Hopgood-Oster, Laura. *Holy Dogs and Asses: Animals in the Christian Tradition*. University of Illinois Press, 2008.
Horowitz, Alexandra. *Inside of a Dog: What Dogs See, Smell, and Know*. Scribner, 2010.
"How to Get Your Dog to Stop Digging." *Humane World for Animals*. https://www.humanesociety.org/resources/stop-dogs-digging.
Humes, Immy. *A Little Vicious*. Doc Tank Inc., DVD. 30 minutes. 1991.
Huspeni, Andrea. "Cesar Millan Just Celebrated 20 Years on TV. Not Everyone Is Happy About It." *This Dogs Life*. June 3, 2024. https://www.thisdogslife.co/cesar-millan-just-celebrated-20-years-on-tv-not-everyone-is-happy-about-it/.
Jackson, Zakiyyah Iman. *Becoming Human: Matter and Meaning in an Antiblack World*. New York University Press, 2020.
Jacobs, G. H. "Evolution of Color Vision and Its Reflections in Contemporary Mammals." In *Handbook of Color Psychology*, ed. A. J. Elliot, M. D. Fairchild, and A. Franklin. Cambridge University Press, 2015.

Jacobs, Joela. *Animal, Vegetal, Marginal: The German Literary Grotesque from Panizza to Kafka*. Indiana University Press, 2025.

Junod, Tom. "The State of the American Dog." *Esquire*, July 14, 2014. http://www.esquire.com/news-politics/a23731/american-dog-0814/.

Kazanjian, David. *The Colonizing Trick: National Culture and Imperial Citizenship in Early America*. University of Minnesota Press, 2003.

Kelley, Raina. "Why Dogs Can't Be Racist." *Newsweek*, July 2, 2010.

Kelsey, David. *Imagining Redemption*. Westminster John Knox, 2005.

Kenny, Glenn. "Heart of a Dog: Enough Time to Hold Love in Your Grasp." Criterion Collection. December 6, 2016.

Kim, Claire Jean. *Dangerous Crossings: Race, Species, and Nature in a Multicultural Age*. Cambridge University Press, 2015.

Koehler, W. R. *The Koehler Method of Dog Training*. Howell Book House, 1962.

Kragie, Andrew. "Last Known 9/11 Search Dog Euthanized in Houston Area." *Chron*. June 6, 2016.

Kuzniar, Alice. *Melancholia's Dog: Reflections on Our Animal Kinship*. University of Chicago Press, 2006.

Lamb, Chris. Ed. *From Jack Johnson to LeBron James: Sports, Media, and the Color Line*. University of Nebraska Press, 2016.

Lee-St. John, Jeninne. "Dog Training and the Myth of Alpha-Male Dominance." *Time*, July 30, 2010.

Leitch, Will. "The Impossible, Inevitable Redemption of Michael Vick." *GQ*, April 18, 2011. http://www.gq.com/story/michael-vick-gq-september-2011-interview.

Levinas, Emmanuel. *Difficult Freedom: Essays on Judaism*. Trans. Seán Hand. Johns Hopkins University Press, 1997.

Lewis, Andy. "Michael Vick Promotes Upcoming Memoir on Dogfighting Scandal on Today." *Hollywood Reporter*, July 18, 2012.

Lyon, David. *Surveillance Studies: An Overview*. Polity, 2007.

Lyon, David, Kirstie Ball, and Kevin D. Haggerty, eds. *Routledge Handbook of Surveillance Studies*. Routledge, 2012.

MacPherson, Sandra. *Harm's Way: Tragic Responsibility and the Novel Form*. Johns Hopkins Press, 2010.

Macur, Juliet. "Given Reprieve, N.F.L. Star's Dogs Find Kindness." *New York Times*, February 2, 2008.

Marcoulesco, Ileana. "Redemption." In *Encyclopedia of Religion*, 2nd ed., ed. Lindsay Jones, 11:7640–42. Macmillan Reference USA, 2005.

Mbembe, Achille. *On the Postcolony.* University of California Press, 2001.
McBride, Keally. *Punishment and the Political Order.* University of Michigan Press, 2019.
McCarthy, Mary. "A Better Life for Michael Vick's Pit Bulls." *The Bark*, October 17, 2012.
McConnell, Patricia. "The Evolution of Play—a Case Study with Skip and Maggie." *The Other End of the Leash* (blog), February 8, 2021.
———. *The Other End of the Leash.* Bantam, 2002.
McHugh, Susan. *Animal Stories: Narrating Across Species Lines.* University of Minnesota Press, 2011.
———. *Dog.* Reaktion, 2004.
Mershon, Katharine. "Animal Rescue." In *Gender: Animals*, ed. Juno Salazar Parreñas, 19–131. Macmillan Reference, 2017.
———. "Are Dogs Part of America's Civil Religion?" *American Religion.* 2020. https://www.american-religion.org/provocations/dogs.
Mettler, Katie. "Firefighters Gave a Final, Farewell Salute to This Old Golden Retriever, the Last 9/11 Rescue Dog." *Washington Post*, June 7, 2016.
Meyer, Eric Daryl. *Inner Animalities: Theology and the End of the Human.* Fordham University Press, 2018.
"Michael Vick Came Back from the Bottom. That's His Real NFL Legacy." *The Guardian*, April 5, 2016.
"Michael Vick's Rehabilitated Dogs Find Homes." *CBS News*, September 20, 2010.
Midgley, Mary. *Animals and Why They Matter.* University of Georgia Press, 1983.
Miller, Reuben Jonathan. *Halfway Home: Race, Punishment, and the Afterlife of Mass Incarceration.* Little, Brown, 2021.
Mitchell, Wendy. "Laurie Anderson Reveals the Inspirations for 'Heart of a Dog.'" *Screen International*, December 18, 2015.
Molloy, Claire. *Popular Media and Animals.* Palgrave Macmillan, 2011.
Moore, Laurence R. *Religious Outsiders and the Makings of Americans.* Little, Brown, 1986.
Morin, Karen M. "Carceral Space: Prisoners and Animals." *Antipode* 48, no. 5 (2016): 1317–36.
Morrison, Toni. *Playing in the Dark: Whiteness and the Literary Imagination.* Harvard University Press, 1992.

Myles, Eileen. *Afterglow (a Dog Memoir)*. Grove, 2017.
Oliver, Mary. *Dog Songs*. Penguin, 2015.
Newman, Judith. "Another Client for Ms. Fix-It." *New York Times*, November 16, 2012.
Omi, Michael, and Howard Winant. *Racial Formation in the United States*. 2nd ed. Routledge, 1994.
Orange, Michelle. "Dog-Seeing Eye: The Cinematic Work of Laurie Anderson." *Virginia Quarterly Review* (Winter 2016): 193–96.
Orsi, Robert Anthony. *Between Heaven and Earth: The Religious Worlds People Make and the Scholars Who Study Them*. Princeton University Press, 2005.
Orlean, Susan. *Rin Tin Tin: The Life and the Legend*. Simon & Schuster, 2011.
Otto, Eckart. "Covenant." In *Encyclopedia of Religion*, 2nd ed., ed. Lindsay Jones, 3:2047–51. Macmillan Reference USA, 2005.
Page, Allison. *Media and the Affective Life of Slavery*. University of Minnesota Press, 2022.
Parry, Tyler D., and Charlton W. Yingling. "Slave Hounds and Abolition in the Americas." *Past & Present* 246, no. 1 (February 1, 2020): 69–108.
Patterson, Charles. *Eternal Treblinka: Our Treatment of Animals and the Holocaust*. Lantern, 2002.
Peterson, Anna. *Being Animal: Beasts and Boundaries in Nature Ethics*. Columbia University Press, 2013.
Peterson, Christopher. *Bestial Traces: Race, Sexuality, Animality*. Fordham University Press, 2013.
Pierce, Jessica. *The Last Walk: Reflections on Our Pets at the End of Their Lives*. University of Chicago Press, 2012.
——. *Run Spot Run: The Ethics of Keeping Pets*. University of Chicago Press, 2015.
Piper, Grant. "Why Do Dogs Dig? 6 Vet-Reviewed Reasons & Solutions." *Dogster*, February 20, 2025. https://www.dogster.com/lifestyle/why-do-dogs-dig.
Piquero, Alex R., Nicole Leeper Piquero, Marc Gertz, Thomas Baker, Jason Batton, and J. C. Barnes. "Race, Punishment, and the Michael Vick Experience." *Social Science Quarterly* 92, no. 2 (2011): 535–51.
Pratt, Mary Louise. *Imperial Eyes: Travel Writing and Transculturation*. Routledge, 1992.

Pryor, Karen. *Don't Shoot the Dog!* Rev. ed. Bantam, 1999.

Puar, Jasbir. *Terrorist Assemblages: Homonationalism in Queer Times.* Duke University Press, 2007.

Quinn, Annalisa. "Book News: Michael Vick Cancels Book Tour Because of Threats." NPR. March 13, 2013.

Ramos-Zayas, Ana Y. "Ordinary Whiteness: Affect, Kinship, and the Moral Economy of Privilege." *Journal of Urban History* 47, no. 2 (2021): 459–64.

Red, Christian. "Trained to Be Killers, Vick's Pit Bulls Now on Death Row." *New York Daily News*, August 30, 2007.

"Redemption." In *The Oxford Companion to Christian Thought*. Oxford University Press, 2000.

Robles, Mario Ortiz. *Literature and Animal Studies*. Routledge, 2016.

Rudy, Kathy. *Loving Animals: Towards a New Animal Advocacy*. University of Minnesota Press, 2011.

———. "Michael Vick, Dog Fighting, and Race." *Duke Today*, August 29, 2007. https://today.duke.edu/2007/08/vick_oped.html.

Samuels, Shirley. *The Culture of Sentiment: Race, Gender, and Sentimentality in Nineteenth-Century America*. Oxford University Press, 1992.

Schade, Victoria. *Who Rescued Who*. Penguin, 2020.

Schaefer, Donovan. *Animal Affects: Animality, Evolution, and Power*. Duke University Press, 2015.

Schilken, Chuck. "Tens of Thousands Object to Michael Vick's Induction Into the Virginia Tech Sports Hall of Fame." *Los Angeles Times*, July 27, 2017.

Schmidt, Michael S. "In the Case Against Vick, Dogs Are Held as Evidence." *New York Times*, August 1, 2007.

———. "Menacing Dogs from Vick Case Await Their Fate." *New York Times*, September 1, 2007.

Schwartz, Marion. *A History of Dogs in the Early Americas*. Yale University Press, 2011.

Schwertfeger, Susanne. "Re-Education as Exorcism: How a White Dog Challenges the Strategies for Dealing with Racism." In *Animal Horror Cinema: Genre, History, and Criticism*, ed. Katarina Gregersdotter, Johan Höglund, and Nicklas Hållén, 126–45. Palgrave Macmillan, 2015.

Shelter Animals Count. "National Animal Welfare Statistics Dashboard." 2024. https://www.shelteranimalscount.org/explore-the-data/data-dashboards/national-animal-welfare-statistics-dashboard/.

Short, Alice. "A Few Words About Pit Bulls." *Los Angeles Times*, July 28, 2008.
Shulman, George. *American Prophecy: Race and Redemption in American Political Culture*. University of Minnesota Press, 2008.
Slattery, Peter. "Last Living 9/11 Rescue Dog Given a Funeral Fit for a Hero." *Daily Beast*. June 7, 2016.
Spiegel, Marjorie. *The Dreaded Comparison: Human and Animal Slavery*. Mirror, 1996.
Strouse, Kathy. *Bad Newz: The Untold Story of the Michael Vick Dogfighting Case*. Dogfighting Investigations LLC, 2009.
Swift, E. M. "The Pit Bull Friend and Killer." *Sports Illustrated*, July 27, 1987.
Tang, Pao-Chen. "Of Dogs and Distractions in Early Cinema." *Early Visual Popular Culture* 15, no. 1 (2017): 44–58.
Torres, Tia. *My Life Among the Underdogs: A Memoir*. William Morrow, 2019.
Travis Agility Group. "About Agility." https://www.austintag.org/about-agility.html.
Tuan, Yi-Fu. *Dominance and Affection: The Making of Pets*. Yale University Press, 1984.
"Tucker Carlson Backs Off 'Execution' Comments About Michael Vick; Host 'Overspoke' Last Week." *New York Daily News*, January 4, 2011; updated January 13, 2019. https://www.nydailynews.com/2011/01/04/tucker-carlson-backs-off-execution-comments-about-michael-vick-host-overspoke-last-week-video/.
Tuveson, Ernest Lee. *Redeemer Nation: The Idea of America's Millennial Role*. Harvard University Press, 1968.
United States of America v. Purnell A. Peace, a/k/a "P-Funk" and "Funk," Quanis L. Phillips, a/k/a "Q," Tony Taylor, a/ka/a "T," Michael Vick, a/k/a "Ookie." 18 U.S.C. §371. 2010. https://www.animallaw.info/sites/default/files/vick_indictment.pdf.
Victor, Daniel. "Mourning Bretagne, a Search Dog and Symbol of 9/11 Heroism." *New York Times*, June 7, 2016.
Vick, Michael. "Associated Materials." Michigan State University Animal Legal & Historical Center. 2007, 2008.
——. *Finally Free: An Autobiography*. Worthy Books, 2012.
Voith, Victoria, et al. "Comparison of Visual and DNA Breed Identification of Dogs and Inter-Observer Reliability." Proceedings of Annual AMVA Convention, Seattle, Washington, July 11–14, 2009.

Wacker, Grant. *America's Pastor: Billy Graham and the Shaping of a Nation.* Harvard University Press, 2014.

——. *Heaven Below: Early Pentecostals and American Culture.* Harvard University Press, 2001.

Wagoner, Zandra. "Kinship Figures, Polluted Legacies, and Recycling: Pragmatic Considerations for Feminist God-Talk." *American Journal of Theology & Philosophy* 28, no. 2 (May 2007): 251–70.

Waldau, Paul, and Kimberly Patton, eds. *A Communion of Subjects: Animals in Religion, Science, and Ethics.* Columbia University Press, 2006.

Walton, Saige. "Other Sides: Loving and Grieving with *Heart of a Dog* and Merleau-Ponty's Depth." *Projections* 13, no. 2 (June 2019): 38–57.

Weaver, Harlan. *Bad Dog: Pit Bull Politics and Multispecies Justice.* University of Washington Press, 2021.

——. "'Becoming in Kind': Race, Class, Gender, and Nation in Cultures of Dog Rescue and Dogfighting." *American Quarterly* 65, no. 3 (2013): 689–709.

——. "Pit Bull Promises: Inhuman Intimacies and Queer Kinships in an Animal Shelter." *GLQ: A Journal of Lesbian and Gay Studies* 21, no. 2–3 (2015): 343–63.

Weil, Kari. *Thinking Animals: Why Animal Studies Now?* Columbia University Press, 2012.

White, Armond. "White Dog: Fuller Vs. Racism." Criterion Collection, November 27, 2008. https://www.criterion.com/current/posts/848-white-dog-fuller-vs-racism.

Will, David, and Peter Wollen, eds. *Samuel Fuller.* Edinburgh Film Festival, 1969.

Williams, Linda. *Playing the Race Card: Melodramas of Black and White from Uncle Tom to O.J. Simpson.* Princeton University Press, 2012.

Williams, Rhys H., Raymond Haberski Jr., and Philip Goff, eds. *Civil Religion Today: Religion and the American Nation in the Twenty-First Century.* New York University Press, 2021.

Wisch, Rebecca F., and Ashley Dillingham. "State Holding Period Laws for Impounded Animals." Michigan State University Animal Legal & Historical Center. 2017. https://www.animallaw.info/topic/state-holding-period-laws-impounded-animals.

Wittmeyer, Alicia P. Q., and Mark Peckmezian. "My Year of Being Very Online About Dogs." *New York Times*, December 20, 2023.

Wolfe, Cary. *Animal Rites: American Culture, the Discourse of Species, and Posthumanist Theory*. University of Chicago Press, 2003.

Woo, Jeremy. "Michael Vick Apologizes for Colin Kaepernick Hair Comments." *Sports Illustrated.com*, July 20, 2017. https://www.si.com/nfl/2017/07/20/michael-vick-colin-kaepernick-hair-apology.

Wyche, Steve. "Colin Kaepernick Explains Why He Sat Down During the National Anthem." NFL.com. August 28, 2016.

Yin, Sophia. "Dominance in Dogs Is Not a Personality Trait." *Cattle Dog Publishing*, September 15, 2009.

Yori, Roo. "An Open Letter to Michael Vick." *Huffington Post*, September 22, 2015, updated December 6, 2017, https://www.huffingtonpost.com/roo-yori/open-letter-to-michael-vi_b_8172720.html.

Zakos, Katharine P. "Violating the Racial Contract: Black Professional Athletes and the Case of Michael Vick." *Howard Journal of Communications* 33, no. 1 (January 1, 2022): 95–113.

INDEX

Abrahamic religions, 118–19
Abu Ghraib, 137–39, 147, 158
Adam and Eve story, 95–96
Adam's Task: Calling Animals by Name (Hearne), 92–93; covenantal theology of dog training, 94–110
Afro-Dog: Blackness and the Animal Question (Boisseron), 11–12, 72, 177n27, 188n19
Afterglow (a dog memoir) (Myles), 15, 124–25, 136–39, 144–51, 158
agility, 112–18, 200n66; as play, 114–15, 117, 200n66
"alpha dog," 81, 90
"alpha male," masculinist and anthropocentric vision of, 91, 121
American Revolution, 124
American Society of Veterinary Behavior, 90
Ammerman, Nancy Tatom, 110, 198n53

Anderson, Laurie, 16, 124–26, 129–36, 139–44, 150–51, 158, 205n27
animals: "absence of linguistic noise," 162; moral understanding of, 44, 95; "*syn-theōria*" used by, 121–22. *See also* dogs; human-animal relationships; interspecies language
animal shelters: incarceration metaphor, 7–8, 40; law enforcement, link with, 155; "redemption" of lost dog, 7, 155, 176n21
animot, 194n24
anthropomorphic language, 95, 186n3
"anthropo-zoo-genetic practice," 113–14
anti–pit bull articles, 183n50
apolitical readings of dogs, 89–90, 192n6
apologies, 24, 28, 33

artistic cocreation/"enrichment" with dogs, 139–40, 206nn34, 35
athletes, Black, constraints on, 50–51
Atlanta, murders of Black children, 58
attacks by dogs, 38–39, 182n47, 189n24. *See also* weaponization of dogs; "white dogs"
attentiveness, 114, 146–47
Augustine of Hippo, 6

Bad Dog: Pit Bull Politics and Multispecies Justice (Weaver), 12, 120–21, 175n17, 176n24
Bauer, Nona Kilgore, 127
Bazin, André, 131
Bekoff, Marc, 114
Bellah, Robert N., 5, 90, 124, 153, 191–92n5, 202n4, 203n7
Bennett, Joshua, 66
Bible: Book of Genesis, 94, 95, 118–19; Hebrew, 7, 13, 98–99, 195; New Testament, 13
Black and brown people: Black-animal relations, 11–12; pit bulls associated with, 2–3; racist tropes of violence, 2–3; responsibility for ending racism placed on, 68, 73, 157. *See also* racialization
Bobby (dog), 138
body language of dogs, 114, 161–62
Boggs, Colleen Glenney, 138

Boisseron, Bénédicte, 11–12, 46, 72, 86, 177n27, 188n19
Bretagne (dog), 123, 124, 150–51, 202nn2, 3
Brooks, Peter, 34
Buddhism, 16, 126, 140, 143, 158, 206n42
Bullet ("pit bull"), 3–4, 5, 174n12
Butler, Judith, 144
Byers, J. A., 114

Calarco, Matthew, 121–22
Calvinism, 16, 93
canine absence, 13, 15, 157
Canine Good Citizen Test, 22, 179n4
canine presence, 15, 94, 97, 125–26, 157–62; and creativity, 108; and death, 148; through covenantal relationship, 97–99, 108, 110
canine redemption narratives: classic, 42–49, 157; failures of, 14, 78–86, *80*, *81*, *82*; helplessness and fear of dog emphasized, 44, 47–49; limits of, 49–52; as literary genre, 4, 13, 23–25, 42, 92, 126, 175n14; as narratively complete and emotionally satisfying narrative, 82; public acceptance required for redemption, 24, 37, 42; "Reclamation" stage, 42, 47; "Redemption" stage, 42–43, 48–49; "Rescue" stage, 42, 43–47; secularized aspects of, 23, 53; subversion of, 124–25; *White*

Dog as, 60–62; white subjects as focus of, 14. *See also The Lost Dogs: Michael Vick's Dogs and Their Tale of Rescue and Redemption* (Gorant); redemption narratives; September 11, 2001, canine redemption narrative

capitalism, 199n60; intertwined with human-animal relationships, 110, 112–13

carceral state, 13–14; broader social forces erased by, 50; evangelical Christian influence on, 10–11. *See also* incarceration

care, politics of, 49

Carlson, Tucker, 181n21

Catholicism, 16, 93, 126; American practice of, 112; figural and literal intertwined, 111–12, 118, 145; in Haraway's thinking, 111–12, 118–20, 145, 198–99n56, 198n55; in Myles's writing, 145

cauda (tail), 162

Cesar 911, 193n13

Cesar Millan: Better Human, Better Dog, 190n1

"chosen people," 7, 175n19

Christianity: and anti-Blackness, 73–75; Calvinism, 16, 93; Last Judgment, 6; Protestant, 5, 53–54, 127–28. *See also* Catholicism; evangelical Christianity; religion

Christian redemption narratives, 5, 42, 53–54; as both religious and political, 4–7, 157; Prince of Darkness (or Satan), defeat of, 6. *See also* canine redemption narrative; redemption narratives

"City of God" (Augustine of Hippo), 6

civil religion, American, 4–5, 90, 202n4; as aspirational, 153–54; racist underpinnings of ignored, 191–92n5; "times of trial," 124, 127; used to justify American self-idolatry, 125, 203n7. *See also* United States

Civil War, 9–10, 124

closed-circuit television (CCTV), 129–30

close reading, 12–13

Clothier, Suzanne, 102–3, 203n9

colonialism, bestiality and bestialization at crux of, 138

commodities, dogs as, 32

communication between animals and humans: breakdowns of, 96, 107, 109, 111; naming, act of, 95–97. *See also* interspecies language

community, strengthened by the return of individual, 24, 37

Companion Species Manifesto (Haraway), 93

confession, 28–35, 153, 156; dogs unable to participate in, 24; sincerity of, 34–35

confusion, experienced by dogs, 43

consent-based training, 121
conversion, 10–11, 197n41; heart-centered language for, 181–82n33, 190n42
Corliss, Denise, 123
covenantal theology of dog training, 197n49; commands as sacred, 98–99; communication breakdown, 96, 107, 109; covenant as term, 195n28; dog's respect for language, 98; fallen world as a given, 107; interspecies language, 94, 98, 103, 110, 120, 157; naming, act of, 95–97; "not fun" for the dog, 102; physical force and pain as part of, 102–7, 109; profane, concept of, 197n40; "secret significance" of dog behaviors, 101–2; stronger and weaker partner roles, 98. *See also* relational redemption
crime: sin linked with, 10–11; US moral panic about, 38; white anxieties about, 2–3, 10–11
Crippens, David, 58
Criterion Collection, 59
Cy-Fair Volunteer Fire Department, 123

Davison, Jon, 55–56, 58
Dayan, Colin, 8, 47, 146–47, 199n59
death: and canine presence, 148; care work as act of religious devotion, 145–46; of dogs in films, 81–82, *82*, 83–84; dying

dogs, caring for, 16, 125–26, 139–44, 158, 206–7n43; euthanasia, 140, 147–48, 179n2; mourning, 143–44; nonredemptive reading of, 149; as preordained, 51; relationship with love, 141–43; scattering ashes, 149–50
"death row," 8
Derrida, Jacques, 194n24
Despret, Vinciane, 113–14, 199n61
DiAngelo, Robin, 65
discomfort, ethics of, 150
dog breeds, racialization of, 9, 21–22, 38–39, 46, 155. *See also* "pit bulls"
dogfighting, 3; domestication and capitalism brought together by, 199n60; football comparison, 31; law enforcement attention to, 38; other forms of cruelty and violence linked with, 38; standard practice for cases, 21, 179n2; violent norms and rituals of, 31–32; witnessed by children, 29–30. *See also* Vick, Michael; Vick dogs; violence
Dog Heroes of September 11th (Bauer), 127
dogs: American family completed by, 5, 54; attentiveness of, 146–47; being seen by, 138, 147; body language of, 161–62; canine absence, 13, 15, 157; as conscious and feeling creatures, 44; erasure of, in service to the

human, 125; infantilization of, 48; interior lives of, 95, 99; not allowed to be a dog, 83–84; as part of the divine order, 94; race not concept in, 85; as symbolic, 15, 51–52, 60, 70–73, 83, 125, 129, 133–34; as symbolic of white anxieties, 2–3, 14–15, 38, 157; tails, 162. *See also* canine presence; canine redemption narrative

Dog's Purpose, A (film), 186n4

dog training, 70, 189n24, 203n9; aversive, 15, 90–92, 102–7, 158; as bridge between theoretical and practical knowledge, 94; consent-based, 121; covenantal theory of, 94–110; dominance-based, 90–93; failures of, 93, 115; family restored through, 15, 91–92, 157; as form of play, 114–15, 117, 200n66; impersonal corrections, 105; naming, act of, 95–97; participation versus refraining, 106–7; philosophy, relationship with, 94–95; posthumanist, postmonotheistic vision, 120–22; redemptive potential of, 98–99; redirecting unwanted behaviors, 101, 106; relational model of redemption, 15–16; as site of religious meaning making and practice, 15–16, 73–74, 100–103, 105–6, 157; talents recognized by trainer, 108–9. *See also* covenantal theology of dog training; relational redemption

Dog Whisperer, The, 89–91, 192n7; mini–dog redemption narratives in, 91

Dombrowski, Lisa, 56

domestication, 110, 112–13, 199n60

dominance-based training, 90–93. *See also* punishment

Dreaded Comparison, The: Human and Animal Slavery (Spiegel), 11

Driscoll, Kári, 209n12

drones, 132, *133*, 134

Dubler, Joshua, 49–50

Dubnicka, Suzanne, 121

Dungy, Tony, 35–36

Edwards, Willis, 58–59

Emberton, Carole, 9–10, 177n30

embodiment in human-animal relationships, 114, 120–21, 199n59; "deeply bodied practice," 121; "queerly affiliative bodyings," 120–21

Eternal Treblinka (Patterson), 11

evangelical Christianity: conversion, heart-centered focus of, 11, 181–82n33, 190n42; courts and prisons influenced by, 10–11; definition of "evangelical," 178n33

exceptionalism, human, 119–20

exorcism, 74

Fall, as linguistic in nature, 96
family, American: 9/11 dogs as part of fire department's, 123; completion of, by dogs, 5, 54; and redemption of dog from shelter, 7–8; restoration of through dog training, 15, 91–92, 157; Vick's faith, family, and football narrative, 25, 26, 35–37; white middle-class, dog breeds associated with, 5, 54
Faust, Drew, 10
films, 185–86n3, 185n1, 186n4; canine redemption narrative in, 53; "cinematic tone poem," 205n27, 207n47; "colorblind" fantasy of, 54; death of dogs in, 81–82, *82*, 83–84; as "greatest educational medium," 62; western-style showdowns, 67, 79; whiteness and anti-Blackness as unmarked categories in, 54, 60. *See also Heart of a Dog* (Anderson); *White Dog* (film)
Finally Free (Vick), 23, 156; dogfighting section, 29–31; Dungy's foreword, 36; "The Fall," 28–35; passive voice in, 33–34; photographs in, 32; "The Redemption," 35–37; "The Rise," 25–28; stages of redemption in, 24–25, 156
Flory, Susy, 127–28
Freud, Sigmund, 143–44
Fuller, Samuel, 14, 54, 56, 62, 83–84

Gary, Romain, 55, 56
Genesis, Book of, 94, 95–96, 118–19
Georgia ("pit bull mix"), 41–42
Giuliani, Rudy, 127
"Given Reprieve, N.F.L. Star's Dogs Find Kindness" (*New York Times*), 41
God: absent from canine redemption narratives, 42; covenant with, 87, 93, 99; dog as, 145–46; dogs as experience of Christ, 199n59; and higher purpose, 128; human dog trainer in position of, 99, 105; secular history, involvement in, 6–7. *See also* religion
Göle, Nilüfer, 135
Goodell, Roger, 36
Good, the Bad, and the Ugly, The (film), 79
Gorant, Jim, 23, 42, 179–80n8
Graham, Billy, 128
Grano, Daniel A., 35, 36
Great Chain of Being, 119
grievable lives, 144
Griffith, Aaron, 10–11
guardians, as term for humans, 117, 201n73
Guenther, Katja M., 155

Hanson, Curtis, 55–56
happiness, 108–9, 197n49
Haraway, Donna, 16, 109, 157, 197n51; Catholicism in thinking of, 111–12, 118–20, 145, 198–99n56, 198n55; religious

language in work of, 110–11; Works: *Companion Species Manifesto*, 93; *How Like a Leaf: An Interview with Thyrza Nichols Goodeve*, 111; *When Species Meet*, 93, 112–13

Hearne, Vicki, 8, 16, 92–93, 121, 157–58, 193nn15, 16; covenantal theory of training, 94–110, 197n49; evidence-based positive training techniques rejected by, 197n41; on public perception of pit bulls, 39

heart, as site of redemption, 11, 181–82n33, 190n42

Heart of a Dog (Anderson), 16, 124–25, 129–36; as "cinematic tone poem," 205n27, 207n47; "good" and "evil" categories resisted in, 136; "horizontal montage," 131; linear narratives rejected in, 130, 136

Hebrew Bible, 7, 13, 98–99, 195

"helping/policing/killing," 155

helplessness, dog's sense of, 44, 47–49, 90

Hingson, Michael, 127–28

Hoffmann, Eva, 209n12

Horowitz, Alexandra, 161–62, 209n17

How Like a Leaf: An Interview with Thyrza Nichols Goodeve (Haraway), 111

human-animal relationships: "active" and "co-shaping," 113; companion species, 120, 197n51;

daily routine and loss of pet, 144; and domestication, 110, 112–13; embodied quality of, 114, 120–21, 199n59; exceptionalism, human, 119–20

human-canine relationships: artistic cocreation/"enrichment," 139–40, 206n34, 35; capitalism intertwined with, 110, 112–13; "command," language of, 98; guardians as term for human, 117, 201n73; as relational process of mutual recognition, 95–96; simplistic account of, 92; stories of redemption as defining cultural script for, 4; systematic factors shaping, 161; unequal power dynamics in, 89, 94, 110, 114, 195n31. *See also* relational model of redemption

humane behavior, destruction linked with, 8

Humane Society of the United States, 22, 25

humor, religion as source of, 144–45

Hurricane Katrina, 3, 174n12

identity formation, 12, 153. *See also* national identity

incarceration, 180n13; animal shelters likened to, 7–8, 40; as answer to doubt about confession, 34–35; as step in redemption narrative, 24, 28–35; Vick as spokesperson for, 35. *See also* carceral state; punishment

individual: animals as, 194n24; burden of proof on, 34, 43; community strengthened by return of, 24, 37; dog as, 45–46, 83–84, 94, 184n61; focus of redemption narrative on, 10–11, 14, 26–28, 33–34, 49, 85, 156; personal accountability of, 26, 33–34, 156
infantilization, of dogs, 48
"inner city" violence, white racist anxieties about, 38
innocence, American myth of, 125
Inside of a Dog (Horowitz), 161–62, 209n17
interspecies connectedness, 11–12, 155, 158–61
interspecies language, 94, 157–58; "absence of linguistic noise," 162, 209n17; body language of dogs, 114, 161–62; "queerly affiliative bodyings," 120–21
interspecies play, 114–15, 117, 200n66

Jasmine ("Sussex 2602," dog), 47, 48, 51

Kaepernick, Colin, 50–51
Katzenberg, Jeffrey, 58
Kilgore, Kevin M., 40
Kuzniar, Alice A., 143–44

language: anthropomorphic, 95, 186n3; commands as act of naming, 108; interspecies, 94, 98, 103, 110, 120, 157–58

Lassie (film), 83, 84
"law-and-order" politics and policing, 2–3
learned helplessness, 90
Leone, Sergio, 79
Letter from Siberia (Marker), 131
Levinas, Emmanuel, 138
Life magazine, 55
linguistic anthropology, 96–97
Lloyd, Vincent W., 49–50
Lolabelle (dog), 126, 131–36, *133*, 139–44, 150–51, 158
Lost Dogs, The: Michael Vick's Dogs and Their Tale of Rescue and Redemption (Gorant), 23, 42–49, 156, 179–80n8; central role of whiteness in, 46; dogs as "Vick-tims" in, 43; dogs distanced from Blackness in, 46–47; public relations work of, 46–47; "Reclamation," 42, 47; "Redemption," 42–43, 48–49; "Rescue," 42, 43–47

Madison, James, 70
Marker, Chris, 131
masculinity, Black, 36
"material-semiotic" process, 93
Mbembe, Achille, 130–31, 204–5n22
melancholia, 143–44
Melancholia's Dog (Kuzniar), 143–44
melodrama, racial, 69, 74
Midnight (dog), 30
Millan, Cesar, 15, 94, 113, 121, 157, 190n1, 192n7, 193n13; on national

unity through dogs, 89–90;
  "rags to riches" life story, 91–92
"millennium," 6, 154
Miller, Reuben Jonathan, 180n13
Moffett, Earl, 1–2, 5, 9, 174n6
Molloy, Claire, 186n3
moral understanding, of more-
  than-human animals, 44, 95
Ms. Cayenne Pepper the Border
  Collie, 94
Myles, Eileen, 16, 124–26, 136–39,
  144–51, 158

NAACP boycott of *White Dog*, 58
"Name of a Dog, The, or Natural
  Rights" (Levinas), 138
naming, act of, 95–97; and
  commands, 108; invocation
  versus label as matter of life and
  death for dogs, 97, 194n25
nation, 6–7, 13; identity of, 4, 16,
  202n4; qualities of dog
  transferred onto, 129; queer,
  feminist, and subversive, 137;
  "redeemer," 5–6, 124–25, 154–55,
  175n19, 202n4; unity through
  dogs, 89–90, 124
National Football League (NFL):
  Black quarterbacks in, 22, 27;
  Kaepernick exiled from,
  50–51
National Society of Film
  Critics, 59
Newport News, Virginia, 25–27,
  180n12; as war zone, 26, 30
New York Times, 41

Obama, Barack, 37
obedience and obeisance, 105
Oliver, Mary, 158–61
oppression, linked between animal
  and human, 11
Orsi, Robert A., 112

Pacelle, Wayne, 183n56
"pack leader" concept, 90
Paramount Pictures, 55–58
"parolees," redemption of, 1–3, 155
pathos, 43
Patterson, Charles, 11
"Percy Wakes Me (Fourteen)
  Today" (Oliver), 158–61
PETA, 184n56
pet ownership statistics, 192n6
Philadelphia Eagles, 37
philosophy, intrinsic relationship
  with dog training, 94–95
Pierce, Jessica, 140
"pit bulls": as "America's dog," 38;
  as "breed" defined by visual
  perception, 38–39; defining, 2,
  38, 174n10; media
  sensationalization of, 2–3; as
  monstrous and criminal, 40–41;
  move toward whiteness as
  precondition for rescue of,
  46–47; racialized, 9, 21–22,
  38–39, 155; reading religion into,
  37–42; said to be both resilient
  and childlike, 3–4; as stand-in
  for all dangerous dogs, 38–39; as
  stand-in for "dangerous" human
  beings, 39. *See also* Vick pit bulls

Pit Bulls & Parolees (reality TV show), 1–4, 9, 155, 173n1
play: canid, 114; dog training as, 114–15, 117, 200n66
Polanski, Roman, 55
politeness, white liberal conceptions of, 69
positive training methods, 197n51
postcolonial theory, 131, 205n22
presence, 2; canine, 15, 94, 97, 110, 125, 157–62; in Catholic practice, 112; seeing the dog, 139–44
Prince of Darkness (or Satan), 6
Protestant Christianity, 5, 53–54; and 9/11 dog narratives, 127–28; Reformation, 6
Puar, Jasbir, 135
punishment, 153; carceral state and logic of, 10–11; in covenantal theology of dog training, 102–7, 109; redemption linked with, 7; US politics of, 49–50; for violation of social norms, 50–51. *See also* dominance-based training; incarceration
"purposelessness," 114

"queerly affiliative bodyings," 120–21

racialization: binary terms of black and white, 72; of dog breeds, 9, 21–22, 38–39, 46, 155; no conception of race in dogs, 85; of "parolees," 1–3, 155; visual perception in racial identification, 38–39; and "white dogs," 55
racism: about Black quarterbacks, 27–28; "canine racism," 55; class status linked to, 76; in football, 180n17; ICE raids, 191n3; unlearning of, 55, 64, 72, 85. *See also* weaponization of dogs
Radical Republicans, 9, 177n29
rape metaphor for forced dog breeding, 41–42, 207n49
"real-life" relationships with dogs, 16
Reamon, Tommy, 26–27
Reconstruction, 9, 154–55, 177n29
Redeemer Nation: The Idea of America's Millennial Role (Tuveson), 5–6, 154, 175n19, 202n4
"redeemer nation," United States as, 5–6, 124–25, 154–55, 175n19, 202n4
redemption: in animal shelter discourse, 7, 176nnn21, 22,155; by and of dogs, 1–2; etymology of, 7, 154; and grief, 144; heart as site of, 11, 181–82n33, 190n42; only traumatized dogs deserving of, 41, 42, 156; public acceptance required for, 24, 37, 42; suffering as precondition for, 5, 10, 14; unredeemed dogs, fate of, 7–8; whiteness associated with, 9–10, 46, 74,

154–55. *See also* covenantal theology of dog training; relational model of redemption

redemption narratives: as about humans, not dogs, 51–52, 129; after Civil War, 9–10; broader social systems erased by, 8–11, 13–14, 26–28, 50, 156; classic human, 23–42; as harmful to humans and canines, 85; individual as focus of, 10–11, 14, 26–28, 33–34, 49, 85, 156; not capable of dealing with legacies of slavery and racism, 85; as retrospective, 25; selective colorblindness in, 27–28; steps in, 23–24; structural injustice avoided in, 26. *See also Finally Free* (Vick)

"Redemption, The" (movement), 154–55

Reed, Lou, 141, 207n44

relational redemption, 15–16, 93, 157; intertwined role of domestication and capitalism, 110; mutual attention required, 117–18; naming, act of, 95–97; new religious narratives needed, 119–20; non-dog and non-animal people not addressed, 195n29; presentness of shared task, 115; through theology of training, 107–8; uneven power dynamics, 78, 89, 94, 110, 114, 195n31. *See also* covenantal theology of dog training; dog training; human-animal relationships; human-canine relationships

religion, 198n53; Abrahamic, 118–19; Buddhism, 16, 126, 140.143, 158. *See* Catholicism; Christianity; civil religion, American; evangelical Christianity; God; sacred, the

retrieving: as sacred, 99; sport of, 106–8, 196n43

Roselle (guide dog), 128–29

Rosie (dog), 126, 136–39, 144–51, 158, 207n49

R+ training, 121

sacred, the, 198n53; dog behaviors as, 99–100; in secular spaces, 111. *See also* religion; *specific religions*

sacrifice, 54; redemptive, of dogs, 44–45

Salty the German Shorthaired Pointer, 94, 99–109, 196n43

sanctimony, 75–78

Schwertfeger, Susanne, 69, 73–74, 77

second chances, 2, 5, 23–37

self: concept of applied to animals, 95; expansion of through naming, 97

"senior" dogs, 3–4

sensory stimulation and deprivation, mixture of, 43

sentimentality, 48, 188n23
September 11, 2001: binary categories of good and evil in discourse of, 136, 203n6, 205n22; disorientation experienced after, 131–32; dogs as symbolic of American vulnerability after, 133–34; "good" and "evil" categories, 136; snapshot metaphor, 135; surveillance heightened by, 129–36
September 11, 2001, canine redemption narrative, 16, 126–29, 148; avant-garde takes on, 124–25; deconstructing, 129–36; dogs as outlet for national unity, 123–24, 151; "Four-Legged 9/11 Heroes" on memorial website, 127; heroism of dogs in, 123, 127–29; qualities of dog transferred onto nation, 129, 151; search-and-rescue dogs present at Ground Zero, 127; as subgenre of dog redemption narrative, 126; tributes geared toward popular audience, 126–27; war crimes, dogs as metonymies for, 16, 137–39, 158. *See also* canine redemption narratives
sin, 10–11, 94, 180n9; slavery as "America's original sin," 9, 70, 189n31

slavery: American failure to address legacy of, 14; as "America's original sin," 9, 70, 189n31; comparison between animals and humans, 11; dog as instrument for white crimes, 70–71. *See also* "white dogs"
South, 9–10, 154–55, 177n30; Radical Republicans, 9, 177n29
Spiegel, Marjorie, 11
sports, dog: agility, 112–18, 200n66; nosework, 97, 194–95n26, 201n71; retrieving, 99, 106–8, 196n43; tracking, 194n26
St. Francis of Assisi, 74, 75
structural problems: avoided in redemption narratives, 8–11, 13–14, 26, 32; evasion of white accountability for, 65, 67–69, 72–73, 78, 85–86
suffering: connection created through, 149–50; "culture of shared," 10; of dogs, 44–45; nonredemptive, 16, 149; as precondition for redemption, 5, 10, 14; racial insufficiency of white tears to end, 53; redemptive sacrifice of dogs, 44–45
surveillance state, 129–36; Black bodies surveilled, 38; closed-circuit television (CCTV), 129–30; drone footage, 132; faulty interpretations of video

footage, 130; new sense of time, 130–31; police state and dogs linked, 138
"*syn-theōria*" (seeing with others), 121–22

tails (*cauda*), 162
talent, 108–9
tears, 63, 75, 188n23
temperament tests, 45
temporality, 130–31; and September 11, 2001, 130–36
Texas Task Force I, 123
Animal That Therefore I Am, The (Derrida), 194n24
theology of dog training. *See* covenantal theology of dog training
Thunder Dog: The True Story of a Blind Man, His Guide Dog, and the Triumph of Trust at Ground Zero (Hingson and Flory), 127–28
time, teleological conception of, 130–31, 204–5n22
Torres, Tia, 1–2, 3–4, 173–74n5, 173n4
torture, from canine perspective, 137–39
"Trained to Be Killers, Vick's Pit Bulls Now on Death Row," 40
transcendence, 110, 149
Trump, Donald, 90, 191n3
trust, 104, 116, 201n71

Tuveson, Ernest Lee, 5–6, 154, 175n19, 202n4

United States: 9/11 dogs as idealized vision of, 124; American dream, 13, 22; "chosen people," 7, 175n19; "culture of shared suffering," 10; federal holidays, 5; innocence, myth of, 125; national project of violence, 155, 191n3; race in binary terms of black and white, 72; as "redeemer nation," 5–6, 124–25, 154–55, 175n19, 202n4; triumphalist narratives, 129, 132; war crimes, dogs as metonymies for, 16, 137–39, 158. *See also* civil religion, American; September 11, 2001 canine redemption narrative

Vick, Michael, 13–14, 156, 179n5, 180nn 9, 12, 18, 181n22; as Black quarterback in NFL, 22, 27–28; broader harms effaced by, 35, 50; cruelty to dogs, participation in, 21, 32, 44–45; defenders of, 22, 32; faith, family, and football narrative, 25, 26, 35–37; narrative frame of redemption applied to, 22–23; public response to case, 39–42; race not mentioned by in book, 26, 32; racist responses to, 22, 46; redemption narrative of, 23–37; return to NFL, 36–37; work ethic and personal accomplishments, 27

Vick dogs, 125, 179n5, 183n56; as bad fighters, 38; dehumanization of, 39–41; held as evidence, 21; as individuals, 45–46; integration of into human homes, 21–22; negative stereotypes as step in preparation for redemption, 41; permanent association with Vick, 43; personification of, 39–42, 47; public response to, 39–42; temperament tests on, 45; "the little red dog," 44–45, 156; understood through redemption frame, 37–42; as "Vick-tims," 22, 43; as "Vick-tory dogs," 22; as victims, 22, 41–43

Vietnam War, 124

Villalobos Rescue Center (VRC), 1–2, 173n2

violence, 109; "immunity" to, 25–26; "inner city," white racist anxieties about, 38; "redeemer nation" and legitimization of, 125, 154–55; torture, from canine perspective, 137–39; US national project of, 155, 191n3. *See also* dogfighting

violence against dogs: aversive dog training, 15, 90–92, 102–7, 158; justifications for, 176–77n26; language of humanity used for, 8

Wagoner, Zandra, 198n55

Walton, Saige, 139

weaponization of dogs, 9, 187n7, 188n19; at Abu Ghraib, 137–39; 147, 158; "canine racism," 55; police state, dogs linked with, 138. *See also* racism; "white dogs"

Weaver, Harlan, 8, 12, 120–21, 155, 175n17, 176n24

West, Kanye, 174n12

When Species Meet (Haraway), 93, 112–13

White Dog (film), 67, 73, 77, 94; as antiracist project, 14, 57–58, 70, 73, 85, 156–57; Black audience response to, 58; character arc, 62; Christianity and anti-Blackness in, 73–75; as classic canine redemption narrative, 60–62; complexity of approach to guilt and innocence, 63–64, 68–69, 77–78; cracks in redemption narrative, 62–69; dangerousness of dog in, 54; didactic mode in, 62; dog as allegorical character in, 60; evasion of white accountability in, 65, 67–69, 72–73, 78, 85–86; failure of as a dog redemption narrative, 84–86, 156–57; failure of redemption in, 78–83, *80*, *81*, *82*; figure of white dog as symbolic, 70–71, 125, 158; final script, 57; Fuller's "nonracist approach," 56, 57; Julie as "audience stand-in," 62; Julie as besieged and innocent white woman, 61–62; literary references in, 70, 187–88n13; NAACP boycott of, 58;

production, reception, and distribution, 55–60; as racist "Jaws on paws," 56; responsibility ending racist violence placed on Black people, 68, 73, 157; VHS and television release, 59; white audience response to, 84–85; white liberals critiqued in, 68–69
"white dogs," 54–55, 63, 65–66, 157, 177n27, 187n7, 188n19, 189n26; continuing legacy of, 55, 66. *See also* weaponization of dogs
whiteness: of dog cultures, 3, 17, 21–22, 93; insufficiency of tears to end racial suffering, 63; pit bull rescue predicated on association with, 46–47; redemption associated with, 9–10, 46, 154–55; as unmarked category in Hollywood films, 54, 60, 67; white anxieties, 2–3, 14–15, 38, 157; "white fragility," 65, 68

white Southerners, 9–10, 154–55, 177n30

white supremacy, 65, 84–85, 154–55

"Who Rescued Who?" bumper stickers, 175n15

Williams, Linda, 69

Williams, Rhys H., 202n4

Winfield, Paul, 58–59

witness, canine, 136–39

worthiness, narratives of, 8, 24, 41, 42, 156

zoopoetics, 209n13

GPSR Authorized Representative: Easy Access System Europe, Mustamäe tee 50, 10621 Tallinn, Estonia, gpsr.requests@easproject.com

www.ingramcontent.com/pod-product-compliance
Lightning Source LLC
Chambersburg PA
CBHW031240290426
44109CB00012B/378